FREE TO LOVE

Louvain Theological and Pastoral Monographs is a publishing venture whose purpose is to provide those involved in pastoral ministry throughout the world with studies inspired by Louvain's long tradition of theological excellence within the Roman Catholic tradition. The volumes selected for publication in the series are expected to express some of today's finest reflection on current theology and pastoral practice.

LOUVAIN THEOLOGICAL & PASTORAL MONOGRAPHS

15

FREE TO LOVE

PAUL'S DEFENSE OF CHRISTIAN LIBERTY IN GALATIANS

by John Buckel

PEETERS PRESS
LOUVAIN
W.B. EERDMANS

ISBN 90-6831-490-4
D. 1993/0602/42

TABLE OF CONTENTS

PREFACE 3

CHAPTER ONE
Freedom's Challenge 7

The Gospel Comes to Galatia 7
  A Roman World 9
  A Counter-Cultural Gospel 12

Destination, Date and Authenticity 16
  Where in the World is Galatia? 16
  By Paul Alone 18
  An Uncorrupted Text 19

Pauline Identity 21
  An Enigma 23
  A Good Friend 24
  A Role Model 26
  An Apostle 27

The Letter 28
  Like No Other 30
  Chaos in Galatia 30
  Paul's Response 34

Concluding Remarks 36
  The Essence of Christianity 36
  Galatians and Revelation 36
  The Challenge of Freedom 37

CHAPTER TWO
Freedom's Spokesperson (Gal 1:1-10) 39

The Proclaimer and the Proclaimed 39
Similar but Different 39
Paul's Christian Identity 41
A Bona Fide Apostle 42
The Divine Message 44

Where Sin Abounded Grace Abounded All the More . . 45
Paradise Lost 45
Original Sin 47
Trapped by Sin 48
The Miracle of Love 49

What God has Joined Together 52
Jesus Christ, Our Lord 52
Thy Will be Done 54
The Gathering 56
The Perfect Gift 56

Let No One Put Asunder 60
The Gospel of Freedom 62
Those Accursed Troublemakers 63

Concluding Remarks 65
Where Two or More are Gathered 65
United We Stand 66
Oblivious to Sin 67
In Defence of Freedom 67

CHAPTER THREE
Surprised by Freedom (Gal 1:11 - 2:14) 69

Amazing Grace 70
Divine Revelation 70
By God's Grace, Kinsfolk 71
From Persecutor to Persecuted 74
Christ Centered 78

Call or Conversion 82
Conversion 82
Call 83
A Faithful Jew 83
Not Anti-Semitic 84
Christianity and Judaism 85

Second to None 87
Peter and Paul 87
First Meeting 88
Second Meeting 88
Third Meeting 91
Apostolic Equality 93

Concluding Remarks 93
Paul and the Galatians 94
Paul and Authority 95
Peter and Paul 95
The Surprise of Freedom 96

CHAPTER FOUR
Faith: The Gateway to Freedom (Gal 2:15-21) . . . 99

Justified by Faith 101

Justification 101
Faith in Christ 103

Not the Law 105
The Call to Holiness 106
Works of the Law 107
Pauline Inconsistency? 109

Why The Law Does not Justify 110
Transgression of the Law 110
Self-Righteousness 112
The Torah is Annulled 115
The Law Condemned Christ 117
A Sociological Approach 119
Inclusion of the Gentiles 123
Salvation Only in Christ 126

Concluding Remarks 129
Christ Makes a Difference 129
The Gift of Justification 130
Freedom through Faith 130

CHAPTER FIVE
The Price of Freedom (Gal 3:1-14) 131

The Wonder of Faith 132
The Blessing of Abraham 134
Trusting Abraham 136

The Curse of the Law 137
Exclusion from Blessing 138
Condemnation not Justification 138

The Failure of the Law 140
Faith and the Law 141
In Principle but Not in Reality 143

Absolved from the Curse 145
Redemption and Liberty 146
Christ Crucified 150
Sacrificial Love 153

From Curse to Blessing 154
Through Christ Alone 154
The Promise of the Spirit 155
A Meaningful Death 156

Concluding Remarks 157
A Proto-Christian 157
Mystery of the Cross 158

CHAPTER SIX
Freed From Captivity (Gal 3:15 - 4:31) 161

The Covenant 162
Captivated By The Law 164
Inferiority of the Law 165
Confining Nature of the Law 166

New Life of Freedom 168
Baptism and the New Testament 168
Theology of Baptism 169
Salvation 171
Transformation 172
Expiation 173
Reconciliation 173

Glorification 175
Sanctification 175
New Creation 176

Neither Male Nor Female 177

Born to be Free 179
Slaves Once More? 180
Abba, Dad 182
Personal Approach 182
By God's Grace, Free 184

Concluding Remarks 186
The Christian Contract 186
Free at Last 187
Foundation of Christian Living 187

CHAPTER SEVEN
Freedom, Love and Responsibility (Gal 5:1 - 6:18) . 189

Christian Freedom 190
Justification and Freedom 191
Freed From 192
Freedom For 193
Happiness 193
Free To 196
Divine Liberty 196
Freedom and the Spirit 197
Spirit vs. Flesh 197
Freedom and Commitment 199
Opponents of Freedom 200

Christian Love 202
Love Is 202

Mutual Self-Giving 203
Unconditional Love 204
Not Agapê 205
Agapê Spirituality 206
Love is the Greatest 206
1 Corinthians 13 208
Charity Begins at Home 209

Christian Responsibility 209
Life in the Flesh 210
Life in the Spirit 211
Personal Responsibility 212

Last Words and Testimony 213

Concluding Remarks 214
Born to Serve 215
The Divine Romance 215
The Holy Family 217
The Demands of Love 217
Ever Vigilant 218
Journey of Faith 219

POSTSCRIPT 221

Zeal for the Gospel 221
The Divine Caretaker 222
Christian Identity 222
Greater Love that This 223
The United Way 224
Mystical Union 225
Giving Your All 226
Joy to the World 226
Realizing a Dream 227

Index of Persons 229

Index of Scriptural References 231

Index of Subjects 239

ABBREVIATIONS

BETL	Bibliotheca ephemeridum theologicarum lovaniesium
BJRL	*Bulletin of the John Rylands University Library*
BNTC	Black's New Testament Commentaries
CBNS	Century Bible. New Series
DNTT	*Dictionary of New Testament Theology*
EerdBib	*Eerdmans Bible Dictionary*
EncylRel	*Encyclopedia of Religion*
EvTh	*Evangelische Theologie*
HBD	*Harper's Bible Dictionary*
HTR	*Harvard Theological Review*
ICC	International Critical Commentary
IThQ	*Irish Theological Quarterly*
IDB	*Interpreter's Dictionary of the Bible*
JAMA	*Journal of the American Medical Association*
JBC	*Jerome Biblical Commentary*
NJBC	*New Jerome Biblical Commentary*
JBL	*Journal of Biblical Literature*
JTS	*Journal of Theological Studies*
LS	*Louvain Studies*
NIGTC	New International Greek Testament Commentary
NICNT	New International Commentary on the New Testament
NTS	*New Testament Studies*
RBib	*Revue biblique*
RSV	Revised Standard Version
SBLDS	Society of Biblical Literature Dissertation Series
SNTIW	Studies of the New Testament and its World
SNTSMS	Society of New Testament Studies. Monograph Series
TDNT	*Theological Dictionary of the New Testament*
WTJ	*Westminster Theological Journal*
WUNT	Wissenschaftliche Untersuchungen zum Neuen Testament
ZNW	*Zeitschrift für die neutestamentliche Wissenschaft*

IN MEMORY

MOST REVEREND EDWARD T. O'MEARA

ARCHBISHOP OF INDIANAPOLIS
1980-1992

PREFACE

"Free at last, free at last, thank God almighty, we are free at last." These words spoken by Martin Luther King at a civil rights demonstration in 1963 expressed his dream of liberty and equality for all human beings, regardless of race, creed, or color. King's cry for freedom continues to ring out. The winds of change that have blown across the former Soviet Union, Eastern Europe, and South Africa, bear witness to the fact that the dream of freedom still captures the imagination of millions of people. For many, this dream seems, to a certain extent, to have been realized.

Nevertheless, the thrill of a new life of liberty has been tempered by the realization that the acquisition of freedom is not without its challenges. More and more people around the globe are becoming increasingly aware of the demands of their newfound liberty and of the sacrifices which are required to retain that liberty. Many have discovered that living in a free society can be rather unsettling. Guidance and direction in this new way of existence is desperately needed.

The dramatic events that have recently taken place on the world stage have made this an ideal time to reflect upon the notion of *Christian liberty*. Twenty centuries ago, Paul, the apostle to the Gentiles, proclaimed that faith in Christ is the key to a life of authentic freedom. Paul was convinced that because of the life, death, and resurrection of Jesus Christ, the barrier of sin, which had previously separated human beings from God and from one another, had come crashing down. As a result, Paul envisioned a Christian society in which there is no distinction between Jew and Gentile, slave and free, male and female. He was well aware of the great demands of Christian freedom. The apostle authored the Letter to the Galatians in order to respond to a community of believers who were experiencing severe difficulties with that liberty which is associated with those who are in Christ. Paul informs the Christians under his care that they have been freed from the enslavement of sin and death so that they might love more fully. By virtue of their unity with the risen Lord, Christians are free to love, in the deepest sense of the word, God, others, and themselves.

Although this book is primarily concerned with the Letter to the Galatians, it also contains information concerning Paul and his theology that is helpful in interpreting his other letters. Ultimately, this monograph is designed for all who are interested in coming to a better understanding of the basic tenets of the Christian faith, as understood by Paul. Accordingly, this book should prove beneficial to a wide variety of people, be they priests, lay persons, religious, or deacons. It will be particularly useful to those whose task, present or future, is to preach and / or teach the word of God. This publication will be a good resource book for bible study groups, religious study classes, and the like. Hopefully, it will help to deepen the reader's appreciation and comprehension of the Christian heritage.

I want to thank Raymond F. Collins and the other members of the editorial board of *Louvain Theological and Pastoral Monographs* for accepting this book for publication. I also wish to express my gratitude to all the professors of the Faculty of Theology at the Katholieke Universiteit Leuven and, in particular, to those in the Department of Biblical Exegesis, who have provided me with a sound theological background. To the staff of the Theology Library in Louvain and at St. Meinrad Seminary, I owe a debt of thanks for the many ways that they have assisted me. My most sincere thanks to the rector of St. Meinrad School of Theology, Eugene Hensell, O.S.B., for allowing me the time to research and write this book. I appreciate the financial assistance that I received from a Faculty Development Grant that has been generously supported by Lilly Endowment Incorporation. I also want to thank Terrence Merrigan, who throughout the writing of this book has proofed the text and offered valuable suggestions. Finally, I wish to express my deepest gratitude to my mother and father, who taught me about faith in Christ long before I studied it in the classroom or read about it in a theological textbook.

CHAPTER ONE

FREEDOM'S CHALLENGE

From the time the gospel of Jesus Christ was first proclaimed, those holding a position of leadership within the Church have often grappled with questions concerning religious freedom. Paul's Letter to the Galatians is the earliest extant Christian document in which such questions are addressed at some length.[1] In this epistle the apostle reflects upon Christian freedom in the midst of an intense discussion concerning justification and the Mosaic law. He summarizes the gospel message clearly and concisely in terms of liberty: "For freedom Christ has set us free" (5:1).[2] Paul's notion of Christian liberty must be understood within the context of love, God's love for humanity as manifested in the person of Jesus Christ and the believer's love for God and neighbor.

The Gospel Comes To Galatia

The events leading up to Paul's writing of Galatians are a story in themselves. In a remote corner of the Roman empire during the reign of Caesar Augustus (Luke 2:1), a teenage girl gave birth to a child destined to change the course of history.[3] Thirty years

[1] Although Paul also deals with issues pertaining to Christian liberty in Romans, the majority of exegetes assume that it was composed after Galatians. See, for example, Gerd Lüdemann, *Paul, Apostle to the Gentiles. Studies in Chronology* (Philadelphia: Fortress, 1984), p. 263.
[2] Biblical quotations are from the RSV.
[3] Paul comments on the significance of the birth of Jesus in Gal 4:4.

later this young woman's offspring, Jesus of Nazareth, went from village to village preaching the good news of liberation and charity. As a result of his bold new teaching Jesus eventually came face to face with the imperial power of Rome and was sentenced to death. Incredible as it may seem, a short time *after* his execution Jesus "appeared" to his disciples and commanded them to herald the gospel to the four corners of the earth (Matt 28:19-20). Thus began the greatest religious phenomenon the world has ever known, namely, the rapid spread of Christianity.[4] Within a short period of time communities centered around the risen Lord were established throughout the empire.

The extraordinary success of the Christian missionaries notwithstanding, the preaching of the gospel often encountered opposition. From the outset those belonging to the "Way" (Acts 9:2)[5] were frequently harassed and even put to death for their religious convictions.[6] Notorious for his antagonism towards the Christian movement was Saul of Tarsus (1:23), usually referred to in the New Testament as Paul, apostle to the Gentiles. In his early years this staunch defender of the Mosaic law attempted to eliminate Christianity. While hunting down the disciples of Jesus so that he might bring them bound to Jerusalem, "spiritual lightning,"[7] as it were, struck Paul. On the road to Damascus Paul had an immediate experience of the risen Christ, who commissioned him to proclaim the good news to the Gentiles. In one of the most dramatic turnarounds ever, the one who aspired to destroy Christianity became its foremost evangelist and theologian. Henceforth the apostle crisscrossed the various provinces of the Roman empire, planting the seeds of faith

[4] See Thomas Bokenkotter, *A Concise History of the Catholic Church* (Garden City, NY: Doubleday, 1979), p. 33. See also Henry Chadwick, *The Early Church* (London: Penguin Books, 1973), pp. 54-73.

[5] See Acts 19:23, 22:4, and 24:14.

[6] See, for example, 1 Thess 1:6. See Luke's account of the martyrdom of Stephen in Acts 7 and of James in Acts 12:1-2.

[7] This terminology has been used by Bokenkotter, *Concise History*, p. 29.

and nourishing Christian communities in places like Thessalonica, Philippi, Corinth, and Galatia.

A Roman World

The age in which the gospel came to Galatia was very different from our own. By this time the Roman empire, for all practical purposes, ruled the world and the emperor ruled the empire. Never before or since has one government controlled such a large geographical area for such a long period of time. At its height the Roman empire encompassed the entire land mass surrounding the Mediterranean and extended from southern Britain to southern Egypt, and from the Atlantic Ocean to the Euphrates River. Defended by more than 150,000 soldiers, the Roman empire brought together an estimated 54,000,000 people of all races and tongues under one political system.[8]

The conditions which existed in this vast domain in the middle of the first century greatly facilitated the spread of a new religious faith.[9] Inhabitants of the empire enjoyed the fruits of the Pax Romana.[10] Political unification and a strong military had brought about comparative peace and stability. Moreover, the empire was proud of its marvelous road system that included 50,000 miles of well-kept highways and of its pirate-free shipping lanes.[11] As a result, individuals, groups, and ideas, could travel the length and breadth of the Roman empire virtually unimpeded. The New Testament bears witness that on numerous occasions Paul and his companions journeyed by land and sea with relative ease.[12] A safe and extensive transportation system

[8] See Robert M. Grant, "Roman Empire" *IDB* 4, pp. 103-109, p. 104.
[9] See Kenneth S. Latourette, *The First Five Centuries* A History of the Expansion of Christianity, Vol. 1, New York, NY: Harper, 1937), p. 8.
[10] See Klaus Wengst, *Pax Romana and the Peace of Jesus Christ* (Philadelphia: Fortress, 1987), for a good presentation of this period of the Roman empire.
[11] See Bokenkotter, *Concise History*, p. 33.
[12] Although the Roman sea lanes were virtually free of pirates, there apparently was still some danger of brigands on the highways. See 2 Cor 11:26.

also enabled the empire to produce an excellent postal system. However, since the official postal system did not carry private correspondence, those desiring to mail personal letters had to make use of private carriers. As he did with the other epistles, Paul must have sent his own envoy to deliver Galatians.[13]

Within the confines of the Roman world the widespread use of an international language allowed people of different ethnic backgrounds to communicate freely. A good deal of the population in Galatia, as well as in all the eastern provinces of the empire, could converse in Greek when the apostle first traversed this territory. Hence Paul could preach the good news to the Galatians and later correspond with them in this language and have no difficulty in being understood.[14] As did the other New Testament authors, the apostle composed Galatians in the type of Greek known as "koine" (meaning common or ordinary). It was the spoken language "of the street," as opposed to the Greek equivalent of the "King's English," that is, the language used for more formal occasions.

Religion seems to have been the very basis of Roman society.[15] A vast array of pagan gods were honored by Rome and her provinces in the New Testament era. It was taken for granted that world domination by the city on the Tiber came about as a direct result of her determination to conform to the will of pagan deities. Therefore paying homage to the numerous gods and goddesses was not only considered a private matter but also a political affair of the state. An extremely important function of the government was to acquire and retain the favor of these divine beings. Political authorities thus made all the necessary arrangements to ensure that sacrifices were

[13] See Phil 2:25.

[14] See Luke T. Johnson, *The Writings of the New Testament* (Philadelphia: Fortress, 1986), p. 27. See Keith Branigan, "Hellenistic Influence on the Roman World" (John Wachr, ed., *The Roman World*. Vol. 1 (New York, NY: Routledge & Kegan, 1987), pp. 38-54.

[15] See Everett Ferguson, *Backgrounds of Early Christianity* (Grand Rapids, MI: Eerdmans, 1987), p. 139.

offered, temples were erected, and games were played on behalf of the gods. All major events were preceded by a religious ceremony. Before a military campaign or a political assembly would commence, for example, animal entrails were examined, flight patterns of birds were observed, and the stars were studied to discern the will of the gods concerning such endeavors.[16] Magic, astrology, and the practice of wearing protective charms were especially popular even among the educated.[17] Paul often encountered these pagan elements in the course of his travels[18] and on at least two different occasions was mistaken for being a god himself (Acts 14:12, 28:6)! The Galatians undoubtedly took part in heathen worship before they came to believe in the Lord Jesus (4:8).

Paul was not alone in assuming that idolatry goes hand in hand with immoral behavior.[19] To be sure lewd conduct and human cruelty cast a dark shadow over the entire Roman empire. Paul's list of unchaste practices in Galatians (5:19-21) illustrates the type of conduct that was all too prevalent at this time. Bloody gladiatorial contests, slavery, and inhumane forms of punishment like flogging and crucifixion all reflect the brutality of the empire. Furthermore, it was not uncommon for an unwanted infant to be left on a trash heap or in some other isolated place to die. As one might expect, Paul refers to the age in which he lived as "evil" (1:4).

[16] See Karl Christ, *The Romans* (Los Angeles, CA: University of California, 1984), p. 159. See Alan Wardman, *Religion and Statecraft Among the Romans* (Baltimore, MD: John Hopkins University, 1982) regarding the importance of religion in the Roman empire.

[17] See Johnson, *Writings*, p. 28. See William H. Stephens, "Religion," *The New Testament World in Pictures* (Nashville, TN: Broadman, 1987), pp. 192-267.

[18] See for example, Acts 16:16, 17:16, 19:19, 24.

[19] See Grant, "Roman Empire," p. 106: "In spite of legislation, and the complaints of moralists like Musonius Rufus and Seneca, the allusions in Martial's epigrams and the wall scribblings at Pompei reflect a way of life against both of which Jews and Christians vigorously protested." See Paul's argumentation in Rom 1:18-32.

A Counter-Cultural Gospel

There was a high degree of stratification in Roman society.[20] First and foremost stood the emperor, the highest authority in the land and the very personification of the Roman empire with all of its might and splendor.[21] Considered to have been called to his position by divine providence, the emperor was regarded as the head of the Roman religion and thus directly responsible for the relationship between the state and the gods. All who held positions of leadership understood their role in terms of carrying out his will. This supreme ruler was even spoken of in terms of "savior" and "lord" (Acts 25:26). Paul's teaching that Jesus Christ is Lord (1:3, 6:18) was undoubtedly viewed as a threat to the pre-eminent authority of the emperor and therefore bound to cause friction with the political authorities. Nero, the well-known tyrant infamous for his cruelty, was probably the emperor at the time that Paul composed Galatians and ultimately responsible for the apostle's martyrdom.[22]

Free persons in the Roman empire had basic rights and were thus in a category radically separated from that of slaves.[23] Those who were free and also had the good fortune to be Roman citizens were further protected by civil law. Non-citizens were merely subject to it. As a citizen of Rome one could not be punished without trial, had the right to appeal to Rome, and was free from degrading forms of punishment.[24] Paul was born a Roman citizen (Acts 22:28) and on several occasions reminded the local civil authorities of this fact. In light of his Roman citizenship, the apostle accused a Roman magistrate of illegal procedure (Acts 22:25) and later exercised

[20] See Ferguson, *Backgrounds*, p. 42.

[21] See Wengst, *Pax Romana*, pp. 46-47. See Fergus Millar, *The Emperor in the Roman World* (Ithaca, NY: Cornell University, 1984), pp. 46-47.

[22] See Edward Schillebeeckx, *Paul the Apostle* (New York, NY: Crossroad, 1983), p. 135.

[23] See Jerome Carcopino, *Daily Life in Ancient Rome* (New Haven, CT: Yale University, 1960), p. 52.

[24] See Ferguson, *Backgrounds*, pp. 48-49.

his legal right to appeal his case before the emperor (Acts 25:10-12). Nevertheless, in his letters the apostle was more apt to focus his attention on those privileges that accompany "heavenly citizenship" (Phil 3:20-21, Gal 5:1) than on those associated with any earthly kingdom. Paul's Roman citizenship would determine the manner in which he was eventually executed. Unlike his master who was crucified, the apostle was beheaded.[25]

Slavery was an ignoble feature of the ancient world.[26] It has been estimated that perhaps one in five persons in the Roman empire was a slave. A number of people were in bondage from the time of their birth, that is, they were born of slave women (4:22-25). Others were enslaved because they had been taken prisoner of war or pronounced guilty of some crime. Still others had become the property of their creditors.[27] Slaves had no legal rights and were subject to the absolute power of their owners. They were not allowed to own property or contract a legal marriage. Because of their work load and the harsh way in which they were often treated, slaves were not expected to live very long.[28] Paul frequently uses terminology in Galatians that is usually reserved for those under subjection (3:23, 4:3, 5:1). Although a freeman in the eyes of the Roman world, the apostle considers himself a "slave" of Christ Jesus (1:10). Surprisingly enough, Paul proclaims in Galatians that for those who are in Christ it makes no difference whether one is slave or free (3:26-28).[29]

[25] See Ferguson, *Backgrounds*, p. 49. Beheading was a swifter form of capital punishment than crucifixion and therefore considered a more merciful form of execution suitable for citizens.

[26] See W.G. Rollins, "Slavery in the New Testament," *IDB* Supplementary Volume, 830-832, p. 830. See Helmut Koester, *Introduction to the New Testament* (Philadelphia: Fortress, 1980), pp. 59-62

[27] See Ugo E. Paoli, *Rome: Its People Life and Customs* (New York, NY: David McKay, 1958), p. 120.

[28] See Ferguson, *Backgrounds*, p. 46.

[29] See Paul's Letter to Philemon regarding the slave Onesimus.

For the most part women in the Roman world had a subsidiary role to play in society. The head male of the family had the power of life and death over his wife, as well as over his children. It was the father who had sole authority to accept or reject a child at birth. He is the one who gave his daughter in marriage regardless of her wishes. Women were denied the privilege of citizenship and their testimony in a court of law was considered inadmissable. Since public justice existed only through the male, he alone was responsible for the offenses committed by his wife and children. A woman was expected to give up her religion for that of her husband and never vice-versa. Adultery committed by the wife was punishable by death while adultery committed by the husband was almost presupposed. By and large all Roman women were under masculine authority for their entire lives.[30] In such a male dominated world, Paul's declaration in Galatians that there is to be no distinction between male and female in the Christian community (3:28) was nothing less than revolutionary.

As many as five million Jewish people lived in the Roman empire at the time Paul authored Galatians. In addition to foreign domination, the poor economic conditions of Palestine had led to the dispersion of the chosen people throughout the Roman world. In many ways they separated themselves from the rest of Roman society and, as a result, were often the object of ridicule. Well known in antiquity for circumcising their male infants and not eating pork, the Jewish people proudly submitted themselves to the dictates of the Mosaic law. Their refusal to dine with non-Jews and to take part in the pagan cult led many Gentiles to believe that the Jewish people were anti-social.[31] Although Judaism was

[30] See Jane F. Gardner, *Women in Roman Law and Society* (Bloomington, IN: Indiana University, 1986), p. 5. See L.F. Cervantes, "Woman," *New Catholic Encyclopedia*, Vol. 14, pp. 991-997, p. 993.
[31] See Chadwick, *Early Church*, pp. 9-23.

but one officially recognized religion among many, it nevertheless held a privileged position. The Jewish people were dispensed from serving in the military and from worshipping Roman gods.[32] Judaism categorized all human beings into one of two highly distinguishable groups: those who were Jews and those who were heathens. Paul repeatedly calls attention in Galatians to specific Jewish customs (e.g., 2:12, 3:10, 5:2) and to those writings held sacred by Judaism (e.g., 3:11-12, 4:22-31). His insistence on the equality of Jew and Gentile within the Christian community (3:28) must have sounded sacrilegious to the Jewish ear.

The more we can "put ourselves into the shoes" of those who lived some 2000 years ago, the better we can appreciate the radical nature and powerful message of Galatians. Assuredly the age in which Paul first preached the gospel to the Galatians differed greatly from our own. Nevertheless on a more fundamental level there are some striking similarities between antiquity and the modern day world. Then, as now, people had to come to terms with a world in which there was alienation and injustice, suffering and death, sin and failure, deteriorating health and broken relationships, boredom and routine. Be it two thousand years ago or today, people yearn for happiness and a meaningful existence in an imperfect world. Proclaiming an invigorating gospel that dealt with such timeless issues, the apostle found receptive audiences in Galatia. Once the Galatians heard and responded to his version of the good news, they viewed themselves, their lives and their mortality in a totally different way. Paul's teaching remains just as revolutionary and forceful today as it was twenty centuries ago.

[32] See Eugene M. Boring, *Revelation*, Interpretation Series (Louisville, KY: John Knox, 1989), p. 12.

DESTINATION, DATE, AND AUTHENTICITY

Where in the World is Galatia?

Paul addresses his letter to the "churches of Galatia" (1:2), Christian communities whose exact location remains ambiguous. The name "Galatia" originally referred to a territory located on the central plateau of Asia Minor (present day Turkey), which was occupied by people of Celtic origin. In 25 B.C.E. this territory was incorporated into the Roman empire and designated as the Province of Galatia. The new Roman province encompassed a much greater area than the old country named Galatia.[33] In Paul's day the term Galatia could be used to indicate either Galatia proper, with its dominant Celtic population (North Galatian theory) or the larger Roman province of Galatia which was inhabited not only by the Celts in the North, but by other peoples farther south as well (South Galatian theory).

There are a number of factors which make the North Galatian theory the more attractive of the two. Paul did not always use the official name of a Roman province in his correspondence to designate a specific location.[34] Moreover, the contents of Galatians suggests that the epistle is being addressed to an exclusively or almost exclusively Gentile audience (4:8, 5:2, 6:12), one which would most likely be located in ethnic Galatia, where we know of no large Jewish settlements. Furthermore, the patristic writings are unanimous in their

[33] For a more detailed analysis of the history of Galatia, see for example, J.B. Lightfoot, *The Epistle of St. Paul to the Galatians* (Cambridge: Macmillan, 1979), pp. 1-17.

[34] In Galatians itself Paul clearly uses the name "Syria" (1:21) and "Judea" (1:22) in the regional sense, and not in the sense of a Roman province. Although Jerusalem belonged to the Roman province of Syria, Paul describes a journey he made *from* Jerusalem *to* Syria. Furthermore, in Gal 1:22 the apostle uses the regional name of Judea and not the Roman designation of Palestine. See, for example, J.A. Fitzmyer, "The Letter to the Galatians," *NJBC*, Vol. 2, pp. 780-790, pp. 780-781.

support of the North Galatian theory. Above all, it seems highly unlikely that Paul would address his readers as "Galatians" (3:1) unless they were all of the same race and language.

The term "Galatia" mentioned in Acts 16:6 and 18:23 is probably used in a similar fashion to that of Gal 1:2 and 3:1, namely, as referring to ethnic Galatia. In the light of the information contained in Acts 18:23 concerning Paul's return visit to Galatia during the third missionary journey, it seems that the apostle founded the churches of Galatia during his second missionary journey (Acts 16:6).[35] This hypothesis coincides with the data given in Galatians that Paul himself established the churches of Galatia and visited these Christian communities on two occasions before he wrote the epistle (4:13). It would therefore seem that Galatians was written sometime during Paul's third missionary journey. If that is the case, then Galatians was probably written about 55 C.E.[36]

By proclaiming the good news in rough and remote Galatia, a relatively sparsely populated region, Paul appears to have broken with his customary practice of preaching the gospel in great metropolitan areas. According to Acts 16:6-7, it was not his original intention to evangelize the mainland. On the contrary, the apostle simply intended to pass through Galatia and Phrygia to Bithynia, to the coast of the Black Sea and its many seaports. As he journeyed through Galatia, however, Paul was evidently forced by illness to discontinue his journey (4:14). While in Galatia he made the best of a bad situation and proclaimed the crucified Christ, professing that the benefits of Christianity come to those who have faith in the risen Lord.[37]

[35] Even though it is not explicitly stated in Acts 16:6 that Paul established a Christian community in the region of Galatia, the declaration in 18:23 that he strengthened the disciples implies that Paul in fact founded a Christian community on his first visit to Galatia (16:6).

[36] See for example, Hans D. Betz, *Galatians: A Commentary on Paul's Letter to the Churches in Galatia*. Hermeneia (Philadelphia: Fortress, 1979), p. 12.

[37] See Schillebeeckx, *Paul*, pp. 14-15.

Paul received a warm reception from the Galatians, who gladly nursed him back to health (4:14). Not long after his return visit the apostle composed our epistle (1:6).

The Letter to the Galatians was originally intended for specific groups of people in Asia Minor who lived in the middle of the first century. However, in view of the fact that the Church eventually incorporated this epistle into the canon of the New Testament, she has deemed that it have a much wider audience. Hence, Christendom finds the theological message of Galatians to have value not only for the churches of Galatia of long ago but also for Christian communities of all times and places, be it Louvain or Rome, New York or Los Angeles, Moscow or Peking.[38]

By Paul Alone

Paul is clearly identified as the author of Galatians in 1:1 and 5:2. Although one could possibly theorize that this letter was written by another person and ascribed to Paul, a number of factors make it difficult to defend such a position: (1) the autobiographical character of chapters one and two; (2) the many comments throughout the letter which indicate that a special relationship existed between the author of Galatians and its recipients, especially in chapter four (4:11-15, 4:18-20); (3) the strong feelings that are conveyed by the author (1:6, 8, 9, 3:1, 5:4, 5:21); (4) the condemnation of Peter (2:11); and, (5) the detailed information about the person of Paul (4:13-14, 6:17). All of these factors make it highly improbable that anyone other than Paul wrote Galatians.[39]

One might also conceivably postulate that, in view of Gal 1:2, the composition of this epistle was a joint effort between

[38] See "Dogmatic Constitution on Divine Revelation," 7: "God has seen to it that what he had revealed for the salvation of all nations would abide perpetually in its full integrity and be handed on to all generations."

[39] See F.F. Bruce, *Commentary on Galatians* NIGTC (Grand Rapids, MI: Eerdmans, 1982), p. 43: "Galatians is the most indubitably authentic of all the Pauline letters."

Paul and "all the brethren" who were with him.[40] However, the use of the first person singular 99 times (including the emphatic use of *egô* no less than 8 times) demonstrates that in fact the composition of Galatians was an individual effort by the apostle himself.

Paul implies that he made use of an amanuensis in writing Galatians (6:11).[41] One might wonder to what extent the scribe influenced the composition of this letter. However, since the vocabulary and the content of the final verses of Galatians (6:11-18) which Paul himself wrote, fit in perfectly with what precedes, it seems more than likely that the amanuensis acted strictly in the role of a scribe and had little, if any, influence on the actual composition of the letter. Moreover, considering the important theological issues that are addressed in Galatians, it seems highly improbable that Paul would have allowed anyone else to compose it in his name. We can rest assured that Paul, the Christian apostle of the first century authored Galatians.[42] That being said, it should be kept in mind that the epistle is included in the Sacred Scriptures. Consequently the Church assures us that its authorship ultimately lies with the Holy Spirit.[43]

An Uncorrupted Text

Even though we are on safe ground in affirming that Paul really composed Galatians, the question nevertheless must be asked if this epistle contains major interpolations. That the

[40] Richard N. Longenecker, *Galatians*, Word Biblical Commentary 41 (Dallas, TX: Word Books, 1990), p. lxi, for example, is open to this possibility.
[41] See 1 Cor 16:21 and Rom 16:22.
[42] See Werner G. Kümmel, *Introduction to the New Testament* (Nashville, TN: Abingdon, 1975), p. 251: "The assumption that Paul assigned to secretaries the formulations of his letters is impossible, in view of the frequent indications of breaks in the spoken word and the uniformity of the specifically Pauline language."
[43] See "Dogmatic Constitution on Divine Revelation," 11: "Those divinely revealed realities which are contained and presented in sacred Scripture have been committed to writing under the inspiration of the Holy Spirit...they have God as their author."

integrity of at least some of Paul's epistles has been doubted is nothing new.[44] Although most New Testament exegetes would deny that the integrity of Galatians is questionable, such a position is not unanimously defended.

J.C. O'Neill has gone against the prevailing trend by insisting that Galatians, as it now stands, was not written by Paul in its totality.[45] According to O'Neill, the problems that one encounters in trying to follow Paul's train of thought in a number of passages in Galatians can be resolved rather simply. Instead of postulating that the apostle was "confused and contradictory," O'Neill prefers to posit that Paul's original text was commented upon and enlarged by "Glossators" who attempted to explain difficulties and fill in the details.[46]

O'Neill's hypothesis regarding the integrity of Galatians creates more problems than it solves. If his thesis were valid, one would expect Paul's line of reasoning in so many passages in Galatians to be much easier to follow. However, this is not the case. Furthermore, the major New Testament manuscripts do not support O'Neill's hypothesis that a drastic rewriting of the original text took place. For these reasons we are dissatisfied with O'Neill's position regarding the integrity of Galatians.[47]

More recently, Joop Smit theorizes that Gal 5:13 - 6:10 was not composed by Paul.[48] According to Smit, this section of Galatians is so different from the rest of the epistle that it cannot have been authored by the same person. Smit's position is at best questionable. Although there may be some

[44] The many exegetes who have addressed the question concerning the integrity of some of Paul's authentic epistles include J. Murphy O'Connor, "Pauline Studies," *RBib* 92 (1985), pp. 456-464.

[45] See J.C. O'Neill, *The Recovery of Paul's Letter to the Galatians* (London: S.P.C.K., 1972), p. 8: "Nobody but Paul could have written Galatians, yet the Galatians we possess is not entirely Paul's."

[46] See O'Neill, *Galatians*, p. 86.

[47] Likewise, for example, J.W. Drane, *Paul: Libertine or Legalist? A Study in the Theology of the Major Epistles* (London: S.P.C.K., 1975), p. 93.

[48] See Joop Smit, *Opbouw en gedachtengan van de brief aan de Galaten*, (Nijmegen: Katholieke Universiteit Nijmegen, 1987), p. 124.

differences in content between Gal 5:13 - 6:10 and the rest of the letter, these differences are not great enough to warrant the conclusion that this section was written by one other than Paul. On the contrary, it is our position that this section of Galatians plays a vital role in Paul's overall strategy. Without a reasonable doubt, Paul authored Galatians as it now stands.

Pauline Identity

What can be said about this towering figure of early Christianity whose name appears in the opening of Galatians and twelve other epistles and about whom one-half of Acts is dedicated? The New Testament vividly portrays Paul as mystic, missionary, and theologian. As one who had an incredible experience of the risen Lord, the apostle is well qualified to be called a mystic.[49] As one who preached the good news of Jesus Christ throughout the known world, he is a missionary without equal. And as one who reflected upon and wrote about the significance of the Christ event, he is theologian *par excellence*.

The author of Acts refers to Paul as a "young man" at the stoning of Stephen (Acts 7:58) while the apostle describes himself as an "old man" near the end of his career (Philmn 9). He was probably born in the first decade of the Christian era in the well known city of Tarsus (Acts 21:39) and martyred about 65 C.E. in Rome. Paul was of Jewish heritage of the tribe of Benjamin, named after the most well-known personality of that clan (Saul). We are informed in Acts that the apostle had a married sister and a nephew who once saved his life (Acts 23:16). Paul was a tentmaker (Acts 18:3) and continued to support himself by this trade even while involved in his apostolic endeavors, though he did not have to do so (1 Cor 9:1-18).

[49] See Bernard McGinn, *The Foundation of Mysticism. Origins to the Fifth Century* (New York: Crossroad, 1991), pp. 69-74.

There is little information in the New Testament regarding Paul's physical appearance. His opponents in Corinth chided the apostle because "his letters are weighty and strong, but his bodily presence is weak, and his speech is of no account" (2 Cor 10:10). It is certainly possible that Paul had a recurring physical ailment (2 Cor 12:7-8, Gal 4:13-16). Interestingly enough, the apocryphal *Acts of Paul* describes the apostle as small in stature, bald headed, bowlegged, of vigorous physique, with a slightly crooked nose and full of grace.[50] Whatever his appearance, the apostle must have possessed a rugged constitution as he worked hard, travelled under adverse conditions in all kinds of weather, endured imprisonment and countless beatings, was often near death, received forty lashes less one on five occasions, was beaten with rods, stoned, shipwrecked and adrift at sea, and the like. (2 Cor 11:23-33).

The apostle was a man well suited for international travel. He apparently had a gift for languages, being fluent in at least three; Greek, Aramaic and Hebrew (Acts 21:40, 26:14). Paul's writings reflect both a classical Greek education and rabbinic training. The apostle functioned equally well in Jewish and Gentile circles, communicating just as freely with the educated as with the uneducated, with the rich as with the poor. He seemed very much at home in all the great cities of the Roman empire. One can easily make a case for supposing that God had good reason for choosing Paul to propagate the Christian faith.

Because of his intimate relationship with the risen Lord, the apostle sensed that it was no longer he who lived but Christ who lived within him (2:20). As a slave of Christ (1:10), Paul felt responsible to him and him alone. His youthful anti-Christian behavior notwithstanding (1:13), Paul understood his whole life in terms of a divine plan unfolding, even from the time he was in his mother's womb (1:15-16). Through Christ Jesus the apostle had received an abundance of God's gifts which he gladly placed

[50] See Bernard Pick, *Apocryphal Acts of Paul, Peter, John, Andrew and Thomas* (Chicago: Open Court Publishing, 1909), pp. 14-15.

at the disposal of those he served. Despite all setbacks and challenges Paul remained confident that God worked through him (2:8). The apostle had absolutely no doubt that the Father was glorified because of his apostolic endeavors (1:24).

Unquestionably *the* watershed experience of Paul's life was his encounter with the risen Lord on the road to Damascus. From that moment on, the apostle was consumed with one desire - to spread the good news of Jesus Christ. His life seemed to have consisted of one ongoing journey, one in which he would speak to anyone who would listen about how good God is and how beautiful life can be for one who believes in Jesus. His evangelical journey which began on the road to Damascus would eventually lead him down the road to Rome. In the capital city of the empire Paul bore witness to Christ in death as he had in life, with great courage and love.

An Enigma

His positive attributes notwithstanding, Paul remains an enigma. He was a devout and zealous Jew, yet had no qualms about possessing citizenship in a brutal and immoral empire. Although of noble birth, the apostle worked as a common laborer and continued to do so despite the demands of an exhausting ministry. He had a great enthusiasm for promoting Christianity but expressed that same enthusiasm in his previous attempts to destroy it. Paul's appearance did not command respect and he lacked skill as a public speaker (2 Cor 10:10, 11:6). Nevertheless his missionary efforts played a major role in the spread of the new Christian faith. Even though the apostle was capable of lofty intellectual insights, he never failed to provide sound pastoral advice for day to day living. Paul had his humble moments (1 Cor 15:9) but was not above boasting (2 Cor 11). He was dead serious about theological concerns yet possessed a good sense of humor (Philmn 11).[51] The apostle was capable of great

[51] In the letter to Philemon the apostle intercedes for his friend Onesimus, a runaway Christian slave whose name in Greek literally means "useful."

warmth and affection but was equally capable of biting sarcasm and vulgarity. He could be short and to the point[52] or long-winded and boring.[53] For all of his shortcomings, however, Paul was always driven by one motive, namely, to preach and uphold the gospel that had been entrusted to him.

The apostle's power to provoke is legion and nowhere is this more evident than in Galatians. Wherever he went, controversy was sure to follow. Although many welcomed Paul and his proclamation of the crucified Christ, this was certainly not a universal response. While some treated him as a heavenly messenger (4:14), others deemed him a "babbler" (Acts 17:18), insane (Acts 18:3), and worthy of death (e.g., Acts 23:14). As a result of his personality and revolutionary teaching he was often in trouble with the authorities. Consequently Paul suffered tremendously at the hands of Jew and Gentile alike, and had the scars to prove it (6:17).

A Good Friend

The New Testament provides ample evidence that the apostle had a special gift for making friends. He went beyond all cultural and religious boundaries by including among his friends Jew and Gentile, rich and poor, slave and free, male and female. As a frequent traveller, Paul was constantly meeting new people. Although a poor public speaker, Paul was undoubtedly a great conversationalist. He must have left new acquaintances spellbound as he preached his gospel of unconditional love and responsible freedom and related to them a plethora of incredible experiences ranging from his first encounter with the risen Lord to being lowered in a basket to escape the wrath of King Aretas (2 Cor 11:32-33). One can easily imagine the eyes of his listeners twinkling as the apostle

[52] See Paul's letter to Philemon.

[53] See Acts 20:6-12. At the celebration of the eucharist in Troas, the apostle spoke into the evening, past midnight until dawn! A young man named Eutychus "sank into a deep sleep as Paul talked still longer."

spoke to them of visions, revelations (2 Cor 12:1-4), and heavenly rapture (1 Thess 4:17). They must have stood in awe as Paul described for them the wonderful miracles that he had personally witnessed (e.g., 1 Cor 12:9-10, Gal 3:5).

The apostle's great capacity for friendship was probably bound up with his ability to inspire, encourage, and challenge. Paul's correspondence indicates that he was a good listener and attentive to the needs of others, having a special place in his heart for the poor (2:10). Cheerfully sharing what little he had with others, Paul's zest for life was contagious. He truly lived life to the fullest. His relationship with Christ seems to have provided him with an almost inexhaustible source of energy and love. The apostle's love for the Son of God was not only an intellectual affair but encompassed his entire being to the very depths of his soul. Paul's great love for Jesus made him bold and compelled him on more than one occasion to "throw all caution to the wind." The apostle celebrated with people when they were happy and empathized with them when they were sad. This first century missionary possessed the rare quality of living out his convictions, whatever the cost might be. In an age of doubt, he had certitude about himself and his mission in life. In a skeptical world, Paul had a keen awareness of the risen Lord and felt intimately bound to that divine presence through faith and love. And in a self-centered society, the apostle was "other" oriented.

Paul was a man of extremes and once he made up his mind about a subject he gave his whole heart, mind, and soul to it. On the flip side of this admirable quality, however, he could sometimes be "bull headed" and uncompromising. We know of at least one instance where this resulted in hard feelings, sharp words, and the parting of ways between the apostle and a fellow missionary (Acts 15:7-8). As spiritual and loving a person as Paul was, he was by no stretch of the imagination sinless. He struggled with his weaknesses (Rom 7:15). Paul attempted to change certain aspects of his life which he found distressing but was powerless to do so, even after long periods of intensive prayer (2 Cor 12:7-10). His failure to improve his situation probably made the apostle more compassionate in dealing with others who also may have had aspects of their lives which they would have liked to have changed but were also helpless to do so. Paul was not discouraged about his imperfections but realized that God often chooses the weak to carry out His will. After all, when good things occur as a result of His grace working through weak people, there is no doubt as to where the power originated - from God (2 Cor 4:7). Paul's faith assured him that Christ's love was stronger than any weakness he might have. The apostle may have felt helpless but he was not hopeless. With a confidence that only comes from divine prompting, the apostle was convinced that he possessed a great treasure within his own "earthen vessel" (2 Cor 4:7). His vulnerability and compassion must have allowed others to draw closer to this larger than life figure.

As Paul was convinced of the immanent return of Christ (e.g., 1 Thess 4:15), he had an intense awareness of the present moment and related to people as if there were no tomorrow. The apostle cared deeply for others and knew what it meant to love and to be loved (e.g., Gal 2:20, 1 Cor 13). He lived a truly liberated existence. It is no great mystery why Paul so readily developed such long and lasting friendships with so many people.

A Role Model

In many ways Paul was an exemplary Christian. His great love for Jesus Christ and God the Father permeates every letter that he wrote. The apostle's life bespeaks a deep and intense spirituality. If his letters are any indication of how Paul conducted his affairs, then he must have begun and ended all endeavors with prayer (e.g., 1 Cor 1:3-4, 16:23). The apostle had a vision of Christianity based on freedom and love. In light of that vision his eyes were ever attentive to the needs of local Christian communities, however remote they might be. Even in the midst of great trials and suffering Paul never despaired nor felt rejected by God but, in fact, detected a divine plan at work (e.g., Rom 8:28). He was well acquainted with the trauma that accompanies the recognition of one's own weaknesses in life. His conviction that divine strength comes from such powerlessness echoes the teaching of his master. The apostle's absolute trust in the one who called him to preach the gospel to the Gentiles enabled him to be at peace despite all adversity and hardship.

Paul never understood his apostolic ministry as a solo effort. On the contrary, the New Testament illustrates that the apostle was very much a "team player." He was always accompanied by fellow missionaries as he traveled throughout the Roman empire preaching the good news. Paul conducted his affairs with the help of an incredible number of co-workers. This is particularly evident in the last chapter of Romans where some twenty-nine of them are listed (19 males and 10 females). The Greek names which are found in Romans 16 are representative of the entire economic and social spectrum.[54]

The apostle frequently refers to his fellow companions in his letters, often by name, and extends greetings on their behalf. Galatians is no exception to this rule as the apostle makes reference to his colleagues in the salutation (1:2) and later specifically mentions Titus (2:3) and Barnabas (2:13). Paul's sense of collaborative ministry is not simply a matter of a personal style nor is it something imposed on him by necessity. Rather, it flows from his faith in Christ and his understanding of the gospel. The apostle's notion of team ministry is rooted in his image of the heavenly Father, namely, the God who gathers all people together, regardless of race or social standing.[55]

An Apostle

Paul was many things to many people, a missionary, a fellow Christian, a man of prayer, a good friend, and a role

[54] See Donald Senior, Convocation Address presented at St. Meinrad School of Theology, St. Meinrad, Indiana in May of 1991, pp. 4-6.
[55] See Senior, Convocation, p. 5.

model. In view of his initial comments in Galatians (1:1), however, he makes it abundantly clear that he considers himself first and foremost an apostle. Paul is God's personal envoy who has been given the task of preaching and defending the gospel.

Via God's activity through Christ Jesus, Paul received a divine revelation that changed his life forever (1:15-16). Like all of God's gifts, this mystifying religious experience was not given to Paul simply for his own sanctification but for the uplifting of the church as well (1 Cor 12). By means of this revelation of Jesus Christ, God Himself had commissioned Paul to proclaim the gospel to the Gentiles. Freed from the burden of his own sins, the apostle was now at liberty to direct his full attention towards the well being of others. As a result of his apostolic calling, he was obligated to both evangelize and to ensure that those who had responded to his preaching remained faithful to the "truth of the gospel" (2:5). In view of these responsibilities Paul felt duty-bound to communicate with those Christian communities under his care that were experiencing difficulties with matters of faith. The churches of Galatia fell into that category.

The Letter

In addition to the theological significance of Galatians, this epistle is also of tremendous importance for its historical value. The letter to the Galatians was composed by a man who, unlike the authors of the four gospels, was not a generation removed from the first followers of Jesus.[56] In fact, Paul was personally acquainted with Peter, James, a relative of Jesus, and John, son of Zebedee. Moreover, Paul was not only familiar with the early

[56] See Kümmel, *Introduction*, for the dating of the various books of the New Testament.

Christian communities, but he even established many of them. In reading the epistles of the apostle one has the impression of looking through a telescope into the distant past. With such a "telescope" one has the opportunity to observe the concerns and issues of some first century Christian communities.

Although personal in nature the letter to the Galatians does not simply function as private correspondence. Nor does it contain mere speculation about theological issues such as justification and moral conduct. Rather, Galatians must be understood as Paul's official response to problems that surfaced in those Christian communities which he himself founded. He addresses the Galatians in an authoritative capacity as a divinely called apostle, with all the rights and responsibilities that accompany such a supernatural appointment. As God's special ambassador Paul was worthy of the Galatians' trust and respect. He would have preferred to address them personally about the matters at hand but, since that was not possible, the apostle allowed the epistle to speak for him (4:20).

The letter to the Galatians indicates that Paul had all the marks of a good teacher. In conveying his theological message to the Galatians, the apostle did not rely on terminology that was normally reserved for esoteric academic discussions (even though the present day reader might be tempted to think so). On the contrary, he used simple ordinary language and referred to some commonly known facts in antiquity. He spoke of legal contracts (3:15), adoption rights (4:1-2), and the market place (3:13a) in a way that he was able to impress upon the Galatians the significance of the life, death and resurrection of Jesus.[57] Like a good teacher, the apostle sometimes repeated himself for emphasis (1:8-9, 2:16), explained an important point in a variety of ways (Gal 3-4), and asked rhetorical questions (2:17, 4:21). Perhaps most importantly, he was aware of the problems that those under his care were experiencing and responded to them firmly but with love.

[57] See also, for example, 1 Cor 3:10-15, 4:9, 9:24-27.

Like No Other

Galatians is truly a remarkable piece of Christian literature. Written in a passionate style, this emotional and intensely personal epistle puts the reader in contact with some of Paul's fundamental theological insights. What is more, it gives us a glimpse of the pre-Christian days of Paul (1:13-14), his first experience of the risen Lord (1:15-16), his early years as a missionary (1:17-24), and his initial contact with the other apostles (2:1-14). From the opening comments of Galatians to its conclusion, Paul wants to jolt and challenge the recipients of the letter, and persuade them to his way of thinking.

One very quickly realizes in reading Galatians that the apostle is infuriated. In contrast to his normal custom, Paul offers no thanksgiving on behalf of his readers after the opening salutation,[58] and in fact expresses dismay at their behavior (1:6). Furthermore, Paul makes a number of fiery comments throughout the epistle indicating that his emotions are running high. "O foolish Galatians! Who has bewitched you" (3:1)? "I am perplexed about you" (4:20)! The apostle's anger drives him to the point of making an almost obscene remark (5:12). Even the final comments of Galatians are those of anger and not of thanksgiving or final greetings (6:17). What were the circumstances which compelled Paul to write such a passionate letter, one containing a fair amount of autobiographical information, and dealing with fundamental elements of the Christian faith?

Chaos In Galatia

A short time after the apostle's most recent visit, the fledgling Christian communities in Galatia were in turmoil. Paul succinctly describes the cause of the confusion: "There are some who trouble you and want to pervert the gospel of Christ" (1:7). Apparently, these "troublemakers"[59] had

[58] See for example, Rom 1:8-15, 1 Cor 1:4-9, Phil 1:3-11, and 1 Thess 1:2-10.
[59] Henceforth, we shall use the terms "troublemakers," "agitators," "opponents of Paul," "adversaries of Paul," and "Judaizers," interchangeably.

unnerved the Galatians by insinuating that they had not yet fulfilled the necessary conditions for obtaining righteousness. The opponents of Paul had coerced the Galatians into believing that justification[60] could *only* be obtained by Gentiles who observed at least part of the Mosaic law (3:2, 3:5, 5:4), in particular those precepts concerning circumcision (5:2-3, 6:12), dietary practices (2:11-14),[61] and the observance of special days (4:10).

As we have noted, the churches of Galatia were founded by Paul himself and composed primarily of Gentile Christians. According to the agitators the apostle had preached to the Galatians a limited and incomplete version of the gospel so that he might attract more converts to Christianity (1:10). These troublemakers evidently accused him of neglecting to inform the Galatians that adherence to the Torah was a prerequisite for obtaining righteousness.

In all likelihood, the adversaries of Paul spoke of justification in terms of becoming a "child of Abraham" (3:7).[62] Only the person who is deemed an offspring of the patriarch participates in the blessing which was promised to Abraham and his descendants (Gen 12:3 and 18:18). Whether or not the Mosaic law was a factor in becoming a descendant of Abraham, that is, obtaining righteousness, was the main point of contention between Paul and his opponents.

There is, within Jewish tradition, a great reverence for the Torah. According to the rabbis, the Torah existed before creation. It is considered as God's most treasured possession, and something so special that the angels tried to keep it from being

[60] We use the expressions "to be justified" and "to obtain righteousness" synonymously.

[61] See Bruce, *Galatians*, p. 19: "Insistence on those [Jewish] food restrictions by some Christians is implied in his [Paul's] account of Peter's withdrawal from table-fellowship with Gentiles at Antioch."

[62] See Drane, *Paul*, p. 24: "The basic issue at question was not the Law and circumcision, but sonship to Abraham, and through him to God himself" (see Gal 3:29 and 4:7).

taken to earth. The people of Israel regard themselves as infinitely precious to God, and central to human history precisely because they have been given and have accepted the Torah.[63] There were marvelous examples of unwavering fidelity to the Mosaic law whereby faithful Jews preferred to suffer an agonizing death rather than ignore the commandments of the Torah (2 Macc 7).

The opponents of Paul undoubtedly appealed to the sacred traditions of Judaism in order to substantiate their claim that the apostle had preached a corrupt rendition of the gospel.[64] First of all, they probably referred to the Abraham narrative, focusing their attention on the fact that God had commanded the patriarch and his male descendants to be circumcised (Gen 17:10-13). Within the context of this epic, it is explicitly stated that whoever is not circumcised breaks the divine covenant and is severed from the chosen people (Gen 17:14). Secondly, the adversaries seem to have quoted Lev 18:5, a passage which contains one of the fundamental doctrines of Judaism. Here it is unequivocally affirmed that obedience to the commandments of the Mosaic law is a *sine qua non* of justification. Moreover, Paul's adversaries presumably cited Deut 27:26 in order to warn the Galatians that non-observance of the Torah results in a curse. Thirdly, the troublemakers may have referred to the two children of Abraham: Isaac, son of Sarah; and Ishmael, son of Hagar.[65] According to the agitators' way of thinking, those who failed to adhere to the law were likened to the offspring of Hagar, that is, illegitimate heirs of the blessing of Abraham, while those who observed the Torah were

[63] See Eugene B. Borowitz, "Judaism. An Overview," in EncyRel, 8 (1987) pp. 127-148, pp. 135-136, for a presentation of the rabbinic theory of Torah.
[64] The apostle's numerous citations from Scripture may indicate that the opponents of Paul had first used the sacred writings in support of their position.
[65] This hypothesis has been proposed, for example, by C.K. Barrett, "The Allegory of Abraham, Sarah, and Hagar in the Argument of Galatians," Johannes Friedrich, Wolfgang Pöhlmann, and Peter Stuhlmacher, eds. *Rechtfertigung. Fs. Ernst Käsemann* (Tübingen, Mohr, 1976), pp. 1-16, p. 9.

akin to the progeny of Sarah, namely, rightful heirs. Fourthly, the agitators seemingly pointed out to the Galatians that there were numerous ordinances in the Torah which dealt with morality. Hence, Paul's teaching of a "law-free" gospel gives the mistaken impression that immoral conduct is an acceptable form of behavior.

In addition to their Scriptural argumentation, the agitators may have also cast doubt on Paul's account of the gospel by calling into question his apostleship. They were convinced that Paul had learned of the gospel second-hand from the authentic apostles such as Peter, James, and John, "who were reputed to be pillars" (2:9).[66] In the eyes of the troublemakers, Paul was subservient to these real apostles. Considering their allegations against Paul, his opponents may well have gone so far as to say that he was in fact an "enemy" of the Galatians (4:16).

Virtually no specific information about the troublemakers can be found in the epistle.[67] With the exception of 5:10b Paul always refers to the troublemakers in the plural. His comment in 5:10b may indicate that the agitators were led by one unnamed individual. The apostle does not inform the reader where these agitators came from. Moreover, he never explicitly presents the contents of the "other gospel" that was taught by them. The majority of biblical scholars identify the troublemakers as "Judaizers," that is, one group of Jewish-Christians who were persuading the Galatians that the observance of at least some precepts of the law, in particular those concerned

[66] See Ernest Burton, *A Critical and Exegetical Commentary on the Epistle to the Galatians*. ICC (Edinburgh: T. & T. Clark, 1980), pp. liv-lv: The troublemakers depicted Paul as "a man who knew nothing of Christianity except what he had learned from the Twelve, and preached this in a perverted form."
[67] See Gal 1:7, 5:10, 12; 6:12-13. See John Bligh, *Galatians. A Discussion of St. Paul's Epistle* (London: St. Paul, 1969), p. 86, who is probably correct in speculating that although Paul never mentions the troublemakers by name, he nevertheless knew their identity, but did not "believe it wise to name his adversaries, for by doing so he would only encourage ambitious teachers who wish to get themselves talked about."

with circumcision, were necessary in order to obtain righteousness.[68] Inasmuch as Paul makes several references to Jerusalem (1:17, 18; 4:25, 26), mentions the men from James (2:12), and insists that he is not dependent on the apostles in Jerusalem (1:16 - 2:14), it seems that these Judaizers were in some way connected with Jerusalem.

Paul's Response

Paul reacts vehemently to the charges made against his gospel and his apostleship. Pulling no punches, the apostle condemns these troublemakers in the strongest terms (1:8-9) and wishes them bodily harm (5:12).[69] He accuses them of hypocrisy in regard to their preaching (4:17; 6:12-13), drawing attention to the fact that although the agitators persuade others to observe the law, they do not keep the law themselves (6:13). According to the apostle, his adversaries had ulterior motives for coercing the Galatians to accept circumcision (6:12). Moreover, Paul emphatically insists that it is the agitators who preach a perverted gospel (1:7) and that all who acquiesce in this "different gospel" (1:6) turn away from God, are severed from Christ, and have fallen from grace (5:4). Furthermore, the admonishing tone of the epistle and the harsh language that the apostle uses make it obvious that he is not one who "seeks to please others" (1:10).

Although Paul's anger is clearly visible in Galatians, one does, nevertheless, get the impression that he feels very close to its recipients. The apostle reminds the Galatians that it was he who had first preached the gospel to them (4:13), and they had received him "as an angel of God, as Christ Jesus" (4:14). Throughout the letter Paul addresses the Galatians in intimate

[68] See for example Franz Mussner, *Der Galaterbrief* (Freiburg: Herder, 1974) pp. 11-29.

[69] Paul does not appear to follow the advice that he gives to the Christians in Rome. "Bless those who persecute you; bless and do not curse them" (Rom 12:14).

terms (e.g., 1:11),[70] and on one occasion refers to them as "my little children" (4:19).[71] Moreover, Paul shares with the Galatians the deeply personal experience of his encounter with the risen Lord (1:15-16). Considering the affection that Paul has for the Galatians, he seems to be wondering how they, perhaps at the suggestion of the troublemakers, could even consider the possibility that the apostle had become their enemy by preaching to them the gospel which he had received from Christ himself (4:16).

At first sight the fiercely emotional tenor of Galatians may lead one to believe incorrectly that the apostle's arguments are haphazardly arranged and disjointed. However, a more in-depth examination reveals that nothing could be further from the truth. Paul's argumentation is systematic and well thought out, forming a cohesive whole. The letter to the Galatians can be divided into three major sections within which the apostle hammers out his plan of attack.[72] Paul's fundamental objective in the first section of the letter is to defend the authenticity of his apostleship, and gospel, and his independence from the apostles in Jerusalem (1:1 - 2:14). He then demonstrates in a variety of ways that one is justified by faith in Christ apart from the law (2:15 - 4:31). Finally, the apostle informs the Galatians of the consequences of his teaching, demonstrating that, properly understood, it does not promote a life of licentiousness (5:1 - 6:10). This threefold division is anticipated in 1:1-4 where Paul asserts that: (1) his apostleship is of divine origin; (2) salvation comes to us through Jesus Christ, who gave himself for our sins; and, (3) Christ died so that we might be delivered.

[70] Likewise, Gal 3:15, 4:12, 28, 31; 5:11, 13; 6:1, 18.

[71] Paul also refers to the recipients of his letters as "children" in 1 Cor 4:14, 1 Thess 2:11, and Phlmn 10.

[72] In general terms, we concur with a number of biblical scholars, most notably, Betz, *Galatians*, pp. 14-25, who suggest that the influence of Graeco-Roman rhetoric is readily seen in the structure of Galatians.

Concluding Remarks

In light of the fact that circumcision and the Mosaic law are no longer hotly debated issues in Christianity, one might wonder about the relevance of Galatians for the modern day believer. Properly understood, however, the theology of this epistle is not outdated but, in fact, proves to be as current as today's newspaper. Paul's argumentation concerning authority within the church, conflict within the Christian community, freedom, the equality of believers, legalism, libertinism, and the connection between Christianity and Judaism, continue to be as meaningful as ever in a Church that still struggles with such issues.

The Essence of Christianity

"What must one do to become and to remain a Christian?" This fundamental question that Paul was forced to address in Galatians confronts each new generation of Christians. As a result, the apostle's discussion of justification is still of tremendous value in the 20th century and beyond. Paul's argumentation in Galatians acts as a constant reminder to Christians of all times of the crucial importance of the believer's faith in Christ, and everything that this entails. Assuredly Galatians has a part to play regarding our salvation. Interpreted in conjunction with the other books of the Bible, the Church assures us that Galatians is error-free regarding issues pertaining to salvation.[73]

Galatians and Revelation

By incorporating Galatians into the New Testament, the church has officially recognized that it belongs to that body of

[73] "Constitution on Divine Revelation," 11: "Since everything asserted by the inspired authors or sacred writers must be held to be asserted by the Holy Spirit, it follows that the books of Scripture must be acknowledged as teaching firmly, faithfully, and without error that truth which God wanted put into the sacred writings for the sake of our salvation."

sacred literature which she considers as divine revelation. Along with the other books of the Bible, Galatians is believed to reveal the divine personality and the human identity. The belief that Divine revelation cannot be separated from liberation and love is attested to in Galatians. In this epistle the apostle informs us that it was out of love and for love (2:20, 5:13-14) that God revealed to him the essence of Christian faith, namely, that all who have faith in His Son Jesus, the fullness of revelation, would be liberated from the bondage of sin and death.

What is so attractive about sinful humanity that compels God to love us so much? Is it that He has created us in His image and likeness? Is it that opposites attract? Is it that we are so vulnerable and helpless? Ultimately, God probably loves us just because of who we are. In other words, He seems to say to the human race, "I love you because you are you." Whatever the case may be God sees "something special" in each and every human being, regardless of their physical traits, personality quirks, or moral conduct. His love makes us lovable (1 John 4:10). Cured from the blindness of sin, those who have experienced the depths of God's compassionate and merciful love are better equipped to see that "something special" in all of humanity. Without a doubt, God's unconditional and liberating love for humankind comes through loud and clear in Galatians.

The Challenge of Freedom

Paul's letter to the Galatians has had a rather troubled history. Already in New Testament times one inspired author issued a warning about Galatians and the rest of Paul's letters. "There are some things in them [Paul's letters] hard to understand, which the ignorant and unstable twist to their own destruction" (2 Pet 3:16). The passing of time has borne witness that this remark is certainly applicable to the apostle's argumentation in Galatians. Apparently the members of the Christian community to which the letter of James was addressed had a gross misunderstanding of Paul's doctrine of justification by faith alone (Jas 2:18-26, Gal 2:16). Moreover, Marcion, a second century heretic, focused a great deal of his attention on Galatians to support his anti-Jewish teaching. Furthermore, Martin Luther's well known commentary on Galatians contained the essence of Reformation teaching.[74]

Throughout the history of Christianity there have been "troublemakers" who have taken exception to Paul's version of the gospel. It is not at all surprising that, ever since the gospel was first proclaimed, questions have arisen regarding Christian liberty. To be sure, whenever individuals come face to face with divine realities, there will be uncertainty, challenges, and mistakes. The apostle provided much needed guidance for those under his care. He envisioned a church without borders, namely, a Christian community in which there is no racial discrimination, no social or economic distinction, and no gender bias. Christians of every age must wage battle against those forces which seek to frustrate the radical equality that we enjoy by virtue of our unity in Christ. Paul's discussion in Galatians concerning freedom and charity have challenged and will continue to challenge Christians of every era.

[74] See Martin Luther, *A Commentary on St. Paul's Epistle to the Galatians* (London, James Clark, 1953).

CHAPTER TWO

FREEDOM'S SPOKESPERSON (GAL 1:1-10)

The Proclaimer and the Proclaimed

Paul wastes no time in defending himself against the false accusations put forth by the troublemakers. He lets it be known in the first verse of the letter that he has every right to be called an authentic apostle. Disproving the malicious teaching of the agitators, Paul testifies that his authorization to preach the gospel did *not* stem from any human being nor did he receive it by means of a human intermediary. On the contrary, Paul insists that he was appointed an apostle by no one less than Jesus Christ and God the Father. In doing so he illustrates that he was not dependent on the other apostles for the contents of the gospel that he received. In fact, Paul implies that anyone who challenges his authority challenges God Himself! Speaking not only for himself but for his fellow companions as well (1:2), the apostle concludes his initial comments by offering a prayer on behalf of the members of the Christian communities in Galatia (1:3-5).

Similar but Different

The form of the salutation in Galatians (1:1-5) is strikingly similar to that found in other epistles of antiquity.[1] Paul follows the letter writing custom of his day by identifying

[1] See Calvin J. Roetzel, *The Letters of Paul. Conversations in Context* (Louisville, KY: John Knox, 1991), pp. 59-71, who compares and contrasts Paul's writings with other correspondence at this time.

himself and the recipients of the epistle in the opening of Galatians. Likewise, he conforms to the standard practice in the ancient world and accompanies such information with a greeting. This being said, the apostle has adapted traditional epistolatory convention in that he "Christianizes" the salutation.[2] Paul identifies himself and those to whom he is writing in light of their relationship with Jesus Christ (1:1-2), with whom he also associates the gifts of grace and peace (1:3). In the salutation of Galatians, as in the body of the letter, Paul focuses his attention on the person of Jesus Christ. The apostle's remarks in Gal 1:1-5 and throughout the epistle bear witness that he is "Christ-centered" in virtually every aspect of his life.

Although the salutation in Galatians has much in common with that of his other letters, Paul's initial remarks in this epistle are nevertheless unique in regard to content and feeling. He often describes himself as an apostle in the salutation of his letters, but it is only in Galatians that Paul also feels compelled to reveal the conditions in which his apostolic calling took place. Moreover, it is in Galatians alone that Paul refers to his fellow missionaries as "*all* the brethren who are with me" (1:2).[3] Furthermore, the apostle addresses his letter to Christian communities that are located in a region as opposed to a specific city in the salutation of Galatians.[4] Finally, it is only in this epistle that Paul concludes his opening prayer with "Amen."[5] As we shall later see, all of these points have a role to play in the apostle's argumentation.

From the outset, the sharp tenor of the epistle is immediately evident. Paul has scarcely identified himself before he

[2] This occurs in his other correspondence as well. See e.g., Rom 1:1-7 and 1 Cor 1:1-3.
[3] Compare Gal 1:2 with 1 Cor 1:1, 2 Cor 1:1, Phil 1:1, 1 Thess 1:1.
[4] See for example, 1 Cor 1:2: "To the church of God which is at Corinth."
[5] Paul usually concludes his prayers at the *end* of his letters with the term "Amen." See Rom 16:27, 1 Cor 16:24, Gal 6:18, and Phil 4:20.

feels obliged to qualify his apostolic authority (1:1). Strangely enough he affirms his apostleship with a rebuttal (not once but twice), that is, he relates to the Galatians how it was *not* bestowed upon him. Moreover, Paul simply directs his remarks to the members of the churches in Galatia. In itself this is not significant but when compared to the salutations of his other letters it strikes one as being a rather "cold" greeting.[6] The apostle usually refers to the recipients of his epistles in a warm and complimentary fashion, for example, as "beloved of God" (1 Thess 1:4) and "those sanctified in Christ Jesus" (1 Cor 1:2). However, such flattering phraseology is completely lacking in Galatians. The somber and curt salutation in this epistle indicates that Paul is well aware of the seriousness of the situation in Galatia and has not taken it lightly.

Paul's Christian Identity

The first five verses of Galatians contain a wealth of information concerning Paul's self understanding. Unequivocally his fundamental relationship in life is with Jesus Christ, the Son of God. Before he came to believe in Jesus as his Lord and savior, the apostle now recognizes that he was a sinner who belonged to an evil age and was in need of deliverance. Paul speaks of Jesus' salvific death in a personal fashion - Christ died for *our* sins (1:3-4). Likewise the apostle discusses Christ's death in terms of his own liberation (1:4). As fundamental and important as is his relationship with Jesus, it is not exclusive but rather the foundation of all others.

Because of his intimate unity with Christ, Paul discovered new meaning in relating to God as Father. Inasmuch as he has

[6] See William Hendriksen, *New Testament Commentary. Exposition of Galatians* (Grand Rapids MI: Baker, 1969), pp. 29-33.

[7] See John L. McKenzie, "Abba," *Dictionary*, p. 1: Aramaic epistles indicate that the term Abba was a familiar address used by children in referring to their father.

received the Spirit of the Son, the apostle can now address God in a warm and affectionate way, namely, as "Abba!" (4:6)!"[7] The importance of his relationship with the Father through Jesus is reiterated again and again throughout the epistle. Indeed it was the Father's will that the apostle be saved from his sins (1:4). Paul's apostleship ultimately originates with the Father, who called this former enemy of Christianity through grace and revealed the risen Lord to him (1:15-16). The very One who raised Jesus from the dead authorized the apostle to preach to the Gentiles (1:1). Paul's spontaneous prayer illustrates that his main concern is with the Father's glory, and not his own (1:5, 10).

The communal dimension of the apostle's faith is evident in the salutation of Galatians. Paul identifies himself closely with his companions and with those to whom he is addressing his remarks. Together they are all children of God (1:1, 3) and share in the belief that Jesus is their Lord and savior (1:3-4). The one who called Paul through grace also called the Galatians to a new life in Christ (1:1, 6, 15). Like Paul the Galatians have benefitted tremendously from Christ's redemptive act and have been set free from that which had previously enslaved them (1:4). United with his fellow workers in prayer, the apostle implores God to bestow His heavenly gifts of grace and peace upon the Galatians (1:3). Paul acknowledges that the same divine presence which dwells in him abides in all believers by referring to his co-workers, the Galatians, and all who belong to the Christian family as brothers and sisters in the Lord (e.g., 1:3-4, 11). The members of this blessed family are bonded together not by blood but by their faith in Jesus, their mutual possession of the Spirit (4:6), and their common unity with Christ (3:26).

A Bona Fide Apostle

As he does in his other epistles (e.g., 1 Cor 9:1-23), Paul argues a great deal in Galatians about his apostolic status.

Consequently one sometimes has the impression in reading Paul's writings that the only person who honestly believed that he was an authentic apostle was Paul!

There is not the slightest indication in the opening verses of Galatians, or elsewhere, that Paul is undergoing any sort of "identity crisis" as a result of the opponents' attack on his apostolic status. On the contrary, Paul gives the impression of one who has the utmost confidence in his Christian vocation. He informs the Galatians that his apostolic appointment can only be understood in view of Jesus Christ and God the Father, from whom his authority originates.

Apparently the troublemakers in Galatia had established their own criteria for what constituted a legitimate apostle. According to their way of thinking, a true apostle was one who had actually accompanied Jesus from the time of his baptism unto his death, had "seen" the risen Lord (Acts 1:21-22) and had been instructed by him to proclaim the gospel (Matt 28:18-20). If the agitators' criteria for apostleship were valid, then Paul would have flunked the test.

Paul, however, has a somewhat different understanding of what constitutes an authentic apostle. As far as he is concerned, a legitimate apostle is one who has been specifically chosen by God for the task (1:15), has had an immediate experience of the risen Lord (1:16), and has been delegated by the glorified Christ to preach the good news (1:1, 15-16). Using such criteria, Paul has passed the apostolic test with flying colors.

Paul points out to the Galatians that even such distinguished personalities as Peter, James and John recognized that his apostolic status and his authority to herald the gospel were genuine (2:7-10). Although he is well aware that others were apostles before him (1:17), Paul refuses to consider himself inferior to them (2 Cor 12:11). In fact, he boasts that he worked harder than any of the original apostles (1 Cor 15:10)!

Paul has every assurance that he was "called by the will of God to be an apostle of Christ Jesus" (1 Cor 1:1). In light of his apostolic calling, Paul views himself as an "ambassador of Christ" (2 Cor 5:20), "God's co-worker" (1 Cor 3:9), and a "steward of the mysteries of God" (1 Cor 4:1). When he preached the gospel to the Gentiles, such as the Galatians, Paul performed the miraculous signs and wonders that accompany a true apostle (2 Cor 12:12, Gal 3:5). He considers those who have responded to his teaching of the good news as the "seal" of his apostleship (1 Cor 9:2). Without a shadow of doubt the apostle is convinced that he is God's personal envoy. God Himself entrusted Paul with the gospel of freedom and commissioned him to proclaim the good news to the Gentiles (1:16). As the members of the Christian communities in Galatia were predominantly Gentiles, the apostle should be considered as God's personal representative to them.

In a similar fashion, most churches in contemporary society are composed of primarily Gentile Christians. Consequently Paul should also be regarded as God's special envoy to present day believers. Assuredly God often "speaks" to human beings in the most unexpected of ways - like through the voice of a fiery Jewish Christian from far away Tarsus. The almighty continues to communicate his message of liberty and love to us through the writings of this controversial figure.

The Divine Message

The term "apostle" is derived from the Greek word *apostolos*, meaning "one who is sent," "a messenger."[8] Paul was sent by God to the Gentiles in Galatia with a message of good news. What exactly was the content of the apostle's missionary preaching?

First, last, and always, Paul proclaimed the person of Jesus Christ, the Son of God. Interestingly enough the apostle paid little attention to details about the earthly career of Jesus. If we

[8] See Erich von Eicken, et al., "*apostellô*," *DNTT*, I, pp. 126-137.

had to depend on Paul's letters to learn about the historical ministry of Jesus, we would have been left in the dark about his miracles, parables, and much of his teaching. The apostle was content with simply mentioning Jesus' birth (4:4), his Davidic ancestry (Rom 1:3), the Last Supper (1 Cor 11:24-26), and his betrayal (1 Cor 1:23). Paul placed an overwhelming amount of importance on the death and resurrection of Christ.[9] The very heart of the apostle's proclamation of the gospel was that Jesus Christ, the one who had been crucified, has been raised from the dead. Paul was much more concerned with the significance of the Christ event than with basic facts about the life of Jesus.

Where Sin Abounded Grace Abounded All the More

In order to appreciate better the liberating power of the gospel that the apostle proclaimed when he first arrived in Galatia, one must be well acquainted with his understanding of unredeemed humanity. Within this context it is noteworthy that Paul makes a connection between sinful humankind and Adam, the one with whom the first sin is associated (1 Cor 15:22, Rom 5:18-19). A great deal of information about the devastating and divisive effects of sin can be gleaned from the biblical narrative of Adam and Eve (Gen 2-3).

Paradise Lost

In the beginning God created male and female in His own image (Gen 1:26). Like all human beings who followed them, Adam and Eve had "something" within them eternal and infinitely precious, "something" newer than the dawn

[9] See e.g., Rom 3:25, 1 Cor 1:23, and 2 Cor 5:14-15. See James D.G. Dunn, *Unity and Diversity in the New Testament* (2nd ed. London: Trinity, 1990), pp. 21-26, who gives a good presentation of the kerygma of Paul.

and older than the stars, more majestic than the mountains and more expansive than the oceans. Indeed the very source of beauty, truth, and peace resided in their very being. They were a masterpiece of God's creation, enjoying love and freedom.

Adam and Eve were given free rein in the Garden of Eden, with but one exception. They were not allowed to eat of the "tree of the knowledge of good and evil" (Gen 2:16-17). After some time had passed the serpent assured Eve that she and her husband would "be like God" if only they would disregard His explicit command (Gen 3:5). Because of the serpent's suggestion, Eve began to question her own identity and failed to trust the One who had created her. She and her husband were already "like God," that is, made in His divine likeness, but they failed to realize it.

Eve seems to have thought that she was "missing out" on life and so she disobeyed God and ate the forbidden fruit. Sin had entered the world and immediately began to spread. Eve invited her spouse to ignore God's command and likewise eat the tempting fruit (Gen 3:6). It was only then that the first couple realized that they were naked (Gen 3:7).

Whereas Adam and Eve had been completely open with God and each other, concealment was now foremost in their minds. Indeed, love reveals while sin conceals. This troublesome couple hurriedly fashioned some crude garments for themselves because they were ashamed of their nakedness (Gen 3:7). Then Adam and Eve made a futile attempt to hide from God (Gen 3:9). They were both afraid (Gen 3:10). When God questioned Adam about his disobedience, he did not admit guilt nor express sorrow but tried to escape punishment by pointing the finger at Eve (Gen 3:11-12). The sin against God caused friction between the first two human beings.

Adam and Eve were exiled from the garden of Eden and warned that they were in for a life of hardship and sorrow, ending ultimately in death. Every Ash Wednesday the words that God spoke to Adam are repeated: "You are dust and to dust you shall return" (Gen 3:19). The first couple spent the rest of their lives living under accursed conditions (Gen 3:16-19).

Left unchecked, sin multiplied and spread, contaminating all that it touched. Although Adam and Eve committed but a seemingly minor act of disobedience, their son committed murder (Gen 4:8). The descendants of that first couple carried on in the same sinful tradition. Stories of pride, betrayal, hate, rape, mass murder, and the like, are all recorded in the Old Testament (e.g., Gen 34). The history of sin continues. One need not go any further than the daily newspaper to realize that sin remains a dreadful reality in the world.

Original Sin

There is a great similarity in the sin of Adam and Eve and every other sin. Every sin contains elements of disobedience, pride and selfishness. Sin never journeys alone, its travel companions are fear, guilt, suffering, and unhappiness. Generally speaking the effect of every sin is the same: separation - separation of people from God, separation of people from people, and separation of people from themselves (that conflict between good and evil which takes place within each of us). Sin prompts human beings to concentrate exclusively on their own well-being, to the neglect of others. It persuades one to mistrust divine providence. In the final analysis, sin is the very antithesis of love and freedom. The ultimate consequence of sin results in the great curse of humanity; sin swallows up its victims in death.

In view of what has been said, it seems that the first sin of Adam and Eve was, so to speak, the "original sin" while all other sins are "copies." Original sin continues to affect us in a most radical way. As a result of its devastating effects we live in a sin-filled world where, all things being equal, we are prone to sin. Even more tragically, we live in a world where death awaits us all.

Trapped by Sin

Paul's writings contain the most comprehensive theology of sin in the New Testament.[10] He contends that "all have sinned and fall short of the glory of God" (Rom 3:23). According to Paul's way of thinking, it was through Adam's disobedience that all were made sinners (Rom 5:19). Likewise, the first person's transgression led to the condemnation of all humanity (Rom 5:18). Death came into the world through sin and since all have sinned then all die (Rom 5:12). Sin is a dominating force (Rom 6:14) that transforms the sinner into a slave. Left to one's own resources, one is powerless to escape from it. The apostle considers sin as rebellion against God (Rom 8:7) and all who partake in it will come to a dire end (Rom 2:9).

Perhaps the most terrifying aspect of sin is that which is associated with judgment day. Paul teaches that all human beings will be held accountable before God on the last day for their behavior (e.g., Rom 2:6). Those who are steeped in sin will experience a negative judgment. When it comes to discussing punishment for sin, the apostle does not go into great detail but simply refers to "the wrath of God" (e.g., Rom 2:8, 3:5).[11]

Paul's understanding of unredeemed humanity does not make for light reading. In the eyes of the apostle, seemingly everything that is wrong with the world can be attributed to sin. All of our troubles, divisions, difficulties, and even own own mortality are a consequence of it. As difficult as it may be to dwell on such a heavy subject, it is, nevertheless, absolutely necessary to reflect upon the nature of sin. Unless one is truly aware of one's sinful condition and one's helplessness in the face of sin, one can never fully comprehend the good news of Jesus Christ.

[10] See McKenzie, "Sin," *Dictionary*, pp. 817-821, p. 820.

[11] Herman Ridderbos, *Paul. An Outline of His Theology* (Grand Rapids, MI: Eerdmans, 1975), pp. 91-158, presents a rather in-depth examination of the Pauline doctrine of sinful humankind.

The Miracle of Love

Paul brought some great news to the Gentiles in Galatia. Humanity does not have to cope with sin on its own. God has revealed to us that He is not uninterested, uncaring, nor unconcerned about the human condition. In spite of the sinful history of the human race (e.g., Rom 1:18 - 3:18, Gal 1:4) our heavenly Father did not turn his back on humanity nor reject those whom He has created in His own image. Rather, He entered into our world more fully. God sent His only begotten Son into the world so that humankind might be delivered from the tragic effects of sin (4:4). Our freedom was obtained at a great price, namely, the death of Christ (1:4). It is a rare enough occurrence that an individual will die for a good person but Jesus died for us while we were still sinners (Rom 5:7-8). Thus God has demonstrated that His love for humanity is supreme and unconditional. He loves us for our own sake. His love for us does not depend on our love for Him. Despite the corrupt past of the human race, God is free to love.

Divine love assures us that we are not alone. In and through Jesus, God identifies in a most radical fashion not only with those who are victims of oppression, injustice, and maltreatment, but with all of suffering humanity as well. In and through the passion and death of Jesus, God identifies in a very personal way with those who suffer profound loss, with those who suffer perhaps the greatest conceivable human loss - the loss of a child. In the Father of the suffering Lord we see, as it were, the image of ourselves. Moreover, if we take His divine Fatherhood seriously, we ought to acknowledge that in and through the suffering of all who are united with His Son Jesus, God identifies with the frailty of the human race.

As a result of Jesus' salvific death and resurrection, all who believe in him, confess that he is Lord, and are baptized, are saved from their sins. Paul lets it be known that Christian believers are intimately bound to the Son of God. Their unity with Christ has tremendous ramifications. As God has entered the world in a remarkable way through Jesus, Christians enter the "divine world" of our heavenly Father in an extraordinary way through Jesus.[12]

Because of their solidarity with the Lord, those in Christ are also united with other believers.[13] The apostle insists that one's unity with Christ could only be achieved as a member of a Christian community, which he referred to as "church" (1:2). There was no such thing as purely individual adherence to Christ.[14] Christianity by its very nature has communal dimensions.

By means of a profession of faith and baptism, one entered the Christian community and began a new life in Christ. Those who entered this community of faith underwent such a transformation that they could be thought of in terms of being born again, that is, born free. By virtue of their unity with Christ they became, in a very special way, children of God. Just as children in a family reflect certain aspects of their parents in a unique fashion, so each member of the Christian family reflects certain aspects of their heavenly Father in a particular manner.

Life within the Christian community was an entirely new mode of living. It was based on a strict morality, mutual love and the sharing of goods. An intensive life of prayer centered around the celebration of the eucharist was also considered a vital part of Christian living. The eucharist was understood as a liturgical meal which the Lord himself had initiated before his passion and death (1 Cor 11:23).[15] Paul firmly believed that Jesus became present in the consecrated bread and wine.

[12] The author of the Fourth Gospel portrays this in a beautiful fashion by professing that Christians find themselves in the "bosom of the Father" through Jesus (see John 1:18, 13:23).
[13] It is within this context that the apostle speaks of Christians as belonging to the "body of Christ" (1 Cor 12:12).
[14] See Bernard McGinn, *The Foundations of Mysticism. Origins to the Fifth Century* (New York, NY: Crossroad, 1991), p. 63.
[15] See McGinn, *Mysticism*, p. 63.

In fact, the apostle taught that the very body and blood of the Lord were to be found in these sacred elements (1 Cor 11:27). Whenever Christians partook in the Lord's supper they were reminded that Jesus poured out his life in their behalf. Consequently every time the celebration of the eucharist took place, Christians were confronted with a challenge - not only to love God unconditionally as He has loved them but also to love others without reservation. With this in mind, Paul urges his converts "to love your neighbor as yourself" (Gal 5:14, Lev 19:18).

Happily, Christians can rest assured that on the last day they will rise from the dead (1 Thess 4:13-18, 1 Cor 15:51-57). By virtue of their unity with the Lord, those who have been faithful to their Christian commitment have nothing to fear on judgment day. Paul did not envision the day of the Lord as arriving sometime in the dim and distant future. Rather, the apostle was absolutely convinced that within his own lifetime Jesus would return in all of his splendor and glory (1 Thess 4:15, 1 Cor 15:51). Because of this conviction of Paul's, one detects a sense of urgency in the apostle's writings. His letters lead one to believe that the time for unconditional love of God and neighbor is *now*. There may be no tomorrow. Although the second coming of Christ may not soon take place, we cannot be so confident that we will not soon return to him! The sense of urgency remains. We should live every day of our Christian existence as if there were no tomorrow. One day there won't be.

Christians find salvation in the arms of our heavenly Father via the outstretched arms of Jesus on the cross. As members of the Christian community we experience the tremendous love of God in a wonderful manner. So often Christianity is thought of as something which adds burdens to an already burdensome life. Nothing could be further from the truth. Properly understood, Christianity is liberating. The very mark of a Christian is freedom. Those who are united with Christ have been released from the burdens of sin, guilt, and divine punishment. Because of Jesus Christ we look at God in a new light. He is not a distant uninvolved spectator but a loving compassionate Father concerned with our well-being. Because of Jesus Christ we also view ourselves and others in a different light. We and our fellow human beings are considered so precious by God that He sent His Son into the world for our salvation. This should always be kept in mind in our daily lives.

The fantastic news is that good has triumphed over evil. All who are united with Christ benefit from the liberating victory that God has won through the life, death, and resurrection of Jesus Christ. Divine love has overcome sin and its tragic consequences. A fundamental aspect of Paul's teaching is that Jesus' salvific death has nullified the divisive and destructive effects of sin. Even death has been swallowed up in this divine triumph (1 Cor 15:54-55). These reflections on the significance of God's work in Christ are summarized in the salutation of Galatians. The theme of these opening verses is that all comes together in Christ Jesus.

What God Has Joined Together...

Jesus Christ, Our Lord

Paul initiates his discussion in Galatians in the same way that he concludes it, with a reference to Jesus Christ (1:1). The very name of Jesus (literally "the one who saves")[16] reveals the salvific character of his divine mission. It is through Jesus alone that salvation comes. Interestingly enough, Paul's first comments in Galatians regarding the significance of Jesus' death are presented in terms of freedom. Jesus is the one who delivers us from the destructive and divisive effects of sin (1:4).

[16] See Matt 1:21.

Jesus is the very embodiment of the conciliatory nature of the gospel. In his person God and humanity come together. While Paul associates sin with division and discord, he associates Jesus with harmony and peace. Sin had previously kept the Galatians at a distance from God and one other. Having responded favorably to Paul's proclamation of the gospel, however, they were now intimately bound to the Father and to each other because of their unity with Jesus Christ. For those who are in Christ, God is Father, Jesus is brother, and fellow Christians are brothers and sisters in the Lord. Within this family of faith there is no distinction of race, economic status, or gender (3:28). All are one in Christ Jesus.

The word Christ (*Christos*) is not the "family name" of Jesus but a Greek rendition of the Hebrew word "messiah", meaning "anointed."[17] There was a hope in Judaism that a Messiah would come and liberate the chosen people from all oppressive powers.[18] Christians believed that Jesus was the Christ, the one who saved them from the oppressive power of sin and death. Already in New Testament times the term Christian came to be used as a designation for the followers of Jesus Christ (Acts 11:26, 26:28, 1 Pet 4:16). All Christians were united in the belief that the crucified Jesus has been raised from the dead. Whenever Christians call to mind the resurrection of the Lord (1:1), it rekindles within them the great hope that, as Christ Jesus has been raised from the dead, they too will be raised on the last day. Until then, all Christians have a tremendous responsibility to live up to that sacred name which they bear.

Paul's reference to Jesus as "Lord" (1:3), a term sometimes used in connection with the Roman emperor (Acts 25:25-26), was probably a more meaningful designation to the non-Jewish

[17] See Karl H. Rengstorf, "*Christos*," *DNTT*, 2, pp. 334-343.

[18] See R.J. Zwi Werblowsky, "Jewish Messianism," *EncyclRel* Vol. 9, pp. 472-477, p. 472: It was "the Jewish belief that the ultimate salvation of Israel, though wrought by God, would be presided over or realized by a descendant of the royal line of David."

Christians of Galatia than was "Christ." At the time of their baptism, the Galatians solemnly professed that Jesus is Lord (Phil 2:11) and thereby promised to make their relationship with him the number one priority in life. They were convinced that their dreams of happiness and fulfillment were wrapped up in Jesus Christ. All relationships were henceforth to be understood in the light of him. Every major decision was to be made within the perspective of their life-long commitment to Christ. Money, earthly power, status in society, and everything else, took a back seat to this fundamental Christian commitment. In effect the Galatians had promised that, in good times and in bad, for better or for worse, they would live a life which reflected their conviction that Jesus is Lord.

Many Christians in antiquity and throughout history have been forced to endure great suffering and even death because of such a promise (e.g., 1 Thess 1:6). Sometimes it seems that the enemies of Christianity have a better grasp of the radical nature of the belief that Jesus is the sole Lord of one's life than do Christians. Those who are hostile towards Christianity often appear to have a deeper awareness of the fact that there is only room for one king in a person's heart, and all that this implies (Matt 2:1-18, John 19:12-16). Whatever may be the case, all who have pledged to follow in the footsteps of the Lord must keep in mind that Jesus traveled through the "valley of the shadow of death" before he was glorified. As Christians, we are challenged to boldly go where Christ has gone before.

Thy Will Be Done

Paul speaks of Jesus' salvific death in connection with God's will (1:4). It was not by chance that Jesus died on the cross and saved humanity from sin. The crucifixion of Jesus was not just a matter of his being in the wrong place at the wrong time. Nor was the redemptive nature of his death simply a case of God making the best of a bad situation. On the contrary, God sent His Son into the world for the explicit purpose of saving humankind from the catastrophic effects of sin. Paul's reflections in Gal 4:4-5 indicates that he associates God's will with the well-being of humanity.

Unfortunately there has often been gross misunderstanding about the "will of God." It seems that the only time we hear of God's will is in times of death and tragedy. "God's will be done," a woman cries out when she discovers she has cancer. "God's will be done," a man prays when he suffers the loss of a loved one. Rarely indeed do people associate God's will with a festive occasion such as a wedding, the birth of a child, or an anniversary. One sometimes has the impression in hearing people converse that the will of God is a cold law and that the Almighty likes nothing better than to watch people suffer. Nothing could be further from the truth. God's will is that we be outrageously happy in this life and the life to come. It is His desire that we find true happiness and live life to the fullest.

As loving parents want only the best for their children, so too our heavenly Father wants only the best for us. Nevertheless, God has given us a free will and He respects that free will immensely. As much as God wants us to be happy, He allows us the freedom to choose otherwise. Although on occasion it might sometimes seem to the contrary, God is always concerned with our well-being. Fortunately, God does not always let us have our way. Our desires are frequently like that of an infant who wants to play with an electrical outlet. As loving parents refuse their child such an activity because they know the dangers involved, so too our heavenly Father sometimes refuses our requests because He knows the dangers involved. A simple childlike trust in God is necessary to believe that our heavenly Father knows what is best for us. Whenever Christians recite the Lord's prayer, they pray that God's will be done, on earth as it is in heaven (Matt 6:10). According to Paul's way of thinking, it was God's will that humanity be delivered from the divisive effects of sin.

The Gathering

As we have previously mentioned, the apostle addresses his letter to the churches in Galatia (1:2). Many Christians in the modern day world associate the word church with a "building" or a "Christian denomination." The term church comes to us from the Greek word *ekklêsia*, meaning "congregation," "assembly," or "gathering."[19] This Greek word is derived from the verb *kalein*, meaning "to call." In the Greek speaking world the term *ekklêsia* was used to designate a gathering of people who were called together for a specific purpose.[20] In the Septuagint, a Greek rendition of the Hebrew Old Testament, the word *ekklêsia* was often used to translate the Hebrew word *qahal*. The *qahal* was a biblical term used to signify the people of God, that is, Israel.[21] The apostle uses *ekklêsia* (church), to denote the Christian community. Thus he uses in Gal 1:2 a term that originally had Jewish overtones to designate communities made up primarily of Gentile believers. In fact, Paul refers to those who accept his version of the gospel, which hopefully includes the Galatians, as the "Israel of God" (6:16). The apostle views the churches in Galatia as communities of Christian believers who have been called by God via Paul to a new life in Christ. Composed of members who are united by their faith in Christ, these Christian communities are those in which all different kinds of people gather together, regardless of religious or social background, in response to God's invitation.

The Perfect Gift

Paul's introductory comments in Galatians includes a customary benediction. The apostle implores God in Gal 1:3 to bestow the gifts of grace (*charis*) and peace (*eirênê*) upon the

[19] See Lothar Coenen, "*ekklêsia*," *DNTT*, 1, pp. 291-307.
[20] See Raymond F. Collins, *Studies On the First Letter To the Thessalonians* (BETL 66, Leuven: Peeters, 1984), pp. 285-289.
[21] See Collins, *Thessalonians*, pp. 287-288.

recipients of the epistle. This traditional prayer of Paul's (see e.g., 1 Cor 1:3) takes on new meaning in Galatians. The apostle has expanded the conventional greeting of the Greek speaking world (*chairein*: greetings) by adding to it a typical Jewish greeting, a wish for "peace" (*shalom*).[22] The bringing together of these standard Greek and Jewish greetings can be said to symbolize one of the Paul's main objectives in Galatians, that is, to demonstrate that for those who are in Christ there is no distinction between Jew and Gentile.[23] Since this epistle is included in the New Testament, perhaps we can say that the prayer for grace and peace in the salutation of the letter also applies to modern day readers as well as those first century Christians in Galatia.

The apostle's greeting in Gal 1:3 is, in a manner of speaking, a disguised prayer that the Galatians might accept his version of the gospel. Throughout the letter Paul implies that those who reject his understanding of the good news do not enjoy the gifts of grace and peace. He warns the Galatians that all who yield to the teaching of the troublemakers have "fallen from grace" (5:4). Likewise those who call into question Paul's rendition of the gospel experience anything but peace (1:7). Consequently, the apostle's hope that grace and peace come upon the Galatians will only reach fruition, according to his argumentation, if they accept his teaching.

Paul often uses the term "grace" in his writings, a word that is extremely rich in meaning. This term is a translation of the Greek word *charis*, meaning "kindness," "mercy," "good will," "favor," "gift," and "thankfulness."[24] In Paul's letters *charis* also conveys the idea of love, conciliatory compassion, and fidelity.[25] Perhaps the most important aspect of *charis* is

[22] See Betz, *Galatians*, p. 40.

[23] See Paul J. Achtemeier, *Romans* (Atlanta, GA: John Knox, 1985), p. 30.

[24] See Hans-Helmut Esser, "*charis*," *DNTT*, 2, pp. 115-124, p. 115.

[25] See Peter Fransen, *The New Life of Grace* (Tournai: Descleé, 1969), p. 15. Although this book was written in 1969 it still remains a classic work on the theology of grace.

that it is associated with a gift which is freely given for the well-being of the recipient. The word *gratia* is the Latin rendition of *charis* from which is derived the English words "grace," "gracious," and "graceful."

There have been many misconceptions about the Christian understanding of grace. Grace should not be considered as an abstract, impersonal reality. On the contrary, grace should be thought of in a very personable way. Piet Fransen has defined grace as the very presence of God.[26] This notion can be understood better if we examine our relationship with a loved one. A close friend is one with whom we want to share our thoughts, our feelings, our joys and sorrows. As two people share more and more of their lives with one another, it is said that they become "part of one another." This is true to such an extent that when two loved ones are separated for a great length of time, they feel as if a "part of themselves were missing." Furthermore, as the relationship deepens, each person is willing to do more and more to ensure the happiness and well-being of the other.

At a time of God's choosing and at His own pleasure, He communicates Himself to us. We experience His presence within us; we call this "presence" grace. As two friends become part of one another, God also becomes "part of us" in a very real way. This mysterious presence is like the wind. It is easier to explain what it does, than what it is (John 3:8).

Where God's presence exists, His divine qualities also exist, for example, peace, joy, forgiveness and love. It is this divine presence which motivates us to become more loving individuals. Just as two close friends are able to bring out the best in each other, so too does God bring out the best in us through grace. Where God's presence exists, people seek to be reconciled with others. They are more aware of the needs and hardships of others. Where God's presence exists, people seek not

[26] See Fransen, *Grace*, p. 24: "Grace in general can be described as the secret of God's presence in our life."

selfish pleasure but the will of God. As the great light of grace shines on people, they become more aware of their sinfulness. One's complete dependence on the mercy of God is readily seen. Whenever we feel motivated to do a good act, God's grace is at work in us. Whenever we forgive or give alms or think of others first, grace is acting within us. Whenever we are motivated to pray or to do an act of kindness, to console or to help one in need, we are responding to Gods grace within us.

Grace should always be understood as a precious gift from God. As a gift, grace can never be "earned" or "deserved" for it would no longer be a gift. This aspect of grace is readily seen in Paul's account of his call to apostleship, which took place even while he was in the midst of persecuting the church (1:13). Grace has that wonderful ability to transform a person into a more loving individual. God's greatest gift to humanity was that of His Son Jesus, who gave of himself for our sins (1:4). Seemingly the apostle views all good things in terms of grace, for example, the conversion of the Galatians (1:6), his own experience of the risen Lord (1:15), and justification itself (Rom 3:24).

Our heavenly Father has not dealt with the human race as we deserve, thank God! Rather, the divine response to human transgressions has been one of compassion, mercy, and love. Through the person of Jesus Christ who gave of himself for our sins, God has offered humanity true liberty. Christian freedom is God's gift to those who are united with His Son. This amazing gift was meant not only for the uplifting of the individual Christian but for the benefit of others as well. For that reason the apostle presents a whole litany of suggestions in Galatians 5 and 6 to encourage his readers to look out for the well-being of others.

Paul associates the gift of grace in Gal 1:3 with that of peace. Like grace, peace is one of the loving gifts that our heavenly Father bestows on those who are justified (Rom 1:2). The apostle speaks of this divine peace as that which surpasses all understanding and keeps the heart and mind of the believer in Christ Jesus (Phil 4:7). Through His only begotten Son God has reconciled the world to Himself and has entrusted us with a message of reconciliation (1 Cor 5:19). By virtue of their unity with the Lord, Christians are at peace with God, with one another, and with themselves. Indeed those in Christ have been called by God to this heavenly peace (1 Cor 7:15).

In the same way that all loving parents experience great joy in giving to their children, so too does our heavenly Father enjoy immensely presenting gifts to His children. Through Jesus Christ, God has given the world the greatest gift that anyone can give, namely, the gift of Himself. We Christians are invited to respond to God's grace by giving of ourselves to our heavenly Father and to one another. In doing so, we participate in divine love and joy and become, as it were, like God.

Let No One Put Asunder

Paul's temper which has been simmering up to this point comes to a full boil in Gal 1:6. No sooner has he concluded his opening prayer with a solemn Amen, than does the apostle express shock and dismay at the behavior of the Galatians. His astonishment is all the more emphatic in that it stands in sharp contrast to the hallowed doxology of the preceding verse. He can't believe what has been reported to him. As a direct result of the heretical teaching of the Judaizers, the Galatians have called into question the authenticity of Paul's apostleship (1:1) and gospel (1:11). In doing so they have also entertained some serious doubts about their own Christian identity. Were they in fact "full members" of the Christian community? At the prompting of the troublemakers, the Galatians were on the brink of accepting the agitators' corrupt rendition of the gospel, namely, that one must obey at least some of the precepts of the Mosaic law, especially those concerning circumcision and dietary regulations, in order to be justified.

The apostle's comment in 1:7 speaks volumes about the repercussions of the agitators' perverted teaching. The churches in Galatia were rife with confusion, discord and discontent. Perhaps within these Christian communities, two "camps" had formed: those who remained faithful to Paul's version of a "Torah free" gospel and those who did not. If this were in fact the case, there were probably a number of heated debates concerning the requirements for obtaining righteousness. Such emotional discussions would undoubtedly have resulted in misunderstanding and hard feelings. The advocates of the troublemakers' rendition of the gospel may have chided other members of the Christian community, and even looked down upon them, because they did not consider them justified, that is, full-fledged Christians (5:15, 26, 6:3). Whatever the case may have been, the heretical teaching of the Judaizers spread like fire. Apparently all the churches in Galatia had been infected with it (1:2, 5:9). Paul felt compelled to intervene before it spread any further. Furthermore, he had to warn the Galatians that, unbeknownst to them, adherence to the Judaizers' perverted gospel results in tragedy.

For all practical purposes, the apostle confronted the Galatians with a question of tremendous importance. "Do you realize what you are doing?" He informs the Galatians that, in effect, by rejecting his version of the good news they are deserting God the Father, the one who called them to a new life in Christ (1:6). Moreover, by turning to a "different gospel" (1:6) they are turning away from the truth. Having said this, however, Paul quickly corrects himself. In fact, there is no other gospel (1:7).

The apostle confronts the Galatians with a decision of great magnitude. They must choose between Paul's rendition of the gospel and that of the troublemakers. The Galatians must not make the mistake of thinking that this decision is simply a matter of choosing between two equally valid renditions of the good news. On the contrary, it is a choice between truth and falsehood. Furthermore, Paul will argue throughout the course of the letter that all who opt for the troublemakers' heretical version of the good news are cursed (3:10) and destined for corruption (6:8a). On the other hand, those who select the apostle's authentic rendition of the gospel are blessed (3:14) and destined for eternal life (6:8b).

The Gospel of Freedom

Often when twentieth century Christians hear the word "gospel," they immediately think of the writings of the four evangelists, Matthew, Mark, Luke, and John. The word gospel is actually a translation of the Greek word (*euaggelion*), meaning "good news."[27] Although in the Greek speaking world *euaggelion* could refer to all kinds of good news, most of the time it was used in connection with a military victory.[28] For example, after a successful military campaign in which an invading army had been driven back, a messenger from the battlefield would be sent to the citizens of the besieged city with good news, namely, that victory over the enemy had been achieved. Such news was received with great joy and celebration as it meant salvation for the city. It had been liberated.

In view of what has been said, *euaggelion* is an extremely suitable term for describing the significance of the life, death, and resurrection of Jesus Christ. Through him God has triumphed over those enemies which have kept humanity under siege, namely, sin and death. All who are in Christ have been liberated. The gospel of Jesus Christ (1:7) is indeed a gospel of freedom. This is certainly good news and worthy of celebration.

The apostle uses the term *euaggelion* more often than any other New Testament author. Although most of the time it signifies the content of Paul's apostolic teaching (1 Thess 2:2), it can also refer to the activity of evangelization (Gal 2:7, Phil 4:3).[29] The gospel is intimately connected with Jesus Christ

[27] See Gerhard Friedrich, "*euaggelion*," *TDNT*, 2, pp. 721-736.
[28] See 1 Sam 31:9. See also Ulrich Becker, "Gospel," *DNTT*, 2, pp. 107-108.
[29] See Gerhard Friedrich, "*euaggelion*," *TDNT* Vol. 2, pp. 729-735.

(Gal 1:7) and thus brings salvation to those who "hold fast" to it (1 Cor 15:2). The fundamental difference between Paul's version of the gospel and that of the troublemakers had to do with whether or not adherence to the Torah was a factor in obtaining righteousness. Unlike his adversaries, the apostle insisted that one was justified by faith in Christ apart from the Mosaic law. Paul's rendition of the gospel does not result in the separation of people into various groups within the Christian community, depending on one's religious background, social status, or gender (2:12, 3:28). On the contrary, the apostle understands the gospel as that which brings people together in Christ. The church is to be a community of believers free from all such categorizing. The truth of the gospel must be preserved (2:5).

Those Accursed Troublemakers

The apostle deals with the agitators in his own unique way. He first denounces their perverted gospel (1:7) and then passes judgment on them. The sentence that Paul imposes on the troublemakers fits their "crime." Anathema sit (1:8). Since those who yield to the teaching of the Judaizers are cursed (3:10) it is certainly appropriate that Paul should invoke the wrath of God upon these agitators. In order to avoid all doubt concerning the intensity and the severity of Paul's sentence on them, he repeats himself in 1:9. "Let them be accursed!" The apostle is so convinced of the authenticity of the gospel that he first proclaimed to the Galatians that he invokes a curse on anyone who might preach a different version of it, be it the apostle himself, the brethren who are with him, the troublemakers, an angel from heaven, or anyone else (1:8-9)!

Paul does not condemn the agitators simply to mete out divine justice. He also wants to point out to the Galatians in a radical fashion the great danger that is involved in accepting the Judaizers' heretical teaching. Moreover, by pronouncing anathema on the troublemakers, the apostle makes it clear that their teaching is not consistent with the truth of the gospel.

Paul's argumentation demonstrates that being declared righteous is not an irreversible condition. Before the Galatians came to believe in Christ Jesus, they were in a cursed state and in need of redemption. However, all that changed after they responded to the apostle's proclamation of the gospel. By accepting his rendition of the good news they were united with Christ and delivered from their sins. Paul argues that this, too, could change. The Galatians are in danger of reverting back to their pre-redeemed status by giving serious thought to rejecting his version of the gospel.

The apostle sharply distinguishes between the agitators and the Galatians. Even though Paul admonishes the latter for being on the verge of acquiescing to a distorted gospel and even though he invokes a curse on the troublemakers, he does *not* condemn the Galatians. The evidence seems to indicate that Paul does not yet consider the Galatians as apostates. After all, the apostle still refers to the Galatians as members of the church (1:2) and as "brethren" (e.g., 1:11), an often used Pauline term to designate fellow Christians. The brethren are contradistinguished from the "false brethren" (2:4) who oppose the truth of the gospel. This being said, the situation of the Galatians will take a dramatic turn for the worst if they choose to ignore Paul's warning and acquiesce in the corrupt gospel advocated by the agitators.

Paul is not alone in his crusade against the troublemakers' heretical gospel. He has the support of his fellow missionaries. The apostle's reference to the "brethren who are with me" (1:2) may not only indicate that his Christian companions are in the same geographical proximity as he is but also signify that they are "with him" as far as his theological position is concerned.[30] Paul concludes this section of Galatians by

[30] See John Chrysostom, "Commentary on Galatians," *The Nicene and Post-Nicene Fathers*, Vol. 13, edited by Philip Schaff (Grand Rapids, MI: Eerdmans, 1979), p. 4.

responding to an accusation put forth by the Judaizers. From his detrimental remarks aimed at the Galatians and the trouble-makers, it should be obvious that the apostle is not one who is seeking the favor of others (1:10). On the contrary, his primary objective is to seek the favor of God. Paul accomplishes this lofty task by standing up for the truth of the gospel, whatever the cost might be.

Concluding Remarks

The first ten verses of Galatians can be said to act as a prelude to the epistle. Here the apostle introduces the major themes of the letter and sets the tone for his following argumentation. Paul lets it be known that even though Christians enjoy God's gift of freedom, this is not unlicensed freedom. This applies to basic theological convictions concerning the gospel of Jesus Christ and, as he will later demonstrate, to moral conduct (Gal 5 and 6). Those who think otherwise distance themselves from God the Father, the ultimate source of justification, and are cursed. Paul's discussion in Gal 1:1-10 indicates that he has mixed emotions about the Galatians. One should not find it strange that the apostle's deep sense of unity with the Galatians does not prevent him from being extremely upset with them. Intense anger is often an indication of the great love and concern that one human being has for another (Mark 11:15-19).

Where Two or More are Gathered

In view of the fact that present day Christians must cope with all sorts of controversy originating from both the "left" and the "right," one might be tempted to dream of a time when all members of the church were of one accord. Unfortunately, such a time did not exist. Even in Christian communities of the first century the significance and the ramifications of the good news were hotly debated. In this respect, the situation in Galatia was not unique. The church in Corinth, for example, was also suffering from factions and misunderstandings (e.g., 1 Cor 1:11-12). Nevertheless the crisis situation in Galatia is of extreme importance because it dealt with fundamental questions about Christianity.

What must one do to become and to remain a Christian? The question of whether or not one had to observe the Mosaic law in order to be justified threatened to split the entire church in two. All modern day controversies pale in comparison. In light of our past, we should not be at all surprised that "intense discussions" concerning the meaning and ramifications of the gospel often take place within the church - it seems to go with the Christian territory.

United We Stand

Throughout the ages Christians have had to withstand great pressure from many fronts concerning the authentic gospel of Jesus Christ. The very first generation of Christians in Galatia were urged by outsiders to ignore the good news of freedom that had originally been proclaimed to them and to accept a teaching that stood in direct opposition to the gospel. Likewise, every age presents its own serious challenges to the Christian believer. In contemporary society, consumerism, nationalism, racism, secularism, sexism and pragmatism exert a tremendous pressure on people to ignore basic Christian values. Those who have pledged to follow in the footsteps of Jesus are not immune from such pressure.

Christians need the support and encouragement of fellow believers in order to remain faithful to their commitment to Christ. The local church, which is usually referred to as a parish, is of tremendous importance in this respect. It is in the parish setting that the people of God gather together in response to the gospel. Within this sacred community, they are strengthened by the proclamation of the gospel, nourished by the eucharist, and supported by their fellow parishioners. Christians are reminded week after week that they are not alone in the world. United they stand together committed to a life of freedom and love.

Oblivious To Sin

"Don't you realize what you are doing?" This question which Paul, in effect, seems to have directed towards the Galatians is a good topic of reflection for all Christians. The Galatians probably did not realize the ramifications of their behavior, that it was contrary to the truth of the gospel. Sometimes, perhaps the same can be said of our conduct. Paul's letter to the Galatians challenges us to examine our own behavior at home, at work, in the parish community, and so forth, and determine whether it conforms to the gospel message. If not, some modifications in our day to day living need to be made. As Paul's comments in Galatians have demonstrated so well, there are occasions when people are blind to their own mistakes, and need to have them pointed out by others.

In Defense of Freedom

Invested with divine authority, Paul was specifically chosen to proclaim, uphold, and defend Christian liberty. In a very real sense he was God's spokesperson for Christian freedom. Paul therefore had an obligation to clarify the Galatians' vision of Christianity, which had been clouded by the troublemakers' heretical teaching. Despite his disappointment and anger at the behavior of the Galatians, the apostle did not give up on them but instead offered them a second chance. After all, once before he too had made a serious mistake by persecuting Christians and God had dealt with him in a similar fashion.

CHAPTER THREE

SURPRISED BY FREEDOM (GAL 1:11 - 2:14)

Paul realizes that he will never persuade the Galatians to accept his point of view unless he first removes all doubt concerning the legitimacy of his apostleship and his version of the gospel. The troublemakers had raised some serious questions about Paul's apostolic status and accused him of preaching an abbreviated form of the good news which, they claimed, he had received from the authentic apostles. As far as these agitators were concerned, whatever status Paul might have in the church, he was definitely subordinate to those who were apostles before him. Paul counters these charges by placing himself, as it were, on the witness stand. His personal testimony is meant to affirm both his apostolic authority and the divine origin of his rendition of the gospel.

Subsequently the apostle narrates the events surrounding his initial contact with the risen Lord and his first years as a Christian missionary. The intimate details that Paul relates to the Galatians concerning his life story make for fascinating reading. His autobiographical account includes elements of violence, a heavenly encounter, dramatic change, friendship, suspicion and confrontation. With such personal information Paul attests that God Himself called him to be an apostle, entrusted him with the gospel of freedom, and commissioned him to preach the good news to the Gentiles. Although the gospel he proclaimed did not originate from those who were apostles before him, it nevertheless received their full approval.[1] In the midst of this

[1] See William Barclay, *The Letters to the Galatians and Ephesians* (Philadelphia, PA: Westminster, 1976), p. 4.

argumentation, Paul illustrates in a variety of ways that he is on equal footing with the other apostles.

AMAZING GRACE

Divine Revelation

The apostle reiterates in Gal 1:11-12 what he previously asserted in 1:1, namely, that the good news which he first proclaimed to the Galatians had not been taught to him by any human being. On the contrary, Paul testifies that the gospel which he originally preached to them came to him through grace (1:15) by means of a "revelation of Jesus Christ" (1:12).

The term revelation is a translation of the Greek word *apokalypsis*, meaning "unveil," or "uncover." Information brought to light through revelation does not come about by means of logical deduction or inferred reasoning.[2] Rather, such information is directly made known to an individual by means of a disclosure of another party. Divine revelation should be understood in terms of its taking place as a result of God's free initiative rather than a human being's inquiry and discovery.[3] In other words, divine revelation is communicated when God so chooses, rather than when human beings desire it. In the apostle's own words, he was graced with divine communication when "God was *pleased* to reveal His Son to me" (1:16). Paul did not infer from a rational thought process that Jesus was the Son of God nor did the apostle logically deduce that he was to preach Christ to the Gentiles. Instead, the identity

[2] See Wilhelm Mundle, "*apocaluptô*," *DNTT*, 3, pp. 310-317.

[3] See C.F.D. Moule, "Revelation," *IDB*, 4, pp. 54-58, p. 55. See Raymond E. Brown, *A Coming Christ in Advent* (Collegeville, MN: Liturgical Press, 1988), p. 11, who rightly observes that the fundamental understanding of New Testament authors was that "the identity of Jesus was a divine revelation, not a human deduction."

of Jesus, Paul's new apostolic vocation, and the gospel of freedom were revealed to him by God the Father. This revelation was not granted to Paul simply for his own personal salvation. According to Paul's way of thinking, God had the Galatians in mind when He revealed His Son to the apostle. Paul insists that the revelation of Christ Jesus took place *in order that* he might preach the risen Lord to the Gentiles.

As Paul, modern day Christians have been the recipients of divine revelation. It was not through intellectual reasoning that twentieth-century believers came to know about the compassionate and merciful love of God. Nor was it simply logical deduction which lead them to the conclusion that God is their heavenly Father, who sent His only begotten Son Jesus into the world for their salvation. Such divine mysteries have been "revealed" to them through the church, that community of faith whose fundamental role is to proclaim the truth of the Sacred Scriptures to each new generation of human beings.

For many Christians the revelation of divine love, the Fatherhood of God, the salvific importance of Jesus, and the radical equality of all those in Christ came to them as children via their parents. Indeed parents are usually the first to teach their offspring about the wonders and the beauty of the Christian belief. In a very real sense parents can be thought of as "missionaries" in their own right, preaching the gospel to their children by word and example. As transmitters of the Christian faith they play a vital role in the ongoing story of salvation history. The same can be said of those who are involved, in one way or another, with teaching the sacred traditions of the church, be it to grade school children, university students, or other adults interested in their Christian heritage.

By God's Grace, Kinsfolk

As the apostle begins to narrate his life story, he specifically refers to the Galatians as "brethren" (*adelphoi*) for the first time in the letter (1:11).[4] One usually associates the word "brother" in the modern day world with a close blood relative. The term "brethren" could also be used in antiquity to signify a person of common ancestry (e.g., Num 16:10, Deut 15:12). Thus, Jewish people often called their fellow tribesman brethren. In Greek literature this term was not only used to denote a physical brother or close relative but could also designate a friend, companion, or even a fellow human being. Within the religious setting, members of various Gentile cults and fraternities often referred to one another as brethren.[5]

The early Christians can be said to have intensified the use of this term by referring to their fellow Christians as *adelphoi*, "brothers and sisters." They believed that they were bonded together in Christ through grace (1:6) in a way that was much deeper and stronger than any relationship based simply on affinity of blood, friendship, or common religious belief. We have previously noted Paul's conviction that those who have been united with Christ Jesus, the Son of God, have become in a very real sense children of God (1:4). Consequently, as those who have received the Spirit of Christ in their hearts (4:6), Christians are truly brothers and sisters in the Lord.

Most of the time that the apostle writes about "brothers and sisters" in Galatians, he simply has in mind those who belong to the Christian family (e.g., 3:15, 4:12). This, however, is not a hard-and-fast rule. When Paul refers to the co-senders of the epistle as the "brethren who are with me" (1:2), he is not merely referring to his Christian companions in general. Rather the apostle is thinking of his fellow Christian missionaries who are presently journeying with him, and perhaps had accompanied him when he first proclaimed the good news in Galatia.[6]

[4] Paul alluded to the fact that the Galatians are brothers and sisters in the Lord in Gal 1:4.

[5] See John L. McKenzie, "Brother," *Dictionary*, p. 108. See Walther Günther, "*adelphos*," *DNTT*, 1, pp. 254-258.

[6] Paul clearly distinguishes between Christians at large and his Christian travelling companions in Phil 4:21-22. The brethren with Paul may have included Barnabas and Titus (Gal 2:1).

Moreover, Paul mentions James, the "Lord's brother" in Gal 1:19. Here it is obvious that James is a blood relative of the Lord as well as a fellow Christian.[7] Furthermore, the apostle uses the familiar term in a sarcastic sense when he speaks of the "false brethren" in Gal 2:4, namely, those "who slipped in to spy out our freedom."

The harsh tone of Galatians notwithstanding, Paul never forgets that he is addressing his brothers and sisters in the Lord. Even though the apostle must correct the Galatians who have been duped by the troublemakers, he does so with fraternal love. Paul's argumentation in the letter reflects the Christian teaching that all believers are brothers and sisters in Christ, regardless of their pre-Christian standing. That Paul, a man so well steeped in the traditions of Judaism, would refer to Gentiles as brothers and sisters was unthinkable in antiquity. The apostle also followed the Christian custom of addressing even those of a different race and/or social status with familiar language. Such a practice was unheard of in the ancient world. Indeed the Christian doctrine regarding the equality of believers was a bold new teaching.

Through faith and baptism individuals commit themselves to Christ. In doing so they become intimately bound not only to the risen Lord but to the greater Christian family as well. For this reason the use of familiar language to designate fellow Christians is extremely appropriate. As is true for those who are bound together by blood, those who are united in faith realize that they are not necessarily obligated to like all the other members of their Christian family, although this is perhaps the ideal. Nevertheless they are duty bound to look out for their well being (6:10).

[7] It is not clear from the text if James is a full brother of Jesus, a half-brother, or a cousin. In the light of the New Testament teaching on the virginal conception of Jesus (Matt 1:18-25, Luke 1:34) and the Roman Catholic tradition about Mary "ever virgin," it has traditionally been assumed that James was the cousin of Jesus. See Joseph A. Fitzmyer, "The Letter to the Galatians," *JBC*, II, pp. 236-246, p. 239.

Christians must be constantly reminded that all those in Christ belong to the one family of faith, be they black or white, rich or poor, liberal or conservative, ordained or lay. Whatever differences there might be between the various members of the Christian communities, they must never forget that they are all brothers and sisters in the Lord and therefore have a sacred obligation to treat one another accordingly.

From Persecutor to Persecuted

The apostle very matter-of-factly reminds the Galatians of his previous anti-Christian conduct before he came to believe in the risen Lord (1:13).[8] In his youth Paul had sought with tremendous enthusiasm to put an end to Christianity. The apostle does not go into detail as to how he "persecuted the church of God violently and tried to destroy it" (1:13). We do know, however, that the author of Acts paints a rather gruesome picture of Paul's attempt to eliminate Christianity from the face of the earth.

The very first time Paul is mentioned in Acts, he is associated with the persecution of Christians (Acts 7:58-60). In regard to the stoning of Stephen, the first Christian martyr, Paul is said to have been "consenting to his death" (Acts 8:1). Paul demonstrated great zeal in his anti-Christian activities. Entering house after house, he ravaged the church by dragging off Christians and having them committed to prison (Acts 8:3). If he found anyone belonging to the new Christian movement, male or female, he brought them bound to Jerusalem to be punished (Acts 9:1-2, 22:5). Paul even attempted to make the Christians blaspheme (Acts 26:11). So enraged was he with Christianity that Paul persecuted those who pledged allegiance to the risen Lord, even in foreign cities. When the time came to vote on a fitting punishment for the Christians, Paul was in favor of the death penalty (Acts 26:10).

[8] See. Gal 1:23, 1 Cor 15:9, Phil 3:6.

Why was Paul convinced that he "ought to do many things in opposing the name of Jesus of Nazareth" (Acts 26:9)? What exactly was wrong with the Christian movement that induced Paul to torment its members so vehemently?[9] Paul's negative attitude towards Christianity seems rather strange in that this new faith placed a great deal of emphasis on the intense love of God and one's neighbor. The apostle's motivation for his previous anti-Christian behavior may lie in Gal 1:13-14. Here Paul makes a connection between his former persecution of the church and his enthusiasm for "the traditions of my fathers" (1:14).

Paul boasts that he was so well acquainted with these sacred traditions, that he was considered advanced in Judaism beyond many of his own age (1:14). Assuredly whatever complaint one might have against Paul, one could not accuse him of ignorance of the Mosaic law and its rigorous demands. Apparently Paul's understanding of the ramifications of the Christian proclamation had led him to believe that the role of the Mosaic law concerning salvation was put into question.[10] Such a view could not be tolerated by one so extremely zealous for his Jewish heritage.

Early Christianity was readily identifiable by its radical teachings and practices. In the beginning this new movement was primarily composed of Jewish Christians. Hence the primitive church was often viewed as either a sub-community of Judaism or a community on the fringe of Judaism. Whatever, Paul was convinced that Christianity was close enough to Judaism that its teaching posed a serious threat to the sacred traditions of the Jewish people.[11] According to his way of thinking, the Christian message implied that adherence to the Mosaic law was not a prerequisite for obtaining righteousness.

[9] This question is addressed in more detail by Arland J. Hultgren, "Paul's Pre-Christian Persecutions of the Church," *JBL* 95 (1976) pp. 97-111.

[10] For a different opinion regarding the motive for Paul's previous persecution of Christians, see Hultgren, "Persecutions," p. 110.

[11] See Hultgren, "Persecutions," p. 97.

Paul did not seek to destroy Christianity because he viewed it as a competing religion. Rather, Paul firmly believed that his persecution of the church was absolutely necessary in order to uphold the elevated status of the Mosaic law within Judaism. By punishing those whom he considered Jewish apostates, in light of their presumed indifference towards the Torah, Paul undoubtedly wanted to reinforce the Jewish belief that the Mosaic law was of vital importance in obtaining righteousness.

The Christian proclamation of a crucified Messiah may also have been a factor in motivating Paul to take such extreme measures against the church (3:13). To be sure, crucifixion was regarded as an abhorrent, humiliating type of capital punishment, reserved for the most grievous of crimes.[12] Perhaps more importantly for Paul, the Torah pronounces a curse on "every one who hangs on a tree" (Deut 21:23, Gal 3:13). For these reasons the very notion of a crucified Messiah would have been considered blasphemous by Judaism. Whatever prompted Paul to terrorize the church, we can be sure that he did so with a vengeance.

The apostle does not simply mention his former anti-Christian activity as an historical footnote. Quite the contrary, Paul's remarks concerning his violent persecution of the church fit in well with the apostle's overall argumentation in Galatians. The apostle is well aware of the radical nature of the gospel that he proclaims, that is, that one is justified through faith in Christ apart from the Mosaic law (2:16). After all, he had at one time persecuted the church for that very teaching. How paradoxical that in the process of attempting to preserve the elevated status of the Torah by violent means, God made known to Paul that righteousness comes through faith in Christ Jesus without observing the precepts of the Mosaic law.

[12] See, for example, J.L. McKenzie, "Cross," *Dictionary*, pp. 161-162, p. 161: "In Roman literature it [crucifixion] is described as a cruel and feared punishment which was not inflicted on Roman citizens; it was reserved for slaves or for non-Romans who had committed heinous crimes such as murder, robbery and piracy, treason, and rebellion."

By reminding the Galatians of his former anti-Christian endeavors, Paul illustrates in a dramatic fashion that the gospel of freedom which he received came to him through sheer grace. The same can be said of his apostolic authority. Obviously Paul was not deserving of these divine gifts nor was he looking for them. It was through God's free initiative alone that Paul was selected to preach the Torah-free gospel to the Gentiles. Like all Christians, Paul's being declared righteous was not a matter of his deserving or earning it. Rather, his new life in Christ was God's free gift to the apostle.

Paul is the master of sharp contrast. He speaks of violently persecuting the church in one breath and discusses his intensely personal experience of the risen Lord in the next (1:13-16). The apostle acts in a similar fashion throughout the letter. In his opening comments he recites a prayer on behalf of the Galatians (1:4) and then expresses astonishment at their behavior (1:6). The apostle extends a friendly handshake to Peter (2:9) and shortly after condemns him to his face (2:11). Paul notes that the Torah imposed a curse on the crucified Jesus (3:13) and then in the same sentence insists that through Christ a blessing comes upon the Gentiles (3:14). Even in the concluding words of the epistle, Paul warns the Galatians to trouble him no longer (6:17) and then immediately offers a prayer for them (6:18). Such contrasting statements not only capture the readers' attention but also serve to highlight the important points of Paul's argumentation.

After his initial encounter with the glorified Christ, Paul came to realize that his former persecution of the church was fundamentally wrong. He had to cope with a sinful past. This being said, there is no evidence in Paul's letters that he suffered from tremendous guilt as a result of his pre-Christian behavior. Through his first contact with the risen Lord, Paul had experienced the compassionate and merciful love of God the Father. He was now a forgiven man. Whenever the apostle recalled his former attempts to destroy the Christian movement, perhaps he no longer thought of his previous sinfulness. Instead Paul may have called to mind that God had been pleased to reveal His Son to him in spite of his sinful behavior. This memory of God's grace would then have given the apostle reason to rejoice.

Paul had previously sought to put an end to Christianity but it was God who put an end to Paul's anti-Christian activity. In doing so God demonstrated once again that sin does not frustrate the divine plan. He does not allow human mistakes and misunderstanding to get in His way. Although it may at times seem to the contrary, God always takes care of His church.

Christ-Centered

The apostle's description of his first encounter with the glorified Christ in Gal 1:15-16 lacks all the dramatic flair of that which is found in Acts (Acts 9:3-6). Here Paul is portrayed as falling to the ground, seeing a great light from heaven, and actually hearing the voice of Jesus. Using terminology reminiscent of the prophetic writings, the apostle's account of his initial experience of the risen Lord in Gal 1:15-16 is profound in its simplicity. "He who had set me apart before I was born, and had called me through his grace, was pleased to reveal his Son to me, in order that I might preach him among the Gentiles" (1:15-16).[13] With this testimony Paul substantiates his manifesto in Gal 1:1 and 1:11 concerning the divine origin of his apostleship and his God given authority to preach the good news to the Gentiles.

Paul's rather simple and unassuming description of his first encounter with the risen Lord (1:15-16) may unfortunately lead one to overlook the monumental transformation that took place in his life as a result of this incredible experience. One of

[13] See Isa 49:1 and Jer 1:5. Paul's allusion to these distinguished prophets may indicate to what extent he was convinced of his special election and appointment. See Ronald Y. Fung, *The Epistle to the Galatians* NICNT (Grand Rapids, MI: Eerdmans, 1988), pp. 63-64.

the recurring themes in Galatians is that the person of Christ has changed everything. Through grace, Paul had come to view himself, his religious traditions, and his society in an entirely new light. Paul goes so far as to say that whatever he had previously considered important, he now considers as "loss"[14] for the sake of Christ (Phil 3:8).

In view of his encounter with the glorified Christ the apostle dares to compare himself with some of the towering figures in Judaism. Like the great prophetic figures of old, like Isaiah and Jeremiah, Paul considers himself to have been chosen for divine service even before he was born. Thus Paul has reinterpreted his entire existence in view of Christ Jesus. He now thinks of his life in terms of the unfolding of a divine plan. No longer an enemy of the church, he is now an apostle of the risen Lord who has been foreordained to preach the faith he once tried to destroy. Paul recognizes the sudden and unexpected nature of the divine revelation which was granted to him. "As to one *untimely born* he [Christ] appeared to me" (1 Cor 15:8).[15]

Paul's experience of the risen Lord also radically altered the way that he viewed the sacred traditions of his Jewish ancestors. Henceforth it was Christ and not the Mosaic law that played center stage in his life. The apostle now associated justification with Christ Jesus instead of the Torah (2:16). Paul was absolutely convinced that the precepts of the Torah concerning circumcision (5:2) and dietary regulations (2:12) had no role to play in obtaining righteousness. Moreover, like

[14] Paul's statement in Phil 3:8 is borderline vulgarity. The word "loss" in this verse is a translation of *zêmia*, a harsh word meaning "street sweepings," "refuse of the table," or even "excrement." See Frank W. Beare, *A Commentary on the Epistle to the Galatians* BNTC (London: Black, 1959), p. 116.

[15] The expression "untimely born" is a translation of the Greek word *ektrôma*, a term which refers to any kind of premature birth (stillbirth, miscarriage, abortion). It conveys the notion of "that which is out of the ordinary." See Gordon D. Fee, *The First Epistle to the Corinthians* NICNT (Grand Rapids, MI: Eerdmans, 1987), pp. 733-734.

other New Testament authors,[16] Paul reinterpreted the Jewish Scriptures in light of Christ (e.g., 3:16). Even the apostle's outlook on moral behavior has undergone a dramatic change. His motivation for living a virtuous life is now understood in terms of fidelity to the kingdom of God as opposed to obedience to the Torah (5:21). Paul's newfound faith in Christ Jesus also greatly influenced the way in which he envisioned society. The apostle came to realize that, for those who are bound to Christ, not only are previous religious distinctions removed, but all social distinctions as well (3:28).

Paul was also viewed by others in a different light after God had revealed His Son to him. Some members of the synagogue who were aware of Paul's former persecution of the church, were amazed on hearing him proclaim Jesus as the Son of God. "Is not this the man who made havoc in Jerusalem of those who called on this name" (Acts 9:21). As might be expected, many Jewish Christians did not trust Paul. They suspected that his preaching of Jesus Christ was just a ploy to draw out Christians so that he might bring them bound to the authorities (Acts 9:21).

One wonders as to how Paul's family and friends regarded his apparent anti-Jewish behavior as a Christian. No doubt they were shocked and dismayed at the apostle's seemingly blatant disregard for the Torah. Assuredly the Jewish authorities considered Paul as an apostate in view of his proclamation of a Torah-free gospel while civil authorities regarded him as a rabble-rouser in that he frequently stirred up people to a frenzy. For these reasons the apostle was often severely punished by his own people as well as the Roman government (e.g., 2 Cor 11:23-25). Regardless of all opposition, however, the apostle remained faithful to his commitment to Christ and to the gospel of freedom.

Perhaps the best way to describe the fundamental shift that took place in Paul's life is to say that he became

[16] See for example, Matt 1:22-23 and John 19:24.

"Christ-centered" in all things. Like all those who have been called to active ministry in the church, the apostle was involved in a variety of activities. Since he was often travelling, composing letters, settling disputes, answering theological problems, suffering all sorts of hardship, and so forth, Paul's life was varied and hectic. Nevertheless, his life was anything but "scattered." In the midst of his missionary activity and all that this involved, Paul's life remained forever centered on the risen Lord. He viewed all aspects of his life in the light of his relationship with Christ Jesus, the one "who loved me, and gave himself for me" (2:20). Would that all Christians did likewise!

Words can never adequately express the radical change that took place in Paul after the risen Lord had been revealed to him. From a Jewish perspective he shifted his theological position regarding the Torah from that of an ultra-conservative to that of a flaming liberal. Paul's transformation from one who sought to do nothing less than annihilate the Christian movement to one who proclaimed the gospel of Jesus Christ throughout the known world is without parallel in recorded history. To be sure other great historical figures, for example, Augustine and Luther, underwent great change in their lives. Nevertheless their change pales in comparison with that of Paul's. After all, such historical personalities did not attempt to destroy Christianity before their "transformation experience" nor did their ecclesiastical endeavors prove to be so foundational in regard to missionary activity and theological reflection following it.

The apostle was fundamentally convinced that he had actually encountered the risen Lord on the road to Damascus. There is not the slightest hint in his correspondence that he ever doubted this. Moreover, there is absolutely no evidence that Paul was in any way unbalanced, mentally unstable, or had suffered from hallucinations. Just the opposite is true. The apostle's letters indicate that he was a solid and stable individual, a good organizer, capable of making deep and lasting friendships with a wide variety of individuals, and that he always possessed a healthy attitude regarding the well being of others. Not only do his epistles illustrate that he argued in a coherent and rational manner,[17] but they also demonstrate that Paul was capable of making theological insights of the highest magnitude.

The apostle to the Gentiles was a fascinating person who had a intense love for God and His people. After the Son of God had been revealed to him, Paul was so enraptured with the love of Christ that he felt compelled to share that with others. The transforming power of grace is readily seen in the life of Paul. The risen Lord who appeared to Paul so long ago and whose presence the apostle felt so strongly throughout his life, is the same risen Lord to whom all Christians are committed and whose divine presence remains with us still.

CALL OR CONVERSION?

Conversion

How should one describe Paul's initial experience of the glorified Christ: as a "conversion," or as a "call?"[18] Within the church there has traditionally been a preference for the former. The Greek word *metanoia* is usually associated with the notion of conversion.[19] This term not only implies the concept of turning *towards* some reality but also includes the idea of *turning away from* some other reality.[20] In reading the biblical accounts of Paul's Damascus experience,[21] there certainly

[17] A few biblical scholars have been extremely critical of Paul's line of reasoning, arguments, premises, and conclusions. See Heikki Räisänen, *Paul and the Law* WUNT 29 (Tübingen: Mohr, 1983), pp. 13-14.

[18] See Krister Stendahl, *Paul Among the Jews and Gentiles* (Philadelphia, PA: Fortress, 1976), pp. 7-23.

[19] See Jürgen Goetzmann, "*metanoia*," *DNTT*, 1, pp. 357-359.

[20] See Goetzmann, "*metanoia*," pp. 357-358.

[21] See Gal 1:13-16, Acts 9:1-22, 22:4-16, 26:9-18. See Raymond F. Collins, "Paul's Damascus Experience: Reflections on the Lukan Account," *LS* 11 (1986), pp. 99-118.

appears to be good reason to speak of this event in terms of a conversion. At first sight it seems that the Jewish Paul was "converted" to Christianity, that he embraced the Christian faith and renounced Judaism. Undoubtedly the Jewish people considered Paul to have turned his back on Judaism. His negative comments concerning the Mosaic law appear to support this conviction (e.g., 2:16, 3:10). The question remains: Did Paul think of himself as one who rejected his Jewish heritage?

Call

The apostle speaks of his first experience of the risen Lord in terms of a "call" (*kaleô*): God the Father "had called me through his grace" (1:15). Within this context *kaleô* conveys the notion of Paul being "summoned," "designated," "appointed," and "commissioned."[22] In other words, Paul was appointed by God to be an apostle and commissioned for a specific task, namely, to proclaim the gospel to the Gentiles. The apostle's use of the term "call" is well grounded in Judaism. In fact, some of the greatest prophetic figures in the Hebrew Scriptures (Isaiah and Jeremiah) also employed such terminology in describing their summons to speak in the name of Yahweh. There is great deal of similarity between Gal 1:15-16, Isa 49:1, and Jer 1:6.

A Faithful Jew

Even though his Jewish contemporaries undoubtedly viewed him otherwise, the New Testament bears witness that the apostle always thought of himself as one who remained faithful to the sacred traditions of his ancestors. By no stretch of the imagination can he be said to have rejected his Jewish heritage. That a tremendous change took place in the life of Paul as a result of the revelation of the risen Lord is beyond question. However, there also remains a great deal of continuity between

[22] See Lothar Coenen, "*kaleô*," *DNTT*, 1, pp. 271-276.

the "before" and "after" of this overwhelming religious experience.[23] Throughout his life the apostle believed that he still served the one true God of Israel for whom he had previously worked so zealously. Moreover, the author of Acts provides ample evidence that after having come to believe in Christ Jesus, Paul had no difficulty in observing the Mosaic law while in Jewish company (e.g., Acts 21:23-26).

Paul's use of the Hebrew Scriptures is also of crucial importance in determining his outlook on Judaism. The apostle did not discard the sacred writings of Israel but in fact often cited them as having divine authority (e.g., 3:10-13). Paul did, however, reinterpret all of Scripture in the light of Jesus Christ. He even expounded on one of the most basic tenets of Judaism in the light of Christ, namely, the promises of Abraham (3:6-9). Interestingly enough, the apostle often used Jewish terminology to describe Christian realities. For example, he understood justification in terms of the "blessing of Abraham" (3:14) and referred to the church as the "Israel of God" (6:16).

Assuredly, Paul re-examined his attitude toward the Torah in light of Jesus Christ. Moreover, on numerous occasions the apostle made derogatory comments about the Mosaic law's ability to make one righteous. Nevertheless, Paul never rejected nor condemned the Torah *per se*. On the contrary, he claimed that he upheld the law (Rom 3:31) and considered it holy.[24] That the apostle had no qualms about the Mosaic law in itself is also borne out by the fact that he referred to Jesus as one who was born "under the law" (4:4).

Not Anti-Semitic

Although Paul cursed the troublemakers, those Jewish Christians who had attempted to persuade the Galatians that one must observe the Mosaic law to be justified, it is extremely

[23] See Stendahl, *Paul*, p. 7.

[24] In the next chapter we will examine whether or not Paul was consistent in his various comments about the Mosaic law.

important to realize that he *never* condemned the Jewish people nor the Judaic religion! The apostle gives every indication that he has not turned his back on the chosen people but that, in fact, he has shown great concern for them. Paul is quick to point out in Romans 9-11 that God has *not* rejected the Jewish people. In fact the apostle warns the Gentile Christians not to "look down" upon the chosen people. As far as Paul is concerned, the election of the Jewish people is irrevocable. They are "beloved for the sake of their forefathers" (Rom 11:28). Paul ultimately believes that as God has shown mercy on the Gentiles, He will also show mercy on the Jewish people (Rom 11:31-33).

Christianity and Judaism

An examination of Paul's own description of his initial experience of the risen Lord suggests that this event is best understood in terms of a call rather than a conversion. The evidence indicates that, regardless of how others may have viewed him, Paul still considered himself in good standing with Judaism. He was convinced that he had received a new and special calling in God's service. Through Christ Jesus, God the Father had commissioned Paul, as a Jew, to proclaim the gospel of freedom to the Gentiles.[25] The apostle's writings further demonstrate that he did not ignore, abandon, nor denounce Judaism. Rather he reinterpreted the traditions of his ancestors in view of the death and resurrection of Christ Jesus. Paul's argumentation in Galatians implies that Christ is the very fulfillment of Judaism (e.g., 3:16).

The church continues to recognize the strong connection between Judaism and Christianity.[26] Indeed it is no accident that Christendom has brought together the Old Testament and the New Testament in one book. "God, the inspirer and author of both testaments, wisely arranged that the New Testament be

[25] See Stendahl, *Paul*, p. 7.
[26] See "Dogmatic Constitution on Divine Revelation," 14-16.

hidden in the Old and the Old be made manifest in the New."[27] Those who pray the Liturgy of the Hours, with its focus on the Psalms, the Benedictus (Luke 1:68-79) and the Magnificat (Luke 1:46-55) are continually reminded of the importance of the Jewish heritage for the Christian believer.

Unfortunately there has often been a great deal of misunderstanding concerning the Christian attitude towards Judaism. That the Jewish people have suffered untold misery as a result of anti-Semitism is a historical fact. Anti-Semitism is not only a product of our troubled past but continues to rear its ugly head in our present-day world. The New Testament account of the life and writings of the apostle has lead some to believe that the religious roots of anti-Semitism can be traced, in part, to Paul, the first century Christian missionary. They contend that his polemic against the law in Galatians and Romans, along with his charge that a veil has descended over Jewish minds (2 Cor 3:12-18) has made him seem an archenemy of Judaism.[28] Hopefully our discussion in this section has illustrated that Paul had no antagonistic feelings towards Judaism.

Both the apostle's positive attitude toward the Jewish people and the church's teaching that Christianity is rooted in Judaism[29] demonstrate that there is no room for anti-Semitism in the church. The New Testament makes it clear that anti-Semitism is not consistent with the gospel of freedom and its emphasis on Christian charity. Using Jewish terminology Paul instructs those committed to the risen Lord tolove their neighbors as themselves (5:14), whether they are Christian believers or not (6:10).

[27] See "Dogmatic Constitution on Divine Revelation," 16.
[28] See Alan Davies, "Anti-Semitism," *EncyclRel*, 1, pp. 323-330, p. 325.
[29] See Raymond F. Collins, *Introduction to the New Testament* (Garden City, NY: Doubleday, 1983), pp. 37-38, regarding the early Church's awareness of its continuity with Judaism, as well as its distinctive character.

SECOND TO NONE

Peter and Paul

Having established his credentials as a Christian missionary, Paul now responds to the accusation that he is inferior to the other apostles. In his attempt to vindicate himself against this charge, Paul often refers to his previous encounters with Peter, one of the original apostles.[30]

Peter, the son of John and brother of Andrew, was originally referred to as Simon (John 1:40-42). After being called by Jesus to be an apostle, he was given the nickname, Cephas (the Greek transliteration of the Aramaic word *kepha* meaning "rock" or "stone"). Peter is a masculine name derived from the feminine noun *petra* (rock). The names Cephas and Peter both appear in Galatians. The vast majority of biblical scholars would agree that the person whom Paul designates in his letters as Cephas is to be equated with Peter, the chief apostle frequently mentioned in the gospels.[31]

There can be no doubt that Peter had a preeminent position among the original apostles. He is mentioned in the gospels much more often than any other disciple. He is cited first in the New Testament lists of the twelve apostles (Matt 10:2, Mark 3:16, Luke 6:14, Acts 1:13). To him has been entrusted the "keys to the kingdom of heaven" (Matt 16:19). Peter may well have been the first of the twelve disciples to have "seen" the risen Lord (1 Cor 15:5, Luke 24:34). The author of Acts unhesitantly portrays Peter as leader of the apostles immediately after the ascension (Acts 1-12). Indeed, Peter had an elevated status in the primitive church.[32]

[30] See 1:18, 2:7, 9, 11, 14.
[31] See for example, George S. Duncan, *The Epistle of Paul to the Galatians*, (London: Hodder and Stoughton, 1944), p. 31. Bart D. Ehrman, "Cephas and Peter," *JBL* 109 (1990), pp. 463-474, defends the highly unlikely thesis that the one whom Paul refers to as Cephas in his epistles is not to be identified with Peter, one of the twelve apostles.
[32] See McKenzie, "Peter," *Dictionary*, pp. 663-666, p. 663.

Even though there is no reason to believe that Peter had ever visited the churches of Galatia, it may well be that the trouble-makers had associated their version of the good news with this towering figure of early Christianity.[33] In any case, Paul sought to counteract the agitators by informing the Galatians of his three previous encounters with Peter.

First Meeting

Paul brushes aside the erroneous notion that the gospel which he received came to him through Peter or any of the other apostles. He assures the Galatians that immediately after the risen Lord had been revealed to him, he did not confer with those who were apostles before him. On the contrary, Paul was not even in the same region where they resided (1:17). Under oath he affirms that it was not until three years later that he had met any of the original apostles for the first time, that is, Cephas, with whom he visited for fifteen days, and James (1:18-20).[34] The fact that Paul was not yet known by sight to the Christians in Judea bears witness to this sworn statement (1:22). As to the other apostles, it was only fourteen years later that Paul made their acquaintance (2:2).

Second Meeting

Paul acknowledges that on one occasion he went to Jerusalem to confer with the other apostles regarding the gospel that he preached (2:1-2). Nevertheless Paul went there at the prompting of the Spirit and not because his proclamation of the good news was under suspicion. By insisting that he received a revelation to visit Peter and the other apostles in Jerusalem, Paul places this whole matter in the same category

[33] See Raymond Brown, Karl Donfried, and John Reuman, eds., *Peter in the New Testament* (Minneapolis, MI: Augsburg, 1973), p. 25.
[34] Paul also takes an oath in 1 Thess 2:5 and 2 Cor 1:23.

as the reception of his call, apostolic commission, gospel of freedom (1:15-16).[35]

Paul was apparently seeking affirmation from the Christian authorities in Jerusalem for the gospel which he preached to the Gentiles lest somehow he "should be running or had run in vain" (2:2). Even though the apostle had no doubt about the validity of the gospel that he preached, he may have been concerned about whether those Gentiles who had responded to his version of the good news would be recognized by the Jerusalem church.[36] Accompanying him to this gathering of Christian leaders were Barnabas and Titus (2:1).

Unlike Paul, Barnabas is spoken of in an exemplary fashion the first time his name appears in Acts (Acts 4:36-37). Originally known as Joseph, this Jewish Christian, who was surnamed Barnabas by the apostles, was renowned for his great generosity. One has the impression that there existed a strong bond of friendship, as well as faith, between Paul and Barnabas. According to the author of Acts, it was Barnabas who introduced Paul to the other apostles and persuaded them to accept this former persecutor of the church as a Christian disciple (Acts 9:27). Barnabas and Paul spent a whole year together with the Christian community in Antioch, where they "taught a large company of people" (Acts 11:25-26). Along with Paul, Barnabas was entrusted with the task of carrying a monetary collection from Antioch to Jerusalem (Acts 11:29). The Christian prophets and teachers in Antioch selected Paul and Barnabas for further missionary endeavors (Acts 13:1-3). To be sure, Barnabas was a well-known and well-respected Christian missionary in the primitive church, whose reputation was beyond reproach.[37]

[35] See Betz, *Galatians*, p. 85. Paul also had other personal revelations. See, for example, 2 Cor 12:1.

[36] See Bruce, *Galatians*, p. 111: "A cleavage between his [Paul's] Gentile mission and the mother-church [in Jerusalem] would be disastrous: Christ would be divided, and all the energy which Paul had devoted, and hoped to devote, to the evangelizing of the Gentile world would be frustrated."

[37] See F.F. Bruce, *The Pauline Circle* (Grand Rapids, MI: Eerdmans, 1985), pp. 15-22.

Although the name of Titus appears relatively few times in the letters of Paul, it is nevertheless obvious that this Gentile Christian enjoyed the apostle's confidence and appreciation to a high degree.[38] The New Testament book which bears his name implies that Titus became a Christian as a result of Paul's proclamation of the good news (Tit 1:4). Titus was Paul's special envoy to the church in Corinth, a Christian community that was experiencing a plethora of severe problems (2 Cor 7:6-16). This "partner and fellow worker" (2 Cor 8:23) of Paul's is commended by the apostle for his Christian ministry (2 Cor 12:18). The depth of Paul's friendship for Titus is illustrated by his strong feelings for him (2 Cor 2:13, 7:6). Titus' feelings for Paul are mutual (2 Cor 7:13). On one occasion the apostle assigned Titus to be a member of a delegation that was to take a special collection to the Christian community in Jerusalem (2 Cor 8:6, 16-17. As the Christian missionary Barnabas, Titus was a man well-suited for Christian ministry and well-thought of in the early church. The presence of these two Christian companions of Paul in Jerusalem can be said to demonstrate a fundamental aspect of the gospel of freedom that he preaches, namely, that in Christ Jesus, Jew and Gentile come together. The apostle may also have brought the uncircumcised Titus, a Christian convert beyond reproach, as a "test case."[39] The Christian leaders in Jerusalem would surely recognize that the grace of God had been active in the life and ministry of Titus, a Gentile Christian who had done so much for the edification of the church.

In the process of relating the story of his encounter with Peter and the other apostles, Paul informs the Galatians of a situation in Jerusalem similar to their own, where the truth of the gospel had been challenged. The apostle mentions some unnamed "false brethren" (2:4) who had apparently insisted on the necessity of circumcision and perhaps also demanded

[38] See Bruce, *Pauline Circle*, pp. 58-65.
[39] See Bruce, *Pauline Circle*, p. 59.

adherence to the dietary regulations of the Torah. Paul, however, had remained steadfast to the good news that he received and did not even compel Titus, his Gentile companion, to be circumcised. This decision was apparently accepted without question by the other apostles. Paul notes triumphantly that Cephas, James, and John, whom he sarcastically refers to as "those who were reputed to be something" (2:6), added nothing to his understanding of the gospel. He later modifies this statement somewhat by recalling that "they would have us remember the poor" (2:10). The apostle quickly adds, however, that he was already eager to do just that (2:10).

Paul was not alone in drawing a parallel between his missionary activity and that of Peter's. Even those apostles who were reputed to be "pillars" (2:9) recognized that Paul had been entrusted with the gospel to the uncircumcised just as Peter had been entrusted with the gospel to the circumcised.[40] They also agreed with Paul that God had worked through his missionary endeavors among the Gentiles just as the Almighty had worked through Peter's missionary endeavors among the Jews. Furthermore, these so-called pillars of the church perceived the grace that was given to Paul and therefore extended to him "the right hand of fellowship" (2:9). There was a mutual understanding that Paul and his companions would direct their missionary efforts towards the Gentiles while James, Cephas, and John, would direct their efforts towards the Jews.

Third Meeting

Paul's confrontation with Peter and the other Christian leaders in Antioch acts as a grand finale to his argumentation that he is not inferior to those who were apostles before him.

[40] Although these two towering Christian missionaries had directed their respective missionary activities towards two different categories of people, Jews and Gentiles, Paul did not see this as indicative of two different gospels. See Gal 1:7. For another point of view, see James D.G. Dunn, *Unity and Diversity in the New Testament* (Philadelphia, PA: Trinity, 1991), p. 23.

The apostle calls to mind what he considers to be the shameful conduct of Peter at a Christian gathering in Antioch, where both Jewish and Gentile Christians came together for a meal. Peter had no qualms about eating with Gentile Christians. However, when "certain men from James" (2:12) came into their company, he drew back and separated himself from the Gentiles out of fear of the "circumcision party" (2:12). Others were adversely influenced by Peter's example. The rest of the Jews who were likewise present also drew back and separated themselves from the Gentile Christians. Even Barnabas, the dear friend and trusted missionary companion of Paul, was carried away by Peter's conduct and acted in a similar fashion.

Undoubtedly the motive for Peter's behavior at this gathering of Jewish and Gentile Christians was based on his desire to avoid scandal. He probably separated himself from these Gentile believers so as not to offend the Jewish Christians from James who, in accordance with the Mosaic law, objected strenuously to dining with non-Jews. Paul saw things differently. According to his way of thinking, Peter's behavior encouraged a Jewish-Christian apartheid. The apostle realizes that the consequences of Peter's behavior would result in a divided church. This stood in direct opposition to the truth of the gospel, which was divinely intended to bring people together in Christ and not drive them apart.

The apostle did not allow Peter's conduct to go unanswered. Paul lets it be known that he personally condemned Peter to his face because this highly esteemed apostle was obviously in the wrong. Before the other Christian leaders, Paul scolded him for separating himself at table from the Gentiles, although the fisherman from Galilee had not previously thought it necessary to do so. "If you, though a Jew, live like a Gentile and not like a Jew, how can you compel the Gentiles to live like Jews" (2:14)? With this derogatory question, Paul forces Peter to see the ramifications of his past behavior.

Apostolic Equality

These three episodes described by the apostle, which circulate around the figure of Peter, are crucial to his argumentation. Although Paul's apostleship and his version of the gospel did not originate from those who were apostles before him, they were nevertheless officially recognized by the "pillars" (2:9) of the church. Indeed, having received the right hand of fellowship, Paul was treated as an equal by those apostles of such lofty stature as Peter, James and John. Not only was Paul on equal footing with these apostles, but on one occasion he had to publicly correct Peter, the prince of the original apostles, for not acting straightforward about the truth of the gospel. In addition to his previous testimony, this incident makes it clear that Paul is in no way inferior to the other apostles.[41] He has presented a strong argument in support of his conviction that his apostleship, his rendition of the gospel, and his Gentile converts are second to none.

Concluding Remarks

Paul shared his life story with the Galatians in order to win them over to his point of view. Perhaps one of the great lessons of the apostle's autobiographical account is that God intervenes in the most unexpected of ways. Two thousand years later we still marvel at the spectacular turn of events that took place in the life of this fascinating personality of the first century. The apostle has provided a wonderful example of how Christians should gear their lives once they have detected the presence of the risen Lord in their midst. Paul's Christ-centered existence is of particular importance in this regard. He viewed

[41] See Donald Guthrie, *Galatians* CBNS (London: Nelson, 1969), p. 63: When the apostle "actually withstood Peter publicly before the Antioch church, there could not have been a clearer evidence of his apostolic status."

all of life with the spectacles of his Christian faith. Literally everything that he had considered of value before his encounter with the glorified Christ took on secondary importance after this mystifying religious experience.

Although present day Christians may not have had the privilege of receiving a divine revelation of the risen Lord, they nevertheless have their own story to tell of how God the Father revealed His Son to them. Perhaps one can say that all Christian believers are challenged to imitate Paul in his missionary capacity. Those in Christ may not all have the vocation to travel to distant lands and preach the good news but they are called, nevertheless, to proclaim the gospel in their own unique way. All who claim allegiance to the risen Lord herald the gospel to those with whom they have contact. They do so by being faithful in word and deed to their commitment to Jesus Christ in their day-to-day living.

Paul was not pronounced a saint by the church simply because so many miraculous happenings were associated with his life. Rather, Christendom canonized the apostle to the Gentiles for his tremendous faith in Christ and for his great love of God and neighbor. Paul expressed his Christian faith and love for the church in a variety ways, remaining true to his apostolic calling through thick and thin even unto death.

Paul and the Galatians

In the course of narrating the story of his initial experience of the risen Lord and previous encounters with Peter and the other apostles, Paul identifies his situation with that of the Galatians. As those to whom he is addressing his remarks, Paul came to believe in Christ Jesus as his Lord and savior. Moreover, just as the apostle's version of the gospel had been recently threatened by the troublemakers in Galatia, so too had other unnamed agitators in Jerusalem challenged his gospel of freedom. However, unlike the Galatians, Paul was never in danger of giving in to these Judaizers who were apparently insisting on at least the partial observance the Mosaic law. The apostle invites the Galatians to follow his example and stand up for the truth of the gospel which he had first preached to them. In a similar fashion, Paul's courageous defense of the gospel of freedom challenges Christians of all times and places to uphold the truth of the gospel despite all outside pressure to do otherwise.

Paul and Authority

Paul's argumentation in Galatians demonstrates that he has a healthy respect for ecclesiastical authority. As one who has been divinely commissioned to proclaim the good news to the Gentiles he definitely views himself as one who possesses apostolic authority. It is in light of his authorative status that he first preached the gospel to the Galatians and now addresses the crisis situation which they are experiencing. Despite Paul's sarcastic comments about those who were apostles before him and reputed to be something, he ventured to Jerusalem in order to lay down his gospel before these recognized authorities of the church in order to receive their approval. This being said, Paul does not seem to regard human authority as "unreprimandable." He informs the Galatians that if he should ever preach a gospel which contradicted the one he originally proclaimed to them, then he too would be deserving of condemnation (1:8). While defending his rendition of the good news, the apostle does not hesitate to upbraid such a commanding figure of authority as Peter himself for behavior contrary to the truth of the gospel. According to Paul's way of thinking, no human authority, no matter how elevated a status one might have, is above the truth of the gospel.

Peter and Paul

Peter and Paul were two very different individuals. Peter was a simple fisherman with little or no formal academic training who probably felt more at home in small villages. Paul, on the other hand, was a well educated person and a cosmopolitan figure. These two men had, nevertheless, much in common. Both Peter and Paul were called by God in their own unique way. They were authorized to preach the good news of Jesus Christ. They were both men of incredible faith who had an intense love for Christ and his church. Neither of them were afraid to take a stand on an issue once they had made up their mind concerning its validity. The importance that the early church attributed to Peter and Paul is borne out by the great deal of information about them which appears in the New Testament.

Interestingly enough, the various authors of the New Testament were not at all embarrassed at exposing the weaknesses of these two larger-than-life personalities. Peter denied Jesus three times (Matt 26:69-75) while Paul violently persecuted the first Christians. This being said, these two men played a pivotal role in the foundational stages of the church. God selected former sinners to occupy authorative positions in a church composed of sinners. The biblical account of the past failures of these great saints illustrates that Christians should not be discouraged at their own failures. Indeed the New Testament repeatedly illustrates that there is no such thing as a terminal spiritual malady. There is hope for everyone, even the greatest of sinners.

Whatever differences Peter and Paul may have had in Antioch and elsewhere, their unity in faith was manifested by their willingness to live out their Christian commitment unto death. Both suffered martyrdom in Rome under Nero. Ever since, the names of these two apostles have often been linked together. In addition to their sharing a common feast day (June 29), there are hundreds of churches throughout the world jointly named in their honor.

The Surprise of Freedom

Paul must have been surprised by the freedom that God demonstrated in choosing him to herald the gospel while he was still persecuting the church. The apostle must have been equally surprised to discover via divine revelation that justification comes through faith in Christ apart from the Mosaic law. This was indeed a shock for one who had been such a fanatic about the sacred traditions of Judaism, that he persecuted Jewish Christians for their supposedly flippant attitude towards the Torah. Furthermore, the troublemakers in Galatia, the false brethren in Jerusalem, and even the other apostles were undoubtedly surprised by Paul's gospel of freedom which completely bypassed the requirement of observing the Mosaic law in one's attempt to obtain righteousness. More than a few eyebrows were raised by the fervor which Paul demonstrated in defending the radical equality of Jewish and Gentile Christians. The ramifications of Paul's gospel of freedom continue to surprise us still.

CHAPTER FOUR

FAITH: THE GATEWAY TO FREEDOM (GAL 2:15-21)

Confident that he has successfully defended himself against all trumped up charges regarding his status as an apostle, Paul now takes the offensive and attacks head on the "other gospel" put forth by the troublemakers. Whether the apostle's comments about the law in Gal 2:15-21 were directed towards Peter in Antioch, as in Gal 2:14, or whether Paul is simply informing the Galatians about his motivation for admonishing Peter, is unclear. Whatever the case might be, in stark contrast to the teaching of the agitators, the apostle insists that the Torah has absolutely no role to play in obtaining righteousness. In a fashion reminiscent of the repeated thrust of a battering ram, the good news that one obtains righteousness through faith in Christ *alone* is again and again proclaimed by Paul (2:16).

In Gal 2:17-21, the apostle is apparently responding to the Judaizers' accusation that his teaching of justification by faith in Christ alone results in a sinful situation.[1] These troublemakers are convinced that Christians who fail to observe the Torah, namely, those who have responded to Paul's teaching of a Torah-free gospel, are sinners by virtue of their failure to obey the commands of the Mosaic law.[2] If that is in fact the case, according to the agitators' way of thinking, then Paul has, in a

[1] Paul's argumentation in Gal 2:17-21 has been the topic of much discussion. See for example, Jan Lambrecht, "The Line of Thought in Gal 2:14b-21," *NTS* 24 (1977-78), pp. 484-495.

[2] Paul himself seems to imply that the non-observance of the Mosaic law is sinful. See Deut 27:26 in Gal 3:10.

manner of speaking, committed the "crime" of making Christ an agent of sin (2:17)!

The apostle reacts vehemently to these accusations. He emphatically denies that his version of the gospel can in any way be construed as making Christ an agent of sin (2:17c). For Paul, it is the Judaizers who have turned everything upside-down. If the apostle were to build up those things which he had previously torn down, that is, if he were to yield to the agitators and insist on adherence to the Torah as a means to justification instead of standing fast to his position that obedience to the Mosaic law is unnecessary in this regard, then he would be a transgressor (2:18).[3] The apostle supports this claim in the following verses.

Paul's argumentation takes on a more personal nature in Gal 2:19-21. Whereas in the previous verses he had been speaking in the first person plural, he now speaks in the first person singular. The apostle makes the ultimate statement in distancing himself from the mandatory observance of the Torah. As far as Paul is concerned, he has "died to the law" (2:19). The apostle's old life in the law is dead because he now lives "by *faith* in the Son of God who loved me and gave himself for me" (2:20). The way in which Christ "gave of himself" is explained in 2:21, namely, by his death. Paul goes on to say that, unbeknownst to the Galatians, all who seek justification by means of the Mosaic law do the unthinkable. They act as if Christ's salvific death were in vain.

If we are to come to terms with Paul's puzzling statement in Gal 2:18 that it is those who observe the Torah in order to obtain righteousness that are transgressors, we must keep the following considerations in mind. Whatever the apostle may have believed before his experience of the risen Lord, his argumentation in his letters implies that all human beings are

[3] See Daniel C. Arichea and Eugene A. Nida, *A Translators Handbook on Paul's Letter to the Galatians* (New York, NY: United Bible Societies, 1975), pp. 46-49.

sinners and in need of salvation, that deliverance from sin, being declared righteous, can only be achieved through Christ; and that the Mosaic law is incapable of liberating the sinner from the tragic effects of sin. Moreover, Paul's writings indicate that he is absolutely convinced that the manner in which one obtains righteousness is through faith in Christ alone. By virtue of their unity with Christ, those who hold fast to the apostle's version of the gospel are justified and thus no longer regarded as transgressors. Those who reject Paul's rendition of the good news and seek justification through the observance of the Torah, however, behave as if Christ died in vain, nullify the grace of God (2:21), and remain steeped in their sins, that is, they remain transgressors.

Justified By Faith

Justification

Paul uses the term "justification" more often than any other New Testament author to describe the transformation that takes place in the Christian believer as a result of the death and resurrection of Christ. The words "justified" and "righteous" are derivatives of the Greek verb *dikaioô*, meaning "to put into a right relationship," "to acquit," "to set free," and "to declare and treat as righteous."[4] The apostle contends that justification is a free gift of God (Rom 5:17).

We have previously spoken of the tragic situation of unredeemed humanity. As sinners, according to Paul's way of thinking, unredeemed human beings are, in a sense, "enemies of God" (Rom 5:10). They are under condemnation (3:10), in bondage (3:23, 4:8), and destined for corruption (6:8). In addition to suffering the many other wretched consequences of sin,

[4] See Colin Brown, "*dikaiosunê*," *DNTT*, 3, pp. 352-373.

unredeemed human beings will have to encounter the wrath of God on the last day (e.g., 1 Thess 1:10). This is not the case for those who have obtained righteousness.

Paul affirms that those who believe in Christ and have been baptized are justified in the sight of God, that is, they are declared innocent of all wrong doing and set free from sin. They have been liberated from the disastrous consequences of sin and have been reconciled to God by the death of His Son (Rom 5:10). All who obtain righteousness have been placed into a right relationship with God and will reap eternal life (6:8). The apostle's argumentation in Galatians is best understood if one realizes that he closely associates those who are "justified" with those who "receive the Spirit" (3:2), are "children of Abraham" (3:7) "are blessed with Abraham" (3:9), receive the "inheritance" (3:19), are "righteous" (3:21), are "children of God" (3:26), "are Christ's" (3:29a), are "Abraham's offspring" (3:29b), and are "heirs according to the promise" (3:29c).

Justification should be thought of in terms of *responsibility* as well as gift. Although it is not something which can be "earned," justification, nevertheless, demands a response. It calls for daily allegiance and obedience to Christ.[5] The apostle underscores the conviction that justification is not "automatic" by often referring to the last judgment. On that day all people will have to render an account of their lives (e.g., Rom 2:6, 14:10). The apostle warns those Christians under his care that an unfavorable judgment awaits anyone who has not been obedient to the gospel (Rom 2:7-11, Gal 1:8-9).[6] In view of these considerations, some biblical scholars contend that Paul makes a distinction between justification and salvation,[7] that is,

[5] Paul elaborates on the notion of Christian fidelity in Galatians 5 and 6. See Karl P. Donfried, "Justification and Last Judgment in Paul," *ZNW* 67 (1976), pp. 90-110, p. 93.

[6] See 1 Cor 10:1-5, 1 Cor 11:27-29, Gal 6:7-10, Gal 5:19-21.

[7] Most notably, Donfried, "Justification," pp. 90-110.

he speaks of justification as the beginning of the Christian life and of salvation as that which denotes a positive judgment on the last day. Thus, although Paul is convinced that he is justified (2:16), he nevertheless refers to salvation as a "hope" (1 Thess 5:8).

The apostle's discussion concerning justification indicates that the good works which he often encourages Christians to perform should be thought of in terms of a "response." In other words, Christians should not be motivated to perform acts of charity by the misguided attempt to "earn" justification. Rather, they should be prompted by their desire to demonstrate to God the Father that they accept His great gift of justification and thank Him for it.

Faith in Christ

Unlike his Jewish contemporaries who completely identified obtaining righteousness with conformity to the Mosaic law, Paul insisted that it was obtained exclusively through faith in Christ. Many present-day Christians often think of "faith" in terms of a "particular religious denomination." Still others merely equate faith with the creed, that is, the content of what Christians believe. Some people associate this word with a strictly intellectual endeavor. Perhaps it is for these reasons that many feel uncomfortable with Paul's fundamental conviction that justification comes through faith alone. Whatever the case may be, the apostle has a far richer and deeper understanding of faith than that which is conveyed by any of the above notions.

The Greek word *pistis* and its cognates can be translated as "belief," "faith," "faithful," and "trust."[8] Christians are those who have responded to the proclamation of the gospel by coming to believe in Christ Jesus as their Lord and Savior (Rom 10:8-9, 17). They not only believe the message about Jesus Christ but they also trust in and submit themselves to

[8] See Otto Michel, "*pistis*," *DNTT*, 1, pp. 593-605.

him. Those who profess faith in Christ Jesus make a commitment of their whole person to God in Christ.[9]

The apostle does not view faith as a mere intellectual assent. On the contrary, faith involves a vital personal commitment which engages the whole person to Christ in all his/her relations with God, other human beings, and the world. One who professes faith in the risen Lord enters a new mode of existence, namely, a new union with God through Christ (2:20). Like justification, faith is ultimately a gift from God (Rom 12:3). Paul declares that faith in Christ alone is the means by which justification operates. One's faith in Christ Jesus is expressed in and through deeds of love. In the light of this, Paul continually exhorts Christians to practice all sorts of good deeds (e.g., Gal 5:16 - 6:6).[10]

That faith is an indispensable ingredient in justification was not an issue between Paul and the Galatians (2:16b).[11] The issue was whether one obtains righteousness *exclusively* by faith in Christ. The troublemakers had apparently swayed the Galatians into believing that, in addition to faith in Christ, at least the partial observance of the Mosaic law was a prerequisite for obtaining righteousness. In seemingly every conceivable way, the apostle prevails upon his readers to accept his conviction that Gentiles obtain righteousness through Christ by means of faith without observing the Torah.

Paul's numerous comments about Christian faith are still relevant to contemporary Christians. Faith is indeed a very precious gift from God. The believer's faith in Christ must be continually nourished by prayer, both personal and communal, if it is to develop and deepen. Assuredly, the life of faith is meant to be lived out in the context of the Christian community. Although one's faith in the risen Lord certainly involves an intellectual assent to basic Christian beliefs about Jesus

[9] See Joseph A. Fitzmyer, "Pauline Theology," *NJBC* II, pp. 1407-1408.
[10] See Fitzmyer, "Theology," p. 1407.
[11] Paul seems to assume in Gal 2:16b that the Galatians would agree with his comment: "Even we have believed in Christ Jesus *in order to be justified.*"

Christ, it nevertheless entails much more than that. Christian believers are called to demonstrate their faith in Christ in all aspects of their day-to-day living.

Not The Law

Paul's understanding of the law is a subject that must be investigated if we are to comprehend Paul's theology.[12] W.D. Davies has remarked that because of its importance not only in the apostle's letters and in other parts of the New Testament but also in the encounter between Roman Catholicism and Protestantism, the treatment of the law by Paul has been and is one of the most discussed subjects in Christian theology.[13] The fundamental reason why so much discussion has taken place on this topic is that the apostle often reflects on the law within the context of a discussion of justification.

How is it possible that Paul, a Jew and a Pharisee (Phil 3:5), and one well acquainted with the Torah, is able to make so many derogatory comments about the law? First of all, he insists that no one is justified by performing the works of the law (2:16). Then, using language that would have shocked his Jewish contemporaries, the apostle declares that all who rely on these works of the law are under a curse (3:10)! That Paul links one's dependance on the Torah with a curse, instead of justification, seems rather strange in view of his strong Jewish heritage. After all, the Jewish people observe the Mosaic law because they believe that their adherence to it reflects the will of God.

[12] See E.P. Sanders, *Paul, the Law, and the Jewish People* (Philadelphia, PA: Fortress, 1983), p. 3: The problem of Paul's comprehension of the law "must be penetrated if one is to understand Paul's thought, and it is no less crucial for understanding an important moment in the divorce of Christianity from Judaism."

[13] See W.D. Davies, *Jewish and Pauline Studies* (Philadelphia, PA: S.P.C.K., 1984), p. 91.

The Call to Holiness

Generally speaking, there is one essential reason why the Torah demands that the people of Israel observe its ordinances, namely, to ensure that they respond to the divine command and become sanctified.[14] "Be holy for I the Lord your God am holy" (Lev 19:2). The biblical notion of "holiness" is associated with that which has been "set apart," or "removed." Because of their observance of the Mosaic law the chosen people have been set apart from all others in that they have separated themselves from idolatry, secularism, and from the vulgar and the profane.[15]

The specific precepts of the Mosaic law demonstrate how the Jewish people are to become holy. Concern for the *sanctity of the person* is reflected in those ordinances which deal with eating habits, personal hygiene, patterns of dress and speech, sexual relationships, social and business ethics, sexual relationships, and so on. Concern for the *sanctity of time* is emphasized by those regulations which relate to the Sabbath and the various festivals. And the concern for the *sanctity of place* is accentuated by those statutes which pertain to the Temple in Jerusalem and to the synagogue.[16]

Of particular importance are the commandments of the Torah that deal with circumcision and dietary regulations. The observance of those ordinances which relate to circumcision guarantees that one obeys Yahweh's sacred decree to Abraham and his descendants, that is, to circumcise every male child as a sign of God's covenant with His people (Gen 17:10-14). The Jewish people were also well known for following those precepts of the Mosaic law which prohibited eating certain types of food (e.g., pork). Within this context, the terms "clean" and "unclean" were thought of as spiritual and not

[14] See Hayim H. Donin, *To Be a Jew* (New York, NY: Basic Books, 1972), pp. 33-34.
[15] See Donin, *Jew*, p. 37.
[16] See Donin, *Jew*, pp. 35-36.

physical. In other words, by distinguishing between "clean" and the "unclean" food, the observers of the Torah were creating a mind-set for holiness. Learning to distinguish the "clean" from the "unclean" in the realm of food also disciplined them to do likewise in other areas of life, such as the moral, the ethical, and the spiritual realm.[17]

The New Testament bears witness that Jesus himself observed the Torah. He was circumcised (Luke 2:21), often went to the synagogue (e.g., Mark 1:21), visited the temple in Jerusalem (Mark 11:11), and celebrated the feast of passover (Matt 26:17). The same can be said of the original twelve apostles. Nevertheless, in spite of all these positive aspects about the Torah, Paul still insists that the observance of the works of the law is not a mandatory requirement for obtaining righteousness and, in fact, that reliance on such observance results in condemnation. What does Paul intend to signify by the phrase "works of the law" in Gal 2:16 and why does he contend that those who depend on them are not justified but cursed (3:10)?

Works of the Law

The expression "works of the law" (*erga nomou*) appears eight times in the authentic letters of Paul and is unique to the apostle.[18] On every occasion that he uses this phrase he asserts, explicitly or unexplicitly, that justification does not come about through doing them (e.g., 2:16, 3:10).

The "law" which Paul frequently refers to in Galatians is not the legal system in general nor is it the Roman law but is, in fact, the Mosaic law.[19] This is borne out by the numerous references to circumcision (2:3, 5:2, 6:12), the mention of Mount Sinai (4:24-25), the allusion to the Jewish food laws

[17] See Donin, *Jew*, pp. 98-99.

[18] See Gal 2:16 (3x), 3:2, 5, 10, Rom 3:20, 28.

[19] Our discussion of Paul's understanding of the law in Galatians is based, in part, on an enlightening article by Douglas J. Moo, "'Law,' 'Works of the Law,' and Legalism in Paul," *WTJ* 45 (1983), pp. 73-100.

(2:11-14) the various citations from the Torah (e.g., Deut 27:26 in Gal 3:10b), and Paul's reminder that the law came 430 years after God made a promise to Abraham (3:17). There are two instances where Paul speaks of the law in a broader sense.[20] These instances, however, are the exception and not the rule.

Some exegetes have opined that Paul makes a distinction between those statutes of the Torah which deal with the cultic aspect of Judaism and those precepts which are concerned with morality.[21] Those who defend this position maintain that Paul sometimes uses the term law to designate only the cultic ordinances of the Mosaic law. Thus, for example, when the apostle states in Gal 2:19 that he died to the law, he would be referring exclusively to those prescriptions of the Torah which deal with cultic considerations. Paul's frequent mention of circumcision (e.g., 5:2-3) and his indirect reference to Jewish food laws (2:11-14) would seem to substantiate this claim. Nevertheless, other considerations cast serious doubt on the validity of such a position.

Paul gives every indication that he views the Mosaic law as a *single individual whole*. The apostle never uses the plural form of the term law in Galatians nor in any other of his letters. Moreover, Paul's remarks about keeping the *whole law* in Gal 5:3 are significant. The logic of his argument in this verse prohibits a neat distinction between moral and ceremonial law.[22] It is also worth mentioning that the apostle's comments about the law in Gal 3:17 and 3:19 clearly demonstrate that he views the Torah as a complete whole. Furthermore, it would be strange indeed for Paul to warn the Galatians in Galatians 5 against a life of licentiousness had he in fact distinguished the cultic and moral aspects of the law. Only if Paul rejected the law as

[20] See Gal 4:21 and 6:2.

[21] See Heikki Räisänen, *Paul and the Law* (Tübingen: Mohr, 1983), p. 18, where a presentation is made in regards to various exegetes have proposed certain distinctions concerning Paul's use of the term "law."

a *whole* was there a danger of the Galatians lapsing into an immoral life-style. Indeed Paul regards the Mosaic law as a unified whole.

Since Paul understands the Torah as an undivided whole, he is in need of an expression that places a greater emphasis on the "specific precepts" of the Torah. Hence the phrase "works of the law" should be understood as an idiom used by the apostle to denote acts which are performed in obedience to the statutes of the Torah, especially those involving circumcision and dietary regulations.[23]

In Galatians, the expression "works of the law" first appears in 2:16 where Paul emphasizes repeatedly (three times in this verse) that no one obtains righteousness by means of them. Just prior to these remarks concerning the works of the law, Paul alludes to the Jewish dietary laws (2:11-14). Furthermore, previous to his comments in Gal 2:16 the apostle mentions circumcision on six occasions. These factors suggest that when Paul uses the phrase "works of the law," he is referring, in particular, to those acts done in obedience to the commands of the Mosaic law which deal with circumcision and food laws.

Pauline Inconsistency?

One might wonder if the apostle is consistent in his various comments about the Mosaic law. For example, although Paul argues again and again in Galatians against the necessity of being circumcised (e.g., 5:2) and observing the law (e.g., 5:4), he unequivocally states in Gal 5:6 and 6:15 that it really makes no difference whether an individual is circumcised or not!

[22] See Moo, "Law," p. 84: "If this distinction were assumed by Paul, he would have argued to the effect that while the Galatians were obligated to the moral law, circumcision (presumably as aspect of the ceremonial law) was to be excluded. Instead, Paul stresses the unity of the law."

[23] See James D.G. Dunn's interesting study of the "Works of the Law and the Curse of the Law (Gal 3:10-14)" *NTS* 31 (1985), pp. 523-542, in which he refers to such works of the law as "identity markers."

The apostle's remarks in Gal 5:6 and 6:15 suggest that he does not object to the Torah nor to the observance of the works of the law *per se*.[24] Therefore, Paul's assertion that justification cannot be obtained through the law (3:11) does not necessarily imply that those who observe the Torah cannot be justified. It does indicate, however, that no one can be justified *by means of* it (2:21, 3:21). According to the apostle's way of thinking, what is important is *why* an individual desires to observe the Torah. On the one hand, those who wish to perform the works of the law yet realize that they are *not* a means to righteousness, will suffer no ill consequences (apparently the assumption in 5:6 and 6:15). On the other hand, those who observe the works of the law because they are convinced that obedience to the Torah is necessary in order to obtain righteousness, are anathema (5:4).

The question remains: Why does Paul consider the Mosaic law an inadequate means of obtaining righteousness? In order to shed some light on this question, we will present the various positions of New Testament scholars who have offered explanations as to why the apostle affirms that the Torah is not a valid means to justification. The exegetes in this survey have been selected to provide a representation of the many ways of understanding Paul's argumentation regarding the law.

Why the Law Does Not Justify

Transgression of the Law

Ulrich Wilckens contends that under no circumstances whatsoever is the law capable of making one righteous, because no one obeys all of its precepts.[25] This interpretation has been

[24] For an opposing hypothesis, see for example, Gerhard Ebeling, *The Truth of the Gospel* (Philadelphia, PA: Fortress, 1985), pp. 178-179.
[25] See Ulrich Wilckens, "Was heisst bei Paulus: 'Aus Werken des Gesetzes wird kein Mench gerecht'?" and *Rechtfertigung als Freiheit: Paulusstudien* (Neukirchen-Vluyn: Neukirchner, 1974), pp. 77-109; "Zur Entwicklung des paulinischen Gesetzesverständnis," *NTS* 28 (1982), pp. 154-190.

referred to as a "quantitative argument"[26] and has been defended by exegetes since the first centuries of the Christian era.[27] On the basis of Paul's citation of Lev 18:5 in Gal 3:12b (He who does them [the precepts of the law] shall live by them"), Wilckens is convinced that if one obeyed all the precepts of the law, one would obtain righteousness. In upholding this position Wilckens opposes any interpretation which claims that the observance of the law *per se* is sinful. On the contrary, in light of the apostle's reference to Deut 27:26 in Gal 3:10b ("Cursed be every one who does not abide by all things written in the book of the law, and do them"), Wilckens affirms that it is the failure to obey every precept of the Torah that brings forth a curse. It is not the "doing" of the law that engenders a curse but rather the failure to obey the law in its entirety.

According to Wilckens, the apostle maintains that no one is justified by means of the law because everyone has transgressed it. A number of passages in the letters of Paul indicate that he views all people as sinners (e.g., Rom 3:23, 5:12). Moreover, the apostle asserts in Gal 2:17 that "we" Jews who seek justification in Christ "were found to be sinners," and are no different from the Gentiles (Gal 2:15). From the context of this passage Wilckens concludes that since Christ has died for everyone, then everyone must have been in need of redemption from the law's curse (3:13a) because everyone has sinned. The same train of thought is also present in Gal 2:19-21. In view of the fact that everyone has sinned, seeking righteousness by means of the law is futile because the law curses the sinner (Deut 27:26, Gal 3:10b) and is unable to make one

[26] In view of the numerical connotation that the word "quantitative" possesses, this term describes well the argument that no one is justified by means of the law because no one obeys each and every one of its precepts.
[27] See, for example, John Chrysostom, "Homilies on Galatians," *A Select Library of the Nicene and Post-Nicene Fathers of the Christian Church*. Vol. 13, edited by Philip Schaff (Grand Rapids, MI: Eerdmans, 1979), pp. 1-48, pp. 26-27.

righteous (3:21).[28] The law which all have transgressed merely has the function of establishing them as sinners and making known to them that they have sinned (Rom 3:20). Consequently the law offers no hope of salvation. Although it is theoretically possible to be justified by means of the law (Lev 18:5, Gal 3:12), in reality, it is not, because all have transgressed it.

Paul's use of Deut 27:26 in Gal 3:10b and his warning in Gal 5:3 (whoever is circumcised is bound to keep the whole law) provide substantial support for agreeing with Wilckens' hypothesis that, according to the apostle, no one is justified by observing the works of the law because no one obeys the Torah in its entirety. This being said, we remain hesitant that such an explanation reflects Paul's *fundamental* reason for rejecting the Mosaic law as a valid means to obtaining righteousness. In other words, it does not seem likely that the apostle came to believe that one is justified by faith alone simply because he was convinced that no one obeyed each and every precept of the Mosaic law.

Self-Righteousness

Gunther Klein, who belongs to a tradition that was crystallized by Martin Luther, is convinced that there is a more fundamental reason which explains the inability of the law to make one righteous than the mere transgression of it.[29] This "Lutheran" interpretation, which has also been referred to as a "qualitative argument,"[30] claims that *in principle* one cannot

[28] In spite of the Old Testament passages which clearly state that atonement is possible (e.g., Lev 4:22-26), Paul's argumentation in Gal 3:21 implies that the law is not able to redeem one from the curse of Deut 27:26.

[29] See Gunther Klein, "Individualgeschichte und Weltgeschichte bei Paulus," *EvTh* 24 (1964), pp. 126-165, p. 151; and "Sündenverständis und theologia crucis bei Paulus," Erich Dinkler and Carl Andressen, eds., *Theologia crucis - signum crucis* (Tübingen: Mohr, 1979), pp. 249-282.

[30] The qualitative argument maintains that there is an *essentially* different way to obtain righteousness than by means of the law, hence the term "qualitative" argument.

be justified by way of the Torah. According to Klein, righteousness is obtained in a way that has nothing whatsoever to do with the law, that is, by means of faith. Faith and the law are understood as two completely different entities because Scripture testifies that the law is based on "doing" (Lev 18:12, Gal 3:12b) while faith is based on believing. Not only is the attempt to be justified by means of the law futile, it is considered sinful. Those who adhere to the Torah manifest the essence of sin in their very observance of the law because they are relying on themselves for justification and therefore rejecting the grace of God.[31]

Klein finds the key to Paul's understanding of the law in Gal 2:16 and Rom 3:20-22 where it is clearly stated that no one is justified by performing works of the law but only through faith. In order to discern how Paul arrived at this conclusion, it is of the utmost importance to realize that his understanding of sin determines his teaching on the law. Ever since Adam first sinned, human beings have lived in a fallen state and have been corrupted with a self-powered striving to secure their own justification by their own strength. The reason why no one is justified by works of the law is that one must not be allowed to imagine that one is able to obtain righteousness by one's own merit. Human beings can only obtain righteousness when they understand themselves as dependent on God.

Because of its intention to help human beings promote unity with God and themselves, it is true that the law is holy (Rom 7:12). It is also true that the law teaches good things. However, one fails to do them because the commandments only show what one ought to do without giving one the power to do it. The purpose of the law is not to provide a means to justification but rather to reveal sin and provoke despair at one's own sinfulness in order to coerce one into seeking righteousness in Christ. In their sinful condition, however, human beings cannot

[31] See Francis Watson, *Paul, Judaism and the Gentiles* SNTSMS 56 (Cambridge: Cambridge University, 1986), p. 2.

but misconceive this divine intention when they attempt to earn justification by keeping the law. Paul refers to this fundamental sin as "boasting" (Rom 3:27).[32] The law, although holy in itself is perverted by sin. This qualitative understanding of the law results in a paradox: "Doing" the law is regarded as more sinful than "not doing" it.[33] In reality, all who seek justification by means of the law not only refuse God's grace, but also commit the treacherous sin of trying to usurp the place of God.

The validity of much of Klein's argumentation stands or falls on the conviction that Paul places "faith" and "law" in total opposition. But is this in fact the case? In light of biblical citations such as Deut 6:4 it seems obvious that the very observance of the Torah presupposes the concept of faith, that is, faith in God and in His promises. Why would one submit oneself to the demands of the Torah if one did not believe in God and trust in His convenantal promises? Consequently, even though one could confidently state that the apostle distinguishes between the two, one hesitates to agree with Klein that faith and law were considered by Paul to be totally opposed to one another.[34]

The apostle's interpretation of the death of Christ in Gal 3:13 is also significant. Paul's assertion in this verse concerning the way in which "Christ became a curse for us" may indicate that the apostle wants to draw attention to the fact that it is particular transgressions of the law which brings forth the curse of Deut 27:26 (Gal 3:10b). In other words, Christ became a curse in light of one of the precepts of the law (Deut 21:23, Gal 3:13b) and not because he was seeking self-justification through the observance of the Torah. This suggests that

[32] See Watson, *Paul*, pp. 4-5.

[33] See Heikki Räisänen, "Legalism and Salvation by the Law," Sigfred Pederson, ed., *Die paulinische Literatur und Theologie* (Göttingen: Aros, 1980), pp. 63-83.

[34] See Wilckens, "Entwicklung," pp. 168-169, for a more detailed evaluation of Klein's position.

the curse from which Christ redeemed us (3:13a) is associated with the transgressions of the Mosaic law and not with the misguided attempt to justify oneself. For these reasons, we find Klein's thesis regarding the inadequacy of the law to make one righteous unsatisfactory.

The Torah Is Annulled

Hans-Joachim Schoeps proposes that the law is an inaccessible means to justification because the Torah is no longer valid in the Messianic era.[35] Since Paul believed that the risen Lord was the Messiah, the apostle came to recognize that "Christ is the end of the law" (Rom 10:4). The Torah ceases when the Messianic kingdom begins. As far as Schoeps is concerned, Paul must oppose any notion that justification is obtainable by means of the law, because whoever believes that the Torah is still valid denies that Jesus is the Messiah. The old authority of the law and the new authority of the Messiah cannot co-exist.

Schoeps contends that Paul's understanding of the law is the most intricate doctrinal issue in his theology.[36] In order to understand the apostle's various comments about the law, Schoeps insists that the concept of Jesus as the Jewish Messiah must be taken into consideration. In rabbinic literature there existed a widespread opinion that the Torah would lose its validity in the Messianic era. Schoeps has been led to this conclusion on the basis of a number of passages in the Talmud, the writings of Philo, and apocalyptic literature.

The apostle states in Rom 7:1 that "the law is binding on a person only during his life." This assertion by Paul calls to mind the rabbinic interpretation found in Shab 30a and Nidd 61b of the Talmud that: "As soon as a man is dead, he is free from the obligation of the [law's] commands." Paul's

[35] See Hans-Joachim Schoeps, *Paul: The Theology of the Apostle in Light of Jewish Religious History* (Philadelphia, PA: Westminster Press, 1961), pp. 171-175

[36] See Schoeps, *Paul*, p. 168.

conviction that Jesus is the Messiah has led him to the realization that the Messianic age has begun and therefore every Christian believer is now dead to the aeon of the Torah. In the same way that a dead man is free from the obligations of the Torah, so too the Christian believer, dead to the age of the Torah, is free from the law's obligations (Rom 7:6).

Paul has a conception of salvation history which he inherited from the Pharisaic tradition. He maintains that world history can be divided into three phases: 1) the period of chaos [Gen 1:2] lasting from Adam to Moses, 2) the period of the Torah lasting from Moses to the Messiah, when the law ruled human existence; and 3) the period of the Messiah, when the validity of the Torah ceases.[37] It was a commonly accepted belief of the Jewish people that one day a new epoch would begin. What separated Paul from the Jewish people, was his belief that Jesus has risen from the dead and has inaugurated the Messianic era, thereby putting an end to the age of the Torah.

Schoeps is convinced that the apostle does not object to the law as such, but he does object to the present validity of the law. Whoever maintains that the Torah is still in force does not believe that Jesus is the Messiah. Paul uses every argument which demonstrates that the law is incapable of making an individual righteous in order to persuade the Galatians that obedience to the law must be replaced by faith in Christ as a means to justification.

Schoeps is to be commended in his study of Pauline theology for taking into consideration the apostle's Jewish background. Paul did not become the apostle to the Gentiles in a vacuum. His Jewish heritage must have exerted a decisive influence on his understanding of Jesus as Messiah and how the apostle viewed the law in light of the fact that the Messiah had come. We must nevertheless express some doubts about accepting Schoeps' position.

[37] See Joseph A. Fitzmyer, *To Advance the Gospel* (New York, NY: Crossroad, 1981), p. 171.

Paul never explicitly asserts in his writings that the validity of the Torah would cease with the coming of the Messiah. This means either that the apostle did not hold this conviction or that it was such a widely held belief that he felt no need to mention it. Even though Schoeps agrees with the latter opinion, other exegetes are not as certain that the notion that the Torah would have a new status in the age of the Messiah was such a widely-known and widely-accepted belief at the time of Paul.[38] It seems logical to assume that Paul would have appealed to this conviction in one of his discussions about the law in Galatians and/or Romans, if it were indeed such a widely-accepted opinion. In view of this, we are not convinced that there is sufficient evidence to place much credence in Schoeps' position regarding Paul's understanding of the law.

The Law Condemned Christ

Morna D. Hooker upholds the position that Paul's understanding of the law must be interpreted in light of his experience of the risen Christ.[39] From the apostle's point of view, she postulates, even though the Messiah was judged guilty by the law (Deut 21:23, Gal 3:13), God raised him from the dead, that is, vindicated him. Because God has shown his approval of Jesus it must be true that something is drastically wrong with the law which condemned him.

Hooker contends that Paul's objection to the law should be understood in the context of the gospel that he proclaimed. It is evident from the apostle's correspondence that the essence of the good news is that Jesus, the one who had been crucified, has been raised from the dead. After his encounter with the glorified Christ, Paul was forced to admit that the law which he had previously obeyed for so long had imposed a curse on the one whom he now believed to be the Messiah. Assuredly, Deut

[38] See for example, Räisänen, *Paul*, pp. 236-240.
[39] See Morna D. Hooker, "Interchange in Christ," *JTS* 72 (1971), pp. 349-361, p. 351; and "Interchange and Atonement," *BJRL* 60 (1978), pp. 462-481.

21:23 (Gal 3:13) pronounces the full curse of the law on anyone who hangs on a tree. Nevertheless, in raising Jesus from the dead, God has, in effect, declared him righteous and has therefore overridden the negative judgment of the law (Rom 1:3-4, 1 Tim 3:16).[40] In short God has "justified" Jesus. Not only has Jesus been justified outside the law, but he has also been justified in defiance to the law. Consequently the apostle has come to the awareness that it is not on the basis of obedience to the Torah that one obtains righteousness.

According to Hooker, Paul is convinced that the justification of every Christian depends on the justification of Christ. Central to every statement that the apostle makes about obtaining righteousness is the notion that it is effected "in Christ." This does not simply mean that justification is obtained through the agency of Christ but rather that it depends upon believers themselves being "in Christ." Those who are united with Christ are no longer alienated from God nor under condemnation. On the contrary, they share in Christ's condition of being right with God because the life of Christ flows into the life of each Christian. Hence, justification should not be thought of as something which the Christian *possesses* but rather as something which *belongs to Christ*. Those who are in Christ participate in his righteousness.

Considering Paul's Jewish background, Hooker's investigation of Deut 21:23 in Gal 3:13 is indeed a worthwhile undertaking. However, one wonders about the overall validity of her interpretation regarding the apostle's negative comments about the law. Perhaps the greatest shortcoming of Hooker's argument is the paucity of references in the Pauline corpus which support her position. This is particularly noticeable in the letter to the Romans where the apostle also discusses at

[40] Hooker, "Interchange and Atonement," p. 479, admits that the idea of Christ's resurrection as vindication is very rarely spelled out in Paul's letters, yet she is still convinced that this seems to be the logic of the apostle's argument.

length his rejection of the law as a means to justification without mentioning the fact that the Torah was wrong for condemning Jesus.[41] As a result, we do not find Hooker's hypothesis concerning Paul's objection to the law as a valid means to justification very convincing.

A Sociological Approach

In his quest for the correct interpretation of the apostle's declarations about the law, Francis Watson opines that a sociological approach to Pauline theology is the key to a more comprehensible understanding of the apostle's conflict with Judaism and Jewish Christianity.[42] Watson's position is a plea for the relinquishment of the supposition that Paul's negative stance is based on theological insights. The source of the apostle's understanding of the law is to be uncovered in a specific social situation and not in his Damascus experience, his psychological problems,[43] or his discernment of the existential plight of humankind. "The abandonment of parts of the law of Moses was intended to make it easier for Gentiles to become Christians, it helped to increase the success of Christian preaching."[44] The social situation which lies behind Paul's theology of the law is his establishment of Gentile Christian communities distinct and separate from the Jewish community.

Watson insists that the answer to Paul's understanding of the law lies not in the complex theoretical discussion of the Torah found in the Pauline letters but in the history of the early church. Throughout his investigation, Watson uses the working hypothesis that "a text presupposes an existing social situation

[41] See Sanders, *Paul*, pp. 25-26; and Räisänen, *Paul*, pp. 249-251.
[42] See Francis Watson, *Paul, Judaism and Gentiles* SNTSMS 56 (Cambridge: Cambridge University, 1986), p. 19.
[43] Räisänen, *Paul*, p. 229, summarizes the position that Paul's rejection of the law is based on his own experience under the law: "Paul broke down, it was held, under the distressing burden of the law. The demands were too high; Paul, as a very sincere man, was just incapable of fulfilling them."
[44] See Watson, *Paul*, p. 34.

and is intended to function within that situation in ways not necessarily immediately apparent from the text itself."[45] This presupposition can shed a great deal of light on interpreting the controversies between Paul and his Jewish opponents.

Watson initiates his discussion on the apostle's comments about the law by offering some reflections on the dynamics of primitive Christianity, understood in sociological terms as a religious "reform-movement." Watson defines this reform-movement as that which is related to the old religion, drawing much of its content from what has gone before yet rebelling against certain elements of the old, and whose purpose is to transform the old religion. Early Christianity began as a reform-movement within an existing religious community (the Jewish community) and was eventually transformed into a "sect,' that is, a community that had broken away and established itself as an independent entity.

In order that the early church, like all sects, might justify its own existence and ascertain its own distinctive identity, an "ideology" was required. According to Watson, the ideology of every sect, including the early Christian community, is usually composed of at least three specific elements: a *denunciation* of the community's opponents, the use of *antithesis* in which positive statements are made about the members of the sect and negative statements are made about the group from which the sect is separating itself, and a *reinterpretation* of the religious traditions of the community in light of the conviction that the sect is the only legitimate heir to those traditions.[46]

Watson makes a hypothetical reconstruction of the ministry of Paul, based on information contained in the Pauline epistles, and then examines it from a sociological perspective. The apostle's remarks in 1 Cor 9:20, 2 Cor 11:24, Gal 1: 18-24, and 5:11, for example, bear witness that in the early stages of his Christian ministry, he preached the gospel *only* to

[45] See Watson, *Paul*, pp. ix-x.
[46] See Watson, *Paul*, p. 40.

Jews. After a period of time, however, Paul, and others, felt compelled to preach the good news to the Gentiles because the Jews failed to accept the gospel (e.g., Rom 11:11-30). It is obvious that the apostle and other Antiochene Jewish Christians did not require the observance of the Torah from their Jewish converts (e.g., Rom 14:14, 1 Cor 10:25, and Gal 2:3, 12). Paul's assertion in 1 Cor 9:21 describes well his intentions for not demanding the Gentiles to submit themselves to the observance of the law: "To those outside the law I became as one outside the law ... that I might win those outside the law." In other words, so as not to repeat the sad experience of almost total failure in preaching the gospel, the apostle and others set aside some of the demands of the Torah that were most offensive to the Gentiles in order to ensure the success of their missionary activity.[47] Even though it might seem that from Paul's discussion of the law in Gal 2:11 - 5:11 that his motive for dispensing with the Torah was strictly theological, 1 Cor 9:21 clearly indicates that the setting aside of parts of the law was, in fact, based on practical reasons. The apostle simply wanted to remove any obstacle that might discourage the Gentiles from entering the church. As a result of the law-free gospel, the separation of the Christian community from the Jewish community, in which the observance of the Torah played such an integral part, that which had already begun with the rejection of the gospel by the Jews was now complete. Using sociological terminology, it can be said that the religious reform-movement (Christianity) had completely distanced itself from the old religion (Judaism) and, therefore, had been transformed into a sect.

Within this context, Watson discovers in the letters of Paul an "ideology" which legitimized the separation of the church

[47] Watson, *Paul*, pp. 34-35, cites a number of Graeco-Roman authors to demonstrate that the main features of the Jewish ritual law were objects of ridicule in the ancient world. Consequently, the insistence on strict observance of the Mosaic law would have made it very difficult to attract Gentile converts.

from the synagogue. There is the element of *denunciation*. Perhaps the best example of this is found in Rom 2:17-24 where the apostle criticizes the Jews for condemning the idolatry and immorality of the pagans, while at the same time they themselves transgress the law by doing exactly the same things. Moreover, there are elements of denunciation found in Gal 1:8-9 (the Judaizers are cursed), Gal 5:12 (the Judaizers are ridiculed), and Gal 6:13 (the Judaizers are considered cowards). There is the element of *antithesis*. Paul presents numerous antithetical terms in his conflict with Judaism and Jewish Christianity which indicate the ineradicable distinction between the Christian community and the Jewish community; for example, works of the law and faith in Jesus Christ (2:16), the law and Christ (2:21), flesh and Spirit (3:3, 4:29), curse and blessing (3:10, 13), and slavery and sonship (4:1-7). Finally there is the element of *reinterpretation*. An illustration of this point can be found in Gal 3:6-18 where Paul demonstrates that the *true* sons of Abraham are those who have faith in Jesus Christ. These are the members of the Christian community, not those who are circumcised and observe the Torah, as the Jews claimed. Moreover, unlike the Jews, Paul declares that a correct understanding of the law can only be found in the Christian community (2 Cor 3:14-16). Although Judaism holds that the observance of the Torah is a prerequisite for justification, the apostle emphatically asserts that the law is a bringer of sin (Rom 5:20-21), death (2 Cor 3:6-9), and condemnation to those who submit to it (Gal 3:10).[48]

Thus, according to Watson, the apostle's discussion of the law took place in the context of legitimizing the separation of the Christian community from the Jewish community. His negative attitude towards the law did not originally come about as the result of theological reflection. Rather his renunciation of the law was a matter of expediency. The full observance of the law was abandoned in order to make it easier for the Gentiles to become Christians.

[48] See Watson, *Paul*, pp. 46-48.

We wholeheartedly agree with Watson that a proper analysis of any biblical passage should not neglect the historical and social context in which it was written. This being said, several factors make it difficult to accept Watson's position. First of all, there are but a few verses which even remotely suggest that Paul rejected the law as a means to justification because he wanted to make it easier for Gentiles to become Christians and thus enhance his chances for attracting more converts to Christianity. Moreover, even the passages which Watson uses to defend his thesis are not persuasive. For example, there is nothing in 1 Cor 9:21 which disproves the conviction that Paul's understanding of the law is based on his experience of the risen Lord and/or on theological reflection. It is certainly possible that Paul's Damascus experience and/or his theological reflection led him to the conclusion that the observance of the law was not necessary for salvation and thus he was able to say in 1 Cor 9:21 that "I became as one outside the law ... that I might win those outside the law." It should also be noted that in 1 Corinthians 8 Paul gives some advice concerning food offered to idols and bases his advice on theological reflection. This suggests the possibility that Paul's declarations about the law in Galatians are, at the very least, also founded on theological reflections. Consequently, in looking at Watson's position as a whole, we find his interpretation interesting but on the negative side not wholly convincing.

Inclusion of the Gentiles

George Howard argues that Paul's attitude toward the law must be understood in relation to his doctrine of the inclusion of the Gentiles into the kingdom of God.[49] Within this framework, Paul refutes the Torah as a means of obtaining righteousness because the law acts as a restrictive force which separates

[49] See George Howard, "Romans 3:21-31 and the Inclusion of the Gentiles," *HTR* 63 (1970), pp. 23-33; and *Paul: Crisis in Galatia* SNTSMS 35 (Cambridge: Cambridge University, 1979), pp. 46-65.

Jew from Gentile and prevents the universal unity that was destined to come. Through the redemptive death of Jesus, the tyranny of the law came to an end, thereby allowing uncircumcised Gentiles to participate in the blessing of Abraham on equal terms with the Jews.

Howard maintains that the apostle's comments about the law must be interpreted in the light of his missionary activity among the Gentiles. Paul describes his initial experience of the risen Lord in Galatians as a call to become an apostle to and for the Gentiles (Acts 9:15, Gal 1:16). He is therefore forced to grapple with the question of the requirements for the admission of Gentiles to the kingdom of God. The apostle asserts that one does not have to go through Judaism into Christianity because there is a more direct way for the Gentiles to enter the kingdom of God apart from the law, that is, by means of faith.

The notion that the Gentiles would participate in the blessing of Abraham first appears in Gen 12:3 (Gal 3:8): "In you shall all nations be blessed." On the basis of this passage from Genesis, Paul believes that the goal of the law is the ultimate unification of all nations under the God of Abraham. According to Howard, the apostle supports his conviction that God's righteousness is one which envisions all nations, by stating: "Christ is the end of the law, that *every one* who has faith may be justified" (Rom 10:4). *All* who believe in Christ (Gentile and Jew) receive the blessing of Abraham, and thus the promise made to the patriarch in Gen 12:3 (that all nations would be blessed) is fulfilled in and through Christ.[50]

According to Howard, Paul's citation of Lev 18:5 in Rom 10:5 and Gal 3:12b is also noteworthy for our discussion. The apostle proves in these verses that the law's ultimate goal corresponds to the work of Christ in unifying all nations. Lev 18:5 does not declare that the "Jew" or the "Israelite" who keeps the law shall live, but rather the "one" who

[50] See George Howard, "Christ the End of the Law," *JBL* 88 (1969), pp. 331-337, p. 335.

observes the law shall live. Paul interprets Lev 18:5 as affirming that, according to Moses, anyone, be they Jew or Gentile, who practices the righteousness which is based on the Torah shall live by it.

There are still other passages where the theme of the inclusion of the Gentiles clearly appears. On the basis of his interpretation of *pistis Christou* ("faith *of* Jesus Christ" instead of the traditional "faith *in* Jesus Christ") Howard is convinced that a reference to the promise that God made to Abraham can be detected in Rom 3:23.[51] Howard translates this verse: "Righteousness comes to all who believe through the faith of Jesus Christ." We find here an allusion to the fact that Christ has demonstrated his faithfulness to the promise, by his unflinching obedience to the will of the Father even to the point of suffering death on the cross, so that the blessing of Abraham might come upon the Gentiles (3:13-14). As a result, "there is neither Jew nor Greek, there is neither slave nor free, there is neither male nor female; for you are all one in Christ Jesus" (3:28). The promise to Abraham is fulfilled by the faithfulness of Christ in bringing the Gentiles into the kingdom of God.

The troublemakers in Galatia do not realize that God's righteousness is one which includes all nations because they seek to establish their own righteousness to the exclusion of the Gentiles. Paul objects strenuously to their insistence on performing the works of the law as a means of obtaining righteousness because it creates a division in humankind and prevents the universal unity that was promised to Abraham.

Howard has built a strong case for advocating the position that the inclusion of the Gentiles plays an important role in Pauline theology. The fact that the apostle focuses so much attention on the Gentile question in Galatians (e.g., 1:16, 2:1-21, 3:8, 14) certainly suggests that the issue of the inclusion of the Gentiles should not be neglected in the attempt to

[51] See George Howard, "Notes and Observations on the Faith of Christ," *HTR* 60 (1967), pp. 459-465.

discover the correct interpretation of Paul's understanding of the law. Howard's thesis regarding the apostle's negative comments about the law is very close to Paul's fundamental objection to the Torah as a valid means to justification.

Salvation Only in Christ

E.P. Sanders rejects the notion that Paul's fundamental conviction concerning the inability of the law to make one righteous is based on one's incapacity to obey the Torah perfectly and/or on one's misunderstanding of the law, that is, the mistaken belief that one can earn justification by observing the precepts of the law. Sanders postulates that the law is in no way able to make one righteous because justification is only available in Christ and therefore cannot be obtained by means of the law. "What is wrong with the law is that it is not Christ."[52]

Sanders believes that it is of the utmost importance to have a proper understanding of Palestinian Judaism in order to correctly interpret the apostle's various comments about the law. What Sanders refers to as "covenantal nomism" must have been the general type of religion prevalent in Palestine in Paul's time. "By 'covenantal nomism' I [Sanders] intend to describe the view according to which salvation comes by *membership* in the covenant, while obedience to the commandments *preserves* one's place in the covenant" (emphasis by the author).[53] God has freely offered salvation to Israel and has given her the commandments. In response to God's salvific offer, the people obey the commandments to the best of their ability, realizing that the law provides a means of atonement

[52] E.P. Sanders, *Paul and Palestinian Judaism* (Philadelphia, PA: SCM, 1977), p. 551.
[53] See E.P. Sanders, "The Covenant as a Soteriological Category and the Nature of Salvation in Palestinian and Hellenistic Judaism," W.D. Davies and Robert Hamerton-Kelly, eds., *Jews, Greeks and Christians* (Leiden: Brill, 1976), p. 41.

for any transgression of the Torah. God's covenantal promise provides salvation while the intention and the effort to obey the commandments constitute the condition for remaining in the covenant.[54]

If Sanders is correct in his description of Palestinian Judaism, then every hypothesis must be eliminated that attempts to explain the apostle's rejection of the law as a means to justification on the grounds that no one can obey the law perfectly (because atonement is possible) and/or that the observance of the law implies the notion of self-justification (because the observance of the law keeps one in the covenant and is not understood as a means of earning grace).[55]

Sanders is of the opinion that Paul's dismissal of the law as a means to justification results from the most basic conviction of his Christian faith. In Christ, God has provided salvation for all who believe. The apostle clearly asserts in Gal 2:21 and 3:31 that if righteousness could be obtained by means of the law, then Christ's death would not have been necessary. However, God did send Christ for our justification and therefore righteousness cannot be obtained through the law. Paul's reflection on his earlier life in Phil 3:6-9 is also a crucial text for determining the apostle's understanding of the law. The apostle's criticism of his earlier life is not that he was incapable of obeying all the precepts of the Torah, or that he was guilty of the sin of self-righteousness. Instead, he put confidence in something other than faith in Christ.

Had Paul denied that righteousness could be obtained through the law, on the grounds that no one can obey all of its

[54] Sanders, *Paul*, p. 6, speaks of this in terms of "getting in" and "staying in."

[55] See E.P. Sanders, "Patterns of Religion in Paul and Rabbinic Judaism," *HTR* 66 (1973), pp. 455-478, p. 465. Concerning his conviction that the Jews did not seek to earn salvation by their observance of the Torah, Sanders states: "One who stays within the covenant has a share in the world to come. For this reason, there is little or no 'quest for salvation' in Rabbinic literature. The feeling 'I am damned, what can I do to be saved' is one which is notable by its absence."

precepts, and/or that observance of the law implies the notion of self-justification, he would have been more consistent in his objections to the law. On the contrary, there is a great deal of diversity and lack of agreement among the apostle's negative statements about the law. The very diversity and lack of agreement indicate that none of these statements about the law should be regarded as the main source of Paul's rejection of the law as a means of obtaining righteousness.[56]

As far as Sanders is concerned, there is, however, one factor that remains consistent in the apostle's discussion about the law, namely, that righteousness cannot be obtained by means of it. Righteousness is obtained only through faith in Christ. This consistency in the apostle's criticism of the law calls attention to his fundamental reason for rejecting the law as a means to justification: the law is not Christ. The purpose of the law is to consign all things to sin so that righteousness can be obtained on the basis of faith in Christ.

The great number of theologians who have responded to Sanders' position concerning his interpretation of Paul's understanding of the law, testify to the impact that this exegete has had on the study of Pauline theology.[57] Sanders has produced some very strong evidence to support his conviction that the apostle's remarks about the law should be understood first and foremost in the light of his firm belief that Christ died for the salvation of humanity. His research of Palestinian Judaism at the time of Paul, his discussion of numerous and important Scriptural passages, and his own personal reflection, all give credence to Sanders' work. Consequently, we find ourselves, in general terms, to be in agreement with Sanders' position regarding his interpretation of the apostle's

[56] Sanders, *Paul*, p. 151. Sanders posits that the apostle's diverse statements about the law reflect a struggle within Paul to reconcile the fact that God gave the law and that salvation is only obtainable through Christ apart from the law.

[57] See for example, Hans Hübner, *Law in Paul's Thought* (Edinburgh: Clark, 1984), pp. 151-154.

understanding of the law. Paul's major difficulty with the Torah as a viable means to justification is that the law is not Christ. Such a conviction ties in well with the central role that Christ played in the life of the apostle.

Concluding Remarks

In Gal 2:16 Paul comes to the very heart of the trouble-makers' version of the gospel which stands in direct opposition to his rendition of the good news. The Judaizers have insisted that at least some of the precepts of the Torah must be performed in order to obtain righteousness. The apostle reacts to this claim by proclaiming that no one is justified by the works of the law but only through faith in Christ. For the remainder of Galatians 2, as well as in Galatians 3 and 4, Paul presents numerous arguments to substantiate this conviction. Although the apostle demonstrates in a variety of ways that one is justified exclusively by faith in Christ, his fundamental reason for denying the law's ability to make one righteous is that it is not Christ.

Christ Makes a Difference

One of the most remarkable aspects of Paul's new life in Christ was his ability to "rise above his culture." In stating that no one is justified by works of the law but only through faith in Christ, the apostle went against the grain of the most sacred aspect of his Jewish heritage. Assuredly, Paul was not the kind of person who accepted a traditional practice simply because "it has always been done that way." The apostle's reflections throughout the epistle clearly indicate that although Christians are undeniably connected to the past, they are by no means chained to it. Once Paul was convinced that a customary practice (such as demanding that Christians obey some of the statutes of the Mosaic law) contradicted a basic element of the Christian faith (e.g., those who contend that justification came through the law imply that Christ died in vain), he fought it with all his strength. The apostle's discussion in Galatians illustrates that a culture cannot be imposed upon Christians. The apostle's letter to the Galatians is the first Christian writing of some length which refutes the idea that Christianity is to be identified with one particular culture or nation.

The Gift of Justification

Although faith and justification are ultimately free gifts from God, they can never be taken for granted. Those who have committed themselves to the risen Lord are challenged to continually manifest their faith in Christ in word and deed. As is true for all gifts, the best way Christians can show their appreciation for the gift of justification is to use it as it was intended, namely, for their own sanctification and for the sanctification of others. In other words, Christian believers are called to love God and to love their neighbors as themselves.

Freedom Through Faith

Those who believe in Christ Jesus and have been baptized are justified in the sight of God. Paul makes a strong connection in Galatians between justification and freedom. Because of their union with the risen Lord, Christians have been liberated from the destructive effects of sin and are destined for eternal life. Time after time, the apostle argues that the gateway to Christian freedom is through faith in Christ and not by way of the Mosaic law.

CHAPTER FIVE

THE PRICE OF FREEDOM (GAL 3:1-14)

Paul continues his unwavering attack in Gal 3:1-14 on the heretical doctrine of the troublemakers. One who reads these verses for the first time is struck by some rather perplexing elements in the apostle's argumentation concerning the inability of the Mosaic law to make one righteous. For example, in his attempt to persuade the Galatians to accept his point of view, Paul's discussion appears rather disjointed. One moment he poses a series of questions about the past behavior of the Galatians (3:1-5), the next he speaks of the Abraham narrative (3:6-9), and then argues about the curse of the law (3:10-14). Moreover, throughout Gal 3:1-14 the apostle frequently refers to the Hebrew Scriptures. This seems rather peculiar since his audience is probably composed of primarily Gentile Christians and thus, in all likelihood, unfamiliar with these sacred writings. It also seems rather strange that Paul uses Deut 27:26 in Gal 3:10b and Lev 18:5 in Gal 3:12b to ground his thesis that the adherence to the Mosaic law is not required to become a child of Abraham. In their original context, these two passages from the Old Testament appear to *encourage* the observance of the law in order to avoid the curse and to obtain righteousness. Furthermore, it appears that the apostle contradicts himself in the process of defending his Torah-free gospel. Whereas Paul undeniably declares in Gal 3:7 that "people of faith" are children of Abraham, he later asserts in Gal 3:16 that Christ is the *only* offspring of Abraham! With these seemingly contradictory statements in mind, some serious questions arise as to how the apostle's discussion in Gal 3:1-14 should be interpreted.

In our opinion, Paul's argumentation is best understood when the following considerations are kept in mind. The apostle's remarks in this section of the epistle clearly indicate that he is addressing one fundamental question. "What must the Gentiles do to become children of Abraham (e.g., 3:7)?" Although Paul uses many different types of arguments in the epistle to sway the Galatians back to accepting his version of the gospel, the apostle's discussion nevertheless contains a common theme: One becomes a descendant of Abraham through faith apart from the law. Using a plethora of arguments Paul illustrates that, on the one hand, Gentiles participate in the blessing of the patriarch by means of faith in Christ while, on the other hand, it is not possible to become Abraham's heir by means of the Mosaic law. These two aspects of the apostle's argumentation are intertwined throughout Gal 3:1-14.

In all probability, Paul did not simply select at random passages from the Hebrew Scriptures which would validate his position. Rather, his numerous citations from the sacred writings may indicate that the apostle's opponents had first used these very passages to substantiate their rendition of the good news. Paul "turns the tables" on the troublemakers by using these same passages from the Hebrew Scriptures to support his conviction that one is justified exclusively through faith in Christ. In doing so, the apostle demonstrates that the agitators have grossly misunderstood these scripture citations.

A critical examination of Galatians reveals that Paul's reflections on the "children of Abraham" in 3:7 do not, in fact, contradict his comment in 3:16 that Christ is the only heir to the promise of Abraham when interpreted in light of Galatians 3 as a whole. The apostle calls to the Galatians' attention that God made a covenant with Abraham (3:16-17), and because Abraham believed God "it was reckoned to him as righteousness (3:6). Paul points out in Gal 3:16 the significance of the fact that the promises were made to Abraham and his offspring (singular and not the plural "offsprings"). According to the apostle, the offspring clearly refers to Christ. The way that one participates in the blessing promised to the offspring of Abraham, Christ, is through one's relationship with him. Paul assures the Galatians that everyone who has faith in Christ and has been baptized, is united with him (3:26-28) and thus belongs to Abraham's seed (3:29), sharing in the patriarch's blessing and receiving the promise of the Spirit (3:14). It is within this framework that the apostle's comments about the children of Abraham in Gal 3:7 should be understood. One becomes an heir of Abraham, that is, an offspring of the patriarch, by means of faith. In the process of interpreting Paul's argumentation in Gal 3:1-14, it is important to remember that Paul closely associates justification with receiving the Spirit, righteousness, redemption, being a descendant of Abraham and participating in his blessing.

The Wonder of Faith

Paul's declaration in the last verse of chapter two of Galatians acts as a springboard for his argumentation in Galatians 3. The apostle asserts in Gal 2:21 that "if justification were through the law" (the context assures us that it is not) "then Christ died in vain." Paul continues in Gal 3:1-14 to illustrate in a variety of ways, namely, by appealing to the personal experience of the Galatians, Scripture, and logical reasoning, that justification is not obtained by way of the law but through faith in Christ.

The apostle initiates his discussion in Galatians 3 by challenging his audience to recall their initial contact with the good news of Jesus Christ. It is obvious from Paul's derogatory comment in Gal 3:1 (O foolish Galatians") that he is no longer referring to the remarks which he made to Peter in Antioch (2:14b-21). The apostle fires a barrage of questions at the Galatians in Gal 3:1-5 indicating that he is outraged by their behavior. "Who has bewitched you?" "Are you so foolish?" "Did you experience so many things in vain?" The emotional tenor of this passage notwithstanding, Paul's aim is clear. The decisive question that he wants to place before the Galatians is found in Gal 3:2 and 3:5. Did they receive the Spirit by performing works of the law or through faith? The context of this question informs us that the apostle knows perfectly well that the Galatians received the Spirit through faith and, in view of their own personal experience, so should they.

The Blessing of Abraham

Paul's position in Gal 3:6-9 regarding the inadequacy of the Mosaic law to make one righteous is not validated by personal experience as in the previous verses but by Scripture. For the first time in the letter the person of Abraham is introduced. The apostle paints a picture in Gal 3:6 of the circumstances in which the patriarch came to be "reckoned as righteous." Paul gleans from the Abraham narrative a fundamental principle concerning the justification of the Gentiles.

It seems logical to assume that the apostle's discussion involving the patriarch would be more meaningful to the Galatians if they were already familiar with the Abraham narrative. Paul is probably reacting in Gal 3:6-9 to the teaching of the troublemakers who may have first referred to the patriarch in support of their position that circumcision and observance of the Torah play a vital role in becoming a child of Abraham. After all, the Hebrew Scriptures bear witness that God Himself commanded the patriarch and his descendants to be circumcised (Gen 17:10-14). Moreover, there seems to have existed in Judaism the notion that "Abraham is the illuminating example of perfect obedience to the commands of God rendered out of love" and "keeps the whole Torah, as yet unwritten."[1]

[1] See Joachim Jeremias, "*Abraam*," *TDNT*, 1, pp. 8-9.

If we are correct in the assumption that the agitators had originally referred to the patriarch in support of their position, then the Galatians were probably quite surprised that Paul should also point to Abraham to defend his point of view. The apostle outflanks the troublemakers as he demonstrates that they have misinterpreted the sacred writings. Although Abraham had been circumcised, Scripture itself testifies that he was justified on the basis of his faith and not on his being circumcised. Not only was the patriarch declared righteous *before* he was circumcised, but this also occurred 430 years before the Torah came into the possession of Israel (3:17).[2] In effect, Paul is saying to the Galatians that just as their own personal experience illustrates that they received the Spirit *by faith* (3:2-5), so too does Scripture demonstrate that Abraham was justified *by faith*.

Referring to Gen 15:6 (Gal 3:6), the apostle makes known to the Galatians that Abraham was declared righteous by God because he believed. Interestingly enough, Paul also cites this passage from Genesis in Rom 4:3 and comments on it throughout Romans 4. Here the apostle notes that the patriarch believed against great odds that God's promise to him would be fulfilled (Rom 4:18). In spite of Abraham's old body and the barrenness of Sarah's womb, the patriarch did not weaken in faith that he would become the father of many nations (Rom 4:19). That is why Abraham's faith was reckoned to him as righteousness (Rom 4:22). Surely, that which Paul spoke to the recipients of the Roman epistle is also applicable to the Galatians. "The words, 'Abraham's faith was reckoned to him as righteousness' were not written for his sake alone, but for ours also" (Rom 4:23-24).

On the basis of Gen 15:6, Paul concludes in Gal 3:7 that it is people of faith who are children of Abraham. The apostle continues his discussion in Gal 3:8 by referring to the Hebrew Scriptures for the second time in this passage. "And the

[2] See Exod 12:40.

Scripture foreseeing that God would justify the Gentiles by faith, preached the gospel beforehand to Abraham, saying, 'In you shall all the nations be blessed.'" As he is wont to do, Paul personifies Scripture in this verse.[3] His citation from the Hebrew Scriptures, a conflation of Gen 12:3 and 18:18, illustrates that his conviction that people of faith are the legitimate descendants of Abraham should come as no surprise to the Galatians - it was foretold by Scripture. The apostle identifies the content of the "gospel" that was preached beforehand to Abraham as the justification of the Gentiles by faith (3:8a). In doing so, the apostle makes a connection between the promise that was made to Abraham and the gospel that the apostle preaches. There can be no doubt that, in light of the introductory comments in Gal 3:8ab, Paul interprets Gen 12:3 and 18:18 as stating that the Gentiles obtain righteousness by means of faith. The apostle highlights in Gal 3:9 the main point of his discussion about Abraham. Bringing together in this verse the terminology that he used in the preceding ones, Paul insists that "people of faith" (3:7) are "blessed" (3:8) with "Abraham who had faith" (3:6).

Trusting Abraham

In many ways Abraham is an ideal model of one who trusts completely and unreservedly in divine providence. At a relatively late age in life (Gen 12:4) when most people tend not to initiate any new major undertakings, the patriarch quite unexpectedly received a directive from God to begin an entirely new mode of life (Gen 12:1-3). Without protest Abraham left his country and his family and journeyed to an unknown land (Gen 12:4). Having no idea what the future held for him, the patriarch exuded total confidence in God,

Abraham's faith in divine providence withstood the test of time. Some twenty-five years passed before the promise that

[3] See Gal 3:22, 4:30; Rom 4:3, 9:17, 10:11, 11:2.

God had made to him (Gen 17:1, 17-21) even began to be fulfilled, namely, that he would be the father of many nations. During these long years the patriarch demonstrated great perseverance and persistence. There is not the slightest indication in Scripture that Abraham ever lost faith nor considered the possibility of returning home. The patriarch's faith was not in vain. His elderly wife Sarah eventually gave birth to a son (Gen 21:2).

Abraham's faith was put to the ultimate test when God commanded him to give up that which was even more precious to the patriarch than his own life, namely, his beloved son Isaac (Gen 22:1-2). Once again Abraham placed his full confidence in God and took his son Isaac to the mountains to offer him up as a sacrifice. At the last possible moment, however, God intervened and spared the child's life (Gen 23:11-12).

On occasion it seems that our lives parallel that of Abraham. In a manner of speaking life sometimes calls us from the "land of the known" to the "land of the unknown," that is, from the land of good health, happy relationships, financial security, and spiritual consolations to the land of poor health, broken relationships, unemployment, and spiritual grief. Tragically, there are also those occasions in life when we too are compelled to let go of that which is perhaps more precious to us than our own lives, namely, the life of a loved one. In all of this we can learn from Abraham who approached life with a persistent faith in divine providence. Like the patriarch, we too remain confident that God will provide us with the strength to endure all the great "tests" in life.

The Curse of the Law

Although Paul continues to substantiate his position with Scripture in Gal 3:10-14, his argumentation in these verses is concerned with the law and its curse instead of the Abraham narrative.[4] In the previous section the apostle illustrated that it was through faith that one participates in the blessing of Abraham. Now Paul declares in Gal 3:10a that not only does the reliance on works of the law fail to make one righteous, it also results in condemnation. The fivefold occurrence of the term "curse" in connection with the law (3:10a, 10b, 13a, 13b, 13c) suggests that it is an important theme in this pericope.

Exclusion from the Blessing

The biblical notion of curse has been defined as the invocation of harm or injury upon a person (or people), either immediately or contingent upon particular circumstances. One who is cursed is "cut off," isolated, and abandoned to the powers of decomposition and death.[5] Apparently the condition that must be fulfilled in Gal 3:10a in order for one to be under the curse is to "rely on works of the law" for justification. In the light of Paul's statement in Gal 3:9 that men of faith are "blessed," it seems that the apostle uses the term in Gal 3:10a, first and foremost, to indicate "exclusion from the blessing."[6] If we keep in mind that, according to the apostle's way of thinking, Scripture proclaims Christ as the only heir to Abraham's blessing (3:16), and that one, therefore, participates in the blessing of Abraham *solely* through one's union with Christ by means of faith (3:26-29), then it is obvious that whoever is excluded from the blessing should also be considered as separated from Christ (5:4).

Condemnation Not Justification

The apostle calls into question in Gal 3:10 the agitators' interpretation of Deut 27:26, a biblical text that apparently

[4] For a more detailed analysis of Paul's argumentation in Gal 3:10-14, see my "'Curse of the Law.' An Exegetical Investigation of Galatians 3:10-14," Ph.D. dissertation, Louvain, 1988.

[5] See Allen C. Myers, "Curse," *EerdBib*, pp. 248-249. There are numerous examples in the Hebrew Scriptures where a curse is mentioned. See, for example, Gen 3:14-19, Num 5:21-22, Deut 21:23, 27:26.

[6] It is interesting to note that the terms "blessing" and "curse" are also contrasted in both Gen 12:3 and Deut 30:19.

played a vital role in substantiating their position regarding the mandatory observance of the Torah. In its original setting, this passage from Deuteronomy concludes the so-called Shechemite dodecalogue, the twelve curses pronounced by the Levites standing on Mount Ebal (Deut 27:15-26). The first eleven curses are spoken of religious or social misdemeanor while the twelfth is more comprehensive.[7] According to the Hebrew and Septuagintal version of Deut 27:26, a curse is imposed on those who do not abide by "the words of *this law*," namely, the dodecalogue. Thus in its original context, Deut 27:26 was probably understood as an incentive to observe the law. With this in mind, the hypothesis that the troublemakers first used this Scripture passage in support of their position seems all the more plausible.[8]

The agitators had pressured the Galatians into believing that Deut 27:26 threatened anathema on all who did not adhere to the law. Evidently, the Galatians were under the impression that obedience to just a few of the precepts of the Torah constituted them as observers of the Mosaic law. Paul's version of Deut 27:26 (Gal 3:10b), however, sheds new light on this passage.[9] He accentuates the idea that if one is to avoid the law's curse, one must obey each and every precept of the Torah. According to the apostle's understanding of Deut 27:26, the full condemnation of the Torah is imposed on all transgressors. There are no exceptions. Paul's argumentation in Gal 3:10 seems to imply that no one fulfills all the commandments of the

[7] See Bruce, *Galatians*, p. 158. No specific penalty is prescribed for each offense mentioned in Deut 27:15-26. God is called upon, in effect, to execute His curse on the wrongdoer. The curse of Deuteronomy involves exclusion from the covenant-community.

[8] This position is held by, for example, C.K. Barrett, "The Allegory of Abraham," Johannes Friedrich et al., eds, *Rechtfertigung. Festschrift für Ernst Käsemann* (Tübingen: Mohr, 1976), pp. 1-16, pp. 6-7.

[9] Paul's reference to Deut 27:26 in Gal 3:10b is not a direct quotation from the Hebrew or Septuagintal text. The Septuagintal version adds emphasis to the Hebrew text by inserting "everyone" after "accursed" and "in all" after "who not abide." The apostle adapts the Septuagintal version by replacing "in all the words of this law" with "all things written in the book of the law."

law since all people are sinners. Subsequently, he makes the surprising declaration that "all who rely on works of the law are under a curse" (3:10a).

As the Galatians listen to Paul's comments in Gal 3:10 concerning his interpretation of Deut 27:26, they are fully aware that they have not fulfilled *all* the commands of the Torah. This failure to obey the law in its entirety, according to Paul's interpretation, has devastating consequences. It results in a curse. Although the apostle seems to focus his attention on the members of the Galatian churches, he nevertheless states generally in Gal 3:10a that "*all* who rely on works of the law are under a curse." Therefore, we can infer that even those who may be trying to obey all the commands of the Torah, to the best of their ability, fail to obey every one of its statutes and, because of their transgression, are cursed. It is rather paradoxical that one of the very passages from Scripture (Deut 27:26) which may have inspired the Galatians to observe the law to obtain righteousness and avoid the curse, also condemns them in light of their transgressions!

The Failure of the Law

Having demonstrated in Gal 3:10 that dependence on the Torah has dire consequences, the apostle continues to develop his argument in 3:11-12 that the Mosaic law is an inviable means to justification. Once again the apostle focuses his attention on Scripture in order to fortify his position. He grounds his assertion in Gal 3:11a that no one obtains righteousness by means of the law with the citation of Hab 2:4 in Gal 3:11b ("He who through faith is righteous shall live").[10] The prophet

[10] Although the term *zêsetai* in Gal 3:11b can be translated "shall live," the context compels one to interpret this word as designating not merely "continued existence" but rather "justification."

Habakkuk affirms in no uncertain terms that justification comes through faith.

Faith and the Law

Hab 2:4 appears in the New Testament on three different occasions (Rom 1:17, Gal 3:11b, Heb 10:38). In its original setting, this passage is part of God's reply to the prophet's second complaint about the continuing oppression of Judah. The Chaldeans, who depend on their great might for victory, are contrasted with the people of Judah, who depend on God for deliverance. It is made known to the prophet in Hab 2:3-4 that a vision will arrive at the appointed time and make it abundantly clear that Judah's deliverance will not depend on its wealth or power but rather on its fidelity to God.[11]

The Septuagint uses the Greek word for "faith" in Hab 2:4 to translate the Hebrew word for "faithfulness." It is interesting to note that the *Qumran Habakkuk* Commentary, which is based on the Hebrew Text, interpreted Hab 2:4 as referring, in part, to the *faithful* observance of the law.[12] Thus, it is conceivable that Hab 2:4 was first used by the Judaizers in support of their position that one must observe the law in order to be justified.[13] The troublemakers could have pointed out to the Galatians this passage from Habakkuk to prove that Scripture itself testifies that the faithful observance of the Torah is a *sine qua non* for obtaining righteousness.

Viewing Hab 2:4 in a different light, C.H. Dodd maintains that this passage was known in primitive Christian times as a

[11] See Raymond T. Stamm, "The Epistle to the Galatians," *The Interpreters Bible*, 10, pp. 427-593, pp. 506-507; and Joseph A. Fitzmyer, "Habakkuk 2:3-4 and the New Testament," *To Advance the Gospel*, pp. 236-246, p. 242.

[12] See Millas Burrows, *The Dead Sea Scrolls with Translations by the Author* (London: Secker and Warburg, 1956), p. 356, in which the interpretation of Hab 2:4 is as follows: "This means all the doers of the law in the house of Judah, whom God will rescue from the house of judgment because of their labor and their faith in the teacher of righteousness."

[13] See for example, John Bligh, *Galatians* (London, St. Paul, 1969), p. 262.

testimonium to the certainty of Christ's coming.[14] Therefore, Dodd suggests that the contents of this passage were familiar to the Christians of the early Church (including the Galatians). This hypothesis gains further credence by the independent usage of Hab 2:4 in Heb 10:37-38. Dodd correctly observes that Paul's argumentation in Gal 3:11 would be far more effective if Hab 2:4 were known by the Galatians, as well as the apostle, prior to the writing of the epistle. We are open to the possibility that the Galatians were already acquainted with Hab 2:4. The context of Gal 3:11 makes it clear that the apostle does not interpret this passage from Habakkuk as an incentive to observe the Torah, nor as a reference to the coming of Christ, but rather as a declaration about obtaining righteousness: One is justified through faith. With Hab 2:4, Paul indisputably underlines the importance of faith as a means to justification.

The Galatians would have no difficulty in accepting the position that one is justified by faith. They would, however, object to the conviction that one is justified *exclusively* by faith. The Galatians were on the verge of believing that the observance of the Torah was also necessary for obtaining righteousness. They may have assumed that a strong connection exists between faith and law. If they were correct in this assumption, there would be no reason for them not to believe that adherence to the Mosaic law was not a prerequisite for obtaining righteousness and therefore challenge Paul's conclusion in Gal 3:11a. The apostle seems to anticipate this response and sets out to prove in Gal 3:12 that there is absolutely no connection between law and faith. He substantiates his position that "the law does not rest on faith" (3:12a) by referring to Lev 18:5 in Gal 3:12b ("He who *does* them shall live by them"). In this way, Paul drives a wedge between law and faith, two entities which the Galatians may have considered bound together.

[14] See C.H. Dodd, *According to the Scriptures: The Sub-Structure of New Testament Theology* (London: Nisbet, 1952), p. 51.

In Principle But Not in Reality

The passage from Leviticus that Paul refers to in Gal 3:12b contains one of the fundamental doctrines of the Old Testament. Lev 18:5 embodies the spirit of the Torah in that it demands obedience to the precepts of the law as a necessary condition for obtaining righteousness.[15] In its original context, this passage belonged to a section of Leviticus that has come to be known as the "Holiness Code" (Lev 17-26).[16] After God proclaims that "I am the Lord your God" (Lev 18:4), Moses is commanded in Lev 18:5 to say to the people of Israel: You shall therefore keep my statutes and my ordinances (Lev 18:5a), by doing "them" one shall live (Lev 18:5b, Gal 3:12b). Judaism apparently viewed Lev 18:5 in a favorable light because it promises life, that is, justification, to those who keep its commandments. In the light of these considerations, it is certainly possible that the troublemakers in Galatia might have first used Lev 18:5 in support of their position.

The apostle may, at least for the sake of argument, concede the validity of Lev 18:5, that is, if one fulfills the precepts of the Torah, one would obtain righteousness. However, Paul's argumentation in Gal 3:12 in which he differentiates between the law and faith might enable the Galatians to view Lev 18:5 from a different perspective where the emphasis falls not on "the promise of life for those who do the law" but rather on "doing" itself.

With the aid of syllogistic reasoning in Gal 3:11-12, Paul illustrates that every attempt to obtain righteousness by any means other than faith - by means of the law, for example - is doomed to failure. Since one obtains righteousness by means of faith (major premise contained in Gal 3:11b), and since the law has nothing whatsoever in common with faith (minor premise

[15] See Rendall, "Galatians," p. 169.

[16] See Martin Noth, *Leviticus: A Commentary*. OTL (London: SCM, 1965), pp. 127-128.

in Gal 3:12a), then one must logically conclude that no one is justified by the law (Gal 3:11a).

Taken in isolation, Paul's claim in Gal 3:11a could conceivably lead one to believe that he interprets Hab 2:4 as saying that faith is, in principle, the *only* means of obtaining righteousness. This position loses credibility if other factors are taken into account. The apostle's comment in Gal 3:11a cannot be interpreted in isolation. The context of this verse must be respected. We have posited that Paul interprets Lev 18:5 as stating that the law offers righteousness to the one who obeys its commandments. Consequently, it seems that Scripture offers two methods for obtaining righteousness, by way of faith (Hab 2:4, Gal 3:11b) and by way of the law (Lev 18:5, Gal 3:12b). However, if this is in fact the case, then why does Paul categorically deny in Gal 3:11a that no one can be justified by the law?

Paul's citation of Lev 18:5 which validates his conviction that the law does not rest on faith, may provide a clue as to why he is convinced that justification is obtainable through faith and not through the law. Indeed Lev 18:5 may guarantee life to those who observe the law but the apostle's version of Deut 27:26 in Gal 3:10b suggests that only those who fulfill *all* the numerous precepts of the Torah are true observers of the Torah. Moreover, Paul warns the Galatians in Gal 3:10b that Deut 27:26 curses anyone who fails to obey each and every one of the commands of the law. Paul's citation of Lev 18:5 in Gal 3:12b calls attention to the fact that those who rely on works of the law have *not* fulfilled all the precepts of the Torah and have not fulfilled the condition set by Leviticus for obtaining justification - that, indeed, they have fulfilled the condition set by Deut 27:26 for evoking the curse. Paul's declaration in Gal 3:10a makes it evident that he assumes that no one obeys all the regulations of the Torah. For these reasons, the apostle's discussion of the law in Gal 3:11-12 suggests that justification by means of the law is impossible for the Galatians not because "doing" of the law is wrong *per se* but rather because they have not done it in its entirety. Consequently, as far as the apostle is concerned, although the Galatians can, in principle, obtain righteousness by faith and by the law, in reality, they can only be justified through faith.

Absolved From the Curse

It would certainly be understandable if, up to now, the Galatians, who were on the threshold of seeking righteousness on the basis of the Mosaic law, feel somewhat discouraged. Paul has informed them in the previous verses that no one is justified by means of the law and that, in fact, all who rely on works of the law are cursed in light of their failure to abide by all things in the book of the law. Was there no hope for those who stood condemned by the law?

The apostle proclaims the good news in Gal 3:13a: "Christ redeemed us from the curse of the law." Strange as it seems, in Paul's attempt to explain how this took place, he insists in Gal 3:13b that Christ "became a curse for us." As one cannot become a curse in a literal sense, it seems that Paul is using a metonym here to signify that Christ was cursed by the Mosaic law. This hypothesis is further supported by the citation of Deut 21:23 in Gal 3:13c ("Cursed be every one who hangs on a tree"), which implies that Christ was subject to the law's curse since he "hung upon a tree." Such metonmy is not uncommon in the letters of Paul.[17]

Besides Paul's citation of Deut 21:23 in Gal 3:13c, there are several other places in the New Testament where allusions are made to this passage (e.g., Acts 5:30, 10:39). In its original context Deut 21:22-23 is concerned with regulations pertaining to the hanging of a condemned person. If one had committed a crime punishable by death "and he is put to death, and you

[17] See, for example, Gal 2:7 where Paul mentions the "uncircumcised" and the "circumcised" instead of the "Gentiles" and "Jews."

hang him on a tree, his body shall not remain all night upon the tree, but you shall bury him the same day, for a hanged man is accursed by God." Since Jewish law does not prescribe crucifixion as a capital sentence, Deut 21:23 should not, in its original setting, be interpreted as referring to the manner in which a condemned person was executed but only to the display of the corpse after the execution had taken place by some other means.[18] Nevertheless, it is easy to see how this text could be applied to a situation in which a person was condemned to death by crucifixion.[19] Unlike the other Scripture citations that Paul has thus far used, there is no specific reason to believe that the Galatians were already acquainted with this passage from Deuteronomy.

The key to understanding the "curse of the law" in Gal 3:13a lies in 3:10. Assuredly there are a number of similarities between these two verses. In both Gal 3:13 and 3:10 a curse is spoken of in connection with the law, a specific reference is made to Deuteronomy, the Scripture citation is preceded by the introductory formula "it is written" (*gegraptai*) and begins with the word "cursed" (*epikataratos*). In the light of these considerations, it seems logical to assume that the curse mentioned in Gal 3:13a from which Christ redeemed us, is to be identified with the curse mentioned in 3:10a, namely, that which is evoked by the transgression of the Torah. This position is further supported by that the fact that Christ was cursed in view of a specific precept of the Mosaic law (Deut 21:23, Gal 3:13c).

Redemption and Liberty

The term "redeemed" in Gal 3:13a and in 4:5 is a translation of the Greek verb *exagorazô*, meaning "buy back," "set

[18] Josh 8:29 and 10:26 are two examples from the Hebrew Scriptures in which those who were first killed were then hung upon a tree.

[19] John 19:31 probably contains an allusion to Deut 21:23. It is for this reason that the evangelist states that the Jews wanted the body of Jesus to be removed before sundown so as not to violate the Sabbath.

free." In both cases this word is mentioned in connection with the law. Some exegetes contend that Paul's use of *exagorazô* in Gal 3:13a should be interpreted in light of manumission in antiquity.[20]

In Hellenistic times, the word *agorazô* was often used as a term for the buying of slaves. The intensive form *exagorazô* was sometimes used to denote the act whereby the slaves' freedom was obtained. It was possible to purchase the freedom of slaves by paying an appropriate price to the owner. The money was paid by the slaves themselves or by someone else who desired to set them free. After the owner was paid in full, the slaves were declared free persons. Slaves who had gained their freedom in this way were said to be "redeemed."

At times, the process in which slaves purchased their freedom, or had it purchased for them, took place in the context of a pagan ceremony. The money was brought to the temple where the priests, in the name of a deity, bought the slaves from the master. The purchase by the deity was feigned, but the slaves in fact gained their freedom. Some exegetes postulate that Paul's use of the word *exagorazô* in Gal 3:13a should be interpreted in light of this pagan ritual. This approach, however, is not without its opponents.

Stanislas Lyonnet, for example, has challenged the hypothesis that *exagorazô* in Gal 3:13a should be understood in light of Hellenistic manumission.[21] He contends that there is little archaeological evidence which supports the conviction that the term *exagorazô* was used in Hellenistic times in connection with sacred or profane manumission. Moreover, Lyonnet maintains that the liberation of slaves in antiquity is entirely different than the redemption of a Christian. One who has been

[20] See, for example, Donald Guthrie, *Galatians*. The Century Bible, New Series (London: Nelson, 1969), p. 102.

[21] See Stanislas Lyonnet, "The Terminology of 'Purchasing' or 'Acquisition,'" Stanislas Lyonnet and Leopold Sabourin, eds., *Sin, Redemption, and Sacrifice: A Biblical and Patristic Study*. Analecta Biblica 48 (Rome: Biblical Institute, 1970) pp. 104-119, pp. 105-107.

freed by Christ is no longer confined by any bond whereas the freedom of a slave was almost always curtailed by certain conditions. Frequently, freed slaves were, nevertheless, compelled to stay with their former master for an extended period of time, quite often until the death of the master. Lyonnet is convinced that *exagorazô* in Gal 3:13a should be interpreted in view of the Hebrew Scriptures instead of Hellenistic manumission. Paul's frequent allusion to the Hebrew Scriptures in Galatians, especially in Gal 3:10-14 and 4:21-31 seems to confirm Lyonnet's hypothesis.

To be sure, the idea of redemption is not unknown in the Hebrew Scriptures. For example, the terms whereby poor people who had sold themselves into slavery could be redeemed is found in Lev 25:47-55. Relatives of slaves, or the slaves themselves, could pay a fee to the owner at which time the slaves would be set free. Moreover, the possibility of redemption for one who had committed a crime worthy of death is mentioned in Exod 21:30. "If a ransom is laid on him, then he shall give for the redemption of his life whatever is laid upon him." Redemption is also spoken of in terms of liberation from the Egyptians in Exod 6:6. Furthermore, the notion of corporate redemption is also present in the Hebrew Scriptures. Lev 9:1-24 describes a ritual in which a scapegoat is sacrificed so that the people of Israel might be redeemed.[22]

Should *exagorazô* in Gal 3:13a be interpreted in light of the Hebrew Scriptures or in view of Hellenistic manumission? There is insufficient evidence to determine with absolute certainty whether the apostle uses this term in connection with the Hebrew Scriptures or in connection with Hellenistic emancipation of slaves, but the evidence rests slightly in favor of the latter. There are two major obstacles in accepting the hypothesis that *exagorazô* in Gal 3:13a should be interpreted in light of

[22] See the discussion concerning the notion of redemption in the Hebrew Scriptures by Madeleine S. Miller and J. Lane Miller, "Redemption," *HBD*, pp. 605-606.

the Hebrew Scriptures. First of all the term *exagorazô* is only mentioned once in the Septuagint and not in the sense of "redeeming" or "liberating."[23] If Paul had wanted to use a term in Gal 3:13a that would call to mind the concept of redemption in the Hebrew Scriptures, he probably would have used a form of the word *lutroô* (Lev 25:48, Exod 6:6, 21:30).[24] Secondly, we must keep in mind that the Galatians were, in all likelihood, Gentile Christians. Therefore, it seems logical to assume that the Galatians would be more familiar with the concept of manumission in Hellenism than with the notion of redemption in the Hebrew Scriptures. It is true that the Galatians may have been acquainted with certain passages of the Hebrew Scriptures which were probably brought to their attention by Paul's opponents (e.g., 3:10b, 3:12b, 4:21-23). However, there is no specific reason to believe that the Galatians had previous knowledge of those passages from the Hebrew Scriptures that deal with the concept of redemption.

In the context of manumission, we have observed that the one who has been redeemed has been set free from something. Moreover, we have noted that a payment of some sort was required in order to secure one's redemption. In a similar fashion, it seems that Paul associates the notion of redemption in Gal 3:13a with that of freedom. When he asserts that Christ redeemed us from the curse of the law, he is apparently stating that Christ has freed us or has delivered us (1:4) from the law's condemnation. Redemption from the curse of the law is to be understood as being closely related to justification. It is also important for understanding Paul's argumentation to realize that the redemption from the curse of the law was not without cost. Christ had to pay for that freedom (1 Cor 6:20, 7:23).

[23] See Dan 2:8.

[24] See Rom 3:24, 8:23; 1 Cor 1:30.

Christ Crucified

The death of Christ plays a crucial role in Paul's argumentation not only in Gal 3:13 but also throughout the entire letter.[25] Modern day Christians are so far removed from the mind-set of those who lived in the first century, that much of the forcefulness of Paul's discussion in Galatians tends to be lost on the contemporary reader of this epistle. Moreover, contemporary Christians are so accustomed to viewing the crucifix as a sacred object and referring to the day that Christ was killed as "Good Friday," that they often forget the tremendous amount of suffering and humiliation that accompanied this form of capital punishment. As did all the inhabitants of the Roman empire, the Galatians would have regarded the cross as a sign of the most terrible form of capital punishment.

Crucifixion, whereby the victim was nailed or otherwise bound to a cross, was an extremely cruel form of execution.[26] Rome reserved this means of capital punishment for slaves and foreigners. Only those who committed the most atrocious crimes, such as treason, murder, and insurrection, were crucified. In addition to punishing the condemned person, crucifixion was meant to act as a warning to the general public against opposition to the state.

The Roman authorities often used this form of punishment for political terrorists who tried to break away from the empire. Having crushed the slave revolt led by Spartacus, the Romans crucified an estimated 6,000 people on the road from Capua (near Naples) to Rome. Furthermore, according to the historian Josephus, after the siege of Jerusalem in A.D. 70, as many as 500 Jews a day were crucified.

[25] See Gal 1:4, 2:20, 21; 3:1, 13; 6:14.

[26] Our discussion concerning crucifixion in the ancient world is based on a fascinating article by William D. Edwards et al, "On the Physical Death of Jesus Christ," *JAMA* 255 (1986), pp. 1455-1463; and John L. McKenzie's, "Cross," *Dictionary*, pp. 161-162.

One of our scholarship students, Fr. Li Guoliang from Beijing, is greeted by Pope John Paul II in Rome (Dec. 1995).

Découverte de la vie des trappistes à Westvleteren.

mation de leurs prêtres, de leurs religieux et laïcs. Ils espèrent une réponse positive, car il est clair pour eux que provisoirement cela ne peut se faire en Chine.

La Fondation a donc été amenée à lancer un "Programme de formation" en plus de son "Programme pour la recherche et les publications" et de son "Programme de coopération au développement en Chine". La collaboration de la K.U.Leuven et de Louvain-la-Neuve nous est acquise. Nous recherchons d'autres instituts dans nos pays où les candidats, après l'indispensable étude de la langue, pourront entreprendre les études qui leur sont utiles. Ce programme est maintenant la priorité de la Fondation. Nous pensons pouvoir ainsi apporter notre contribution à l'Église de Chine, car déjà dans le passé la Belgique a beaucoup contribué, en Chine même, à la formation des responsables de l'Église: scheutistes, franciscains, soeurs de La Chasse, samistes, A.F.I., lazaristes, soeurs de St-Joseph (Heerlen), soeurs F.M.M., etc. Mais aussi beaucoup de prêtres et de laïcs chinois sont venus chez nous - surtout depuis le P. Lebbe - et recevaient une formation spécialisée à l'Université Catholique de Louvain et dans d'autres instituts. Le temps où nos missionnaires exerçaient leur activité en Chine est complètement révolu. L'Église chinoise, qui se dirige maintenant de façon autonome, appelle ses anciens amis à collaborer sur un terrain spécialisé: la formation.

Cela signifie réellement une "Nouvelle Mission de Chine" pour notre temps. La Mission s'appelle mainte-

Under normal circumstances, those who had been sentenced to death by crucifixion were forced to carry their cross along a public road to the place of execution (John 19:17). In view of traditional Roman practice, the cross carried by Jesus was probably not the entire cross but only the crossbeam. The upright beam was usually left permanently at the execution ground, with the crossbeam being attached at each particular execution. A sign indicating one's crime was usually worn around the neck and later posted above the victim on the cross (John 19:19). Before being bound to the cross, one was completely stripped of one's clothing. This was meant to add to the humiliation of the punishment. Most of the time, the clothing of the condemned person went to the soldiers as a gratuity (John 19:23). The hands (or wrists) and feet of the victim would then be tied and/or nailed to the cross.

Ropes were frequently used to bind the arms, legs, and belly of the condemned person to the wood. Consequently, one was not free to move and thus experienced great difficulty in coping with heat, sweat, insects, and the like. It was standard procedure to slightly elevate the victim a foot or two above the ground. Thus, Jesus was crucified low enough for an onlooker to offer him a vinegar-filled sponge that was put on a reed (John 19:29). While on the cross, the unfortunate victim was often mocked and ridiculed by others (Matt 27:39-43).

Crucifixion was an agonizingly slow death. This was due, in part, to the fact that no vital organs were damaged by the nails that affixed the victim to the cross. Once a person was firmly bound to a cross, a cramping of the muscles took place. Since the lack of movement decreased the flow of blood in the lungs dramatically, air could enter the lungs but could only be expelled with a tremendous amount of effort. Only by pushing one's self up on one's feet, which obviously resulted in terrific pain as the feet were nailed to the cross, could one expel the air. As the body grew ever weaker, one had less and less strength to lift oneself up and thus experienced even greater difficulty in breathing. A crucified person eventually suffocated. Crucifixion was, in the full sense of the word, "excruciating" (from the Latin word *excruciatus*, i.e., "out of the cross").[27]

Suffering from fatigue, cramped muscles, hunger and thirst, the condemned person often endured intolerable pain for days before death mercifully occurred. Thus, Pilate and the Roman soldiers were surprised that Jesus expired so quickly (e.g., Mark 15:44). Why was it that Jesus died after a relatively short time on the cross?

In accordance with Roman law, one who had been sentenced to death was first scourged. Tied to a pillar, the condemned person was beaten severely by slaves. Roman scourging was frequently so severe that the victim who was flogged often died as a result of it. Inasmuch as the number of times that one was to be whipped was not limited, it usually continued until the slave who administered it tired or until the flesh of the condemned person hung down in bloody shreds. There were a variety of methods of scourging. Sometimes the victim was simply beaten with rods (Acts 16:22). Other times the condemned person was beaten with a whip (Acts 22:24). According to Matthew and Mark, the scourging of Jesus was of the worst kind (*fragellion*). A whip consisting of knotted cords weighted with pieces of metal or bone was used on Jesus (Matt 27:26; Mark 15:15). There is a distinct possibility that Jesus died but after a few hours because of the intensity of the scourging. The fact that he did not have the strength to carry his cross to Calvary (Matt 27:32) gives further credence to this theory.

Jesus' death on the cross involved unthinkable physical pain. Moreover, he must have also experienced a great deal of emotional trauma. Even before he was arrested, Jesus seems to have had an inkling of the suffering that was in store for him (Matt 26:38: "My soul is very sorrowful, even to death."). His closest companions deserted him when he needed them the

[27] See Edwards, "Physical Death," p. 1461.

most, including one who betrayed him and another who three times denied even knowing him. Jesus may also have *felt* abandoned by God Himself (Mark 15:34, Ps 22:1: "My God, my God, why hast thou forsaken me"). Nevertheless, in spite of his great physical, emotional, and spiritual pain, Jesus continued to put his trust in God. According to the third evangelist, the last words of Jesus on the cross demonstrated his tremendous faith in divine providence. "Father, into thy hands I commit my spirit" (Luke 23:46).

Paul underscores his conviction in Gal 3:13 that the liberation from the curse of the law which Christ has obtained for us did not come easy. Not only did Christ suffer a terrible death but he also endured the curse of Deut 21:23 so that we might be redeemed. The apostle may want to place before the eyes of the Galatians (3:1) the consequences of their belief that one must observe the works of the law in order to be justified. They act as if the crucifixion of Jesus served no purpose (2:21).

Sacrificial Love

Our primary focus, concerning the death of Jesus, should not be on the intense suffering and anguish that he experienced but rather on the great love that God has shown for humanity by allowing His Son to die for us (John 3:16). What value we must have in the eyes of God that He considers us worth undergoing such tragedy. In our attempt to grapple with the suffering and death of Jesus, we also grapple with the "human condition," namely, that every human being must cope with pain, hardship, and the harsh reality of death. The resurrection of Jesus (1:1) demonstrates that suffering and death do not have the final word. God's all-encompassing love changes everything. The crucifixion of Jesus is now understood in terms of redemption instead of tragedy. Because of the resurrection of Jesus, we no longer look upon the cross as a instrument of torture but rather as a sign of divine love.

From Curse To Blessing

There is a remarkable change in mood as Paul's argument progresses from Gal 3:13 to 3:14. After a three-fold mention of curse in Gal 3:13, the apostle's emphasis on the blessing of Abraham in 3:14 seems like a breath of fresh air. Much of the terminology that Paul uses in Gal 3:1-13 reappears in 3:14. He makes a connection in this verse between Christ - the blessing of Abraham - the promise of the Spirit - and faith. The apostle's main objective in Gal 3:14 is to illustrate the results of Christ's redemptive death: so that the Gentiles might participate in Abraham's blessing (3:14a), and more specifically, so that Paul and the Galatians might receive the Spirit through faith (3:14b). The apostle's use of the term "faith" refers to "faith in Christ" (2:16, 3:22).

Through Christ Alone

Paul's remarks in Gal 3:13a intimate that Christ must play an important part in the Galatians' attempt to obtain righteousness. Redemption from the law's curse, which Christ has obtained for us, goes hand in hand with being blessed. The apostle explicitly pronounces in Gal 3:14a Christ's contribution to the process of justification. It is *in Christ* that the blessing of Abraham might come upon the Gentiles. Rather surprisingly, the apostle feels no need to demonstrate how it came about that the one who was so closely associated with a curse in Gal 3:13b is now associated with a blessing in 3:14a. Nevertheless, Paul's comments in this verse do suggest that through Christ the Gentile Christians of Galatia are no longer in a cursed condition; rather, they are in a blessed one.

The apostle brings to light in Gal 3:14 the condition that is necessary for obtaining righteousness. Paul's argumentation in this verse indicates that he does not simply declare that all Gentiles participate in the blessing of Abraham but only those who seek justification through Christ. The condition set forth in Gal 3:14a which must be fulfilled in order to be blessed is placed side by side with the condition set forth in 3:10a for being cursed. The apostle's discussion in these verses makes it clear that all who rely on works of the law for justification are cursed (because no one obeys all the commands of the Torah) while those who seek justification through Christ are blessed.

The Promise of the Spirit

Paul does not speak in Gal 3:14b of the blessing of Abraham, which was probably but a vague concept to the Galatians. Instead, the apostle refers to something that they are much more familiar with and in fact have experienced - the reception of the Spirit. Paul calls attention to the fact that the Galatians began their Christian life with the Spirit (3:3). He associates the possession of the Spirit with the working of miracles (3:5). The mention of the Spirit in Gal 3:14b more than likely reminds the Galatians of the question that he put to them in 3:2 concerning how they came to possess the Spirit. Paul's comments in this verse imply that the Galatians had received the Spirit by hearing with faith and not by observing the works of the law.

The apostle's declaration in Gal 3:14 is not the first time in the epistle that the apostle makes a connection between the Spirit and Abraham's blessing. He associates the notion of the "blessing of Abraham" with "justification" in Gal 3:6-9 and seems to link the concept of "justification" with "reception of the Spirit" in 3:5-6. On no occasion in the letter does Paul explain to the Galatians why he believes the blessing of Abraham is connected with receiving the Spirit.[28] He seems to take

[28] Richard B. Hays is one of the few exegetes who has addressed the question as to why Paul makes such a close connection between "Abraham's blessing" and the "reception of the Spirit." See *The Faith of Jesus Christ. An Investigation of the Narrative Substructure of Galatians 3:1 - 4:11*, SBLDS 56 (Chico, CA: Scholars Press, 1983), pp. 210-212.

it for granted. What is rather puzzling about the apostle's discussion in this regard is that it appears to play a crucial part in his argument. If the Galatians accepted Paul's claim that one who receives the Spirit participates in the blessing of Abraham, they would probably realize that, in light of their own personal experience, Abraham's blessing had already come upon them (implication in 3:2 in conjunction with 3:14b). Moreover, they would no doubt realize that it came upon them because of their faith and not because they performed the works of the law (3:2, 5).

Obviously the Galatians were not originally aware that the reception of the Spirit was associated with Abraham's blessing or they would not have been tempted to adhere to the Torah in order to become children of Abraham. Since Paul does not deem it necessary to prove to the Galatians that the blessing of Abraham and the promise of the Spirit, that is, the reception of the Spirit, are synonymous expressions, he apparently does not believe that he will be challenged on this point. Although Paul does not substantiate his conviction that one who receives the Spirit participates in the blessing of Abraham, it is nevertheless quite evident how it fits into his argument that the observance of the works of the law is not a prerequisite for becoming a child of Abraham. The personal experience of the Galatians illustrates that they have previously received the Spirit and have thus already participated in the blessing of Abraham, although they did not realize it, in light of their faith and not by virtue of their adherence to the Torah.

A Meaningful Death

Paul's allegations in Gal 3:14 illustrate that the death of Christ did in fact serve a purpose, that the Gentiles, and specifically the Galatians, might receive the Spirit through faith. According to the apostle's line of reasoning in Gal 2:21, if Christ did not die in vain then it must be true that justification does not come about through the law. Paul's declaration in Gal

3:14 that the Gentiles might participate in the blessing of Abraham through faith, reiterates his conviction in 3:9 that people of faith are blessed. Furthermore, the apostle's emphasis on faith in Gal 3:14b concurs with his citation of Hab 2:4, which demonstrates that one is justified by faith. What had been foreseen by Scripture (3:8) has now become a reality.

Concluding Remarks

Paul attempts to win back the Galatians to his point of view in 3:1-14 by arguing with material that, for the most part, was already known to them. First of all, the apostle defends his negative stance towards the law as a viable means to justification by relying heavily on the personal experience of the Galatians (3:1-5). He then turns his attention to Abraham, that great figure of faith in the Hebrew Scriptures (3:6-9). In the process of doing so, Paul demonstrates that his conviction that Gentiles are justified by faith alone is not simply a personal concoction. On the contrary, it was foretold by Scripture (3:8). Subsequently the apostle refers again to the sacred writings to validate his position and cites passages with which the Galatians were probably familiar, namely, Deut 27:26 (3:10b), Lev 18:5 (3:12b), and perhaps Hab 2:4 (3:11b). Paul's allusion in Gal 3:13 to the death of Christ also plays an essential part in his discussion. Hence the apostle leads the Galatians to accept his version of the gospel by appealing to that which they were already well-acquainted. Although Paul uses such material, he provides his own particular emphasis to illustrate that one is justified exclusively through faith in Christ.

A Proto-Christian

The apostle focuses on the fact that, like Abraham, the Gentile Christians of Galatia participate in the blessing through faith apart from the law. In a manner of speaking, Paul presents the patriarch as the forerunner of the Christian believer. Abraham had to respond to the divine initiative in order to be blessed. Likewise, the Galatians must respond to the divine initiative (in Christ) in order to be justified. That Paul considers the patriarch as the precursor of the Christian believer is underscored in Gal 3:8. Both Abraham and the Galatians respond to the divine initiative by means of faith without adhering to the Torah.

Mystery of the Cross

Perhaps no where else is the divinity and humanity of Jesus Christ so evident as when he hung upon the cross on that first "Good Friday." In and through his suffering, his sense of isolation, and his death, the Son of God identified fully with the human situation in a most dramatic fashion. Even so, the divinity of Jesus shone through because of his willingness to place full confidence in his heavenly Father when all seemed lost, and his desire to forgive those who were responsible for his death (Luke 23:34). Can we not say that the vertical dimension of divinity and the horizontal dimension of humanity came together in the person of the crucified Christ?

Paul makes a strong connection between the death of Jesus and obtaining righteousness. Indeed, it is because of the crucifixion of Christ that those who believe in him might participate in the blessing of Abraham through faith. We have previously noted that before the condemned were bound to the cross, they were first stripped of their clothing. Interestingly enough, it is by one's clothing that one's nationality, social status, profession, and gender, are often indicated. As Jesus hung naked on the cross, all such distinctions were removed. He was, in a very real sense, a "universal person." Perhaps this is a divine sign that the benefits of Christ's death are meant for all humanity.

Paul's reflections on the passion and death of Jesus in Gal 3:13-14 demonstrate that suffering and death can have tremendous value. The power of God is such that He can transform even these horrendous realities into a blessing. After all, Christ's crucifixion had redeeming value. This is not to say that unnecessary human suffering should not be avoided at all costs. Just the opposite is true, those who imitate Jesus and promote the kingdom of God have a sacred duty to eliminate all needless suffering. Nevertheless, human beings sometimes encounter situations in which suffering is unavoidable. When this occurs, Christians can follow the example of Jesus who, even when all seemed hopeless, trusted in God completely that somehow such suffering could have meaning and value.

Because of the suffering and death of Jesus, it is readily seen that life's tragedies, which human beings must occasionally endure, should not necessarily be understood as divine punishment. Even the beloved Son of God underwent the tragedy of crucifixion and the intense agony and abuse which accompanies this form of capital punishment.

Reflections on the death of Christ by the various New Testament authors indicate that Jesus was free to love, even in the midst of the tragic situation on Calvary. Through his sacrificial love, redemption from the law's curse, freedom from sin, has been obtained. Paul argues that Christian liberty is never to be taken for granted. Rather, our freedom, which was anticipated in the Abraham narrative, should always be treasured as a precious gift, one that was obtained for us at a great price, namely, the death of Christ.

CHAPTER SIX

FREED FROM CAPTIVITY (GAL 3:15-4:31)

Paul still has plenty of ammunition to carry on his assault against the heretical teaching of the troublemakers. Should there be any doubt about his position concerning the law's deficiency to make one righteous, the apostle offers yet more evidence in Gal 3:15 - 4:31 that one is justified by faith without performing the works of the law. As in Gal 3:1-14, Paul's discussion in this section of the epistle first strikes one as being a rather disorganized collection of material. In his quest to disprove the agitators' version of the gospel, the apostle begins with an example from everyday life (3:15-18), then reflects on the purpose of the law (3:19-22), refers to several well-known facts about the status of a slave and of a free person (4:1-2), offers some personal testimony (4:12-20), and concludes with a rather lengthy interpretation of the biblical narrative about the two sons of Abraham (4:21-31). A more in-depth examination of these passages reveals, however, that several factors link Paul's seemingly haphazard arguments together in a cohesive whole.

In the process of demonstrating that faith, not the law, is the fundamental ingredient for obtaining righteousness, the apostle speaks of justification in terms of "an inheritance from Abraham" (3:16). With this in mind, it is readily seen why Paul uses terminology associated with the legal realm concerning the rights of a legitimate heir. The apostle refers to a person's will and to contractual obligations regarding such a legal agreement (3:15). Paul follows these remarks with some reflections on "Abraham's will," namely, the blessing which God promised not only to the patriarch but to his legal heirs as well (3:16-18). The apostle's argumentation concerning the rightful beneficiaries of Abraham's inheritance provide Paul with the opportunity to offer some interesting insights about the official status in the Roman empire of those who are children of free persons, that is, legitimate heirs to their parents' estate, and of those who are children of slaves, that is, offspring who have no legal rights of inheritance (4:1-2). This discussion eventually leads to the apostle's reflections on the two children of Abraham, one born of a free woman and one born of a slave (4:21-31).

In the midst of this discussion, Paul presents some autobiographical information regarding his first contact with the Galatians (4:12-20). The apostle wonders aloud how the Galatians could challenge his law-free version of the gospel which they had so readily accepted when he first preached it to them. "Have I then become your enemy by telling you the truth" (4:16)? One senses the depth of feeling that Paul has for the Galatians, even as he chastises them for their being in danger of yielding to the agitators' rendition of the good news.

Although his argumentation in Gal 3:15 - 4:31 is varied, the apostle is, nevertheless, consistent in his belief that one becomes a legitimate heir to Abraham by means of faith without observing the law. Paul remains persistent in demonstrating the overriding importance of faith and the secondary nature of the Torah. Moreover, the apostle invariably associates faith with freedom and with those who are the rightful heirs to Abraham's blessing while he affiliates reliance on the law with slavery and with those who are illegitimate heirs to the patriarch's inheritance.

The Covenant

In his attempt to discredit the false teaching of the Judaizers, Paul calls to mind an evidently well-known datum from the legal realm. Once a will has been validated, no one can add to or take away from it (3:15). The Greek term *diathekê*, which appears in this verse, is usually translated as a "will" or "testament" but in the Septuagint it normally means "covenant."[1] The apostle's argument in the following verses demonstrates that he is making a comparison between the covenant that God made with Abraham and a person's will.

Paul presents the conditions of "Abraham's will" in Gal 3:16, namely, that "the promises were made to the patriarch and to his offspring." The apostle spells out the ramifications in Gal 3:18a of the conviction that the inheritance is obtained by the law. If that should be the case, then it would no longer be by a promise (Rom 4:14). Those who profess that one must observe the works of the law in order to participate in the blessing of Abraham conduct themselves as if the conditions of the covenant with Abraham have been changed. The apostle, however, reminds the Galatians in 3:18b that, in fact, God gave the inheritance to Abraham by a *promise*. Anyone who insists that the inheritance is obtained by the law instead of by the promise, is attempting to annul the covenant that God had previously made with Abraham and, as the apostle has demonstrated in 3:15-17, this cannot be done.

The main point that Paul wants to bring out in his argumentation is found in Gal 3:17 ("this is what I mean"). The terms of the divine contract that God made with Abraham cannot be annulled by the Torah, which did not even come into the possession of Israel until some four centuries later. The unstated, but nevertheless insinuated, conclusion of 3:18, as well as of 3:15-18, is that inheritance does not come about by the law. If one is not allowed to alter a human legal agreement once it has been certified, then it is all the more obvious that one is not permitted to revise a divine contract once it has

[1] Betz, *Galatians*, pp. 155-156, notes that it is not at all clear which kind of testament that Paul has in mind in Gal 3:15. Is it Greek, Roman, or Jewish? There are difficulties with each position.

been ratified. The apostle's observation that the law came such a considerable length of time after God made a promise to Abraham is also meant to further distance the patriarch from the Torah.

As we have previously mentioned, Paul expounds in Gal 3:16 on the significance of the fact that the promises were made to Abraham and his offspring (singular and not the plural "offsprings"). Despite the apostle's comments in Gal 3:29 and Rom 4:18, which indicate that he realizes that the singular form "offspring" can refer to many descendants, Paul assumes that this term in Gal 3:16 refers to one, and only one, descendant, namely, Christ.[2] The apostle apparently feels no need to substantiate his Christocentric interpretation of Gen 12:7.[3] According to Paul's way of thinking, the way that one becomes a legal heir to Abraham's inheritance is exclusively through Christ. In sharp contrast to the agitators' teaching that only those who are bound to the Mosaic law receive the inheritance, the apostle insists that it is those who are united with Christ that "are Abraham's offspring, heirs according to the promise" (3:29).

Captivated By The Law

One can almost hear the Judaizers' grumbling over Paul's derogatory comments about the law. "Why would God have given the Mosaic law to the chosen people in the first place unless He had intended it to be a valid means of making one a legal heir to Abraham's blessing?" The troublemakers may also have queried that the apostle's negative stance towards the

[2] See Robert Yates, "St. Paul and the Law in Galatians," *IThQ* 51 (1985), pp. 105-124, p. 112: "The rabbis would understand Paul's use of the singular of 'seed' to refer to one person, but for them that person would be Isaac."
[3] Paul's method of arguing in Gal 3:16 may reflect a rabbinic style of biblical interpretation.

Torah not only suggests that the law serves no purpose but also implies that it stands in direct opposition to the promises of God. Such a thought would have seemed absurd to them in view of the fact that God Himself gave the Torah to the Jewish people.

Inferiority of the Law

Paul seems to anticipate such a reprisal against his understanding of the Mosaic law by asking the rhetorical question in Gal 3:19a. "Why then the law?" As he sees it, the Torah was never designed to be a viable means of obtaining righteousness. The apostle first supports this conviction by illustrating that the law has only secondary importance. He mentions in Gal 3:19b that it was simply *added* "because of transgressions" (3:19b). Moreover, the time of the Mosaic law *was limited*, it was valid until the coming of Christ (3:19c). Paul further demonstrates the subordinate nature of the Torah by drawing attention to the indirect way in which it was given. Unlike the promise to Abraham, which was ratified by God Himself (3:17), the Mosaic law was *mediated* by the angels and not given directly by the Almighty (3:19d).[4] The intermediary to whom the apostle is referring in Gal 3:19c is undoubtedly Moses (Exod 20:19, Deut 5:5, 23-27). Not only does Paul highlight the temporary nature of the Torah in Gal 3:19-20, but he also illustrates its indirect association with God.

A word needs to be said about the apostle's conviction that the law was added "because of transgressions." What exactly does Paul intend to convey with this expression? Several interpretations regarding the meaning of this phrase have been proposed, namely, (1) "to check transgressions," (2) "to reveal transgressions for what they are, namely, violations of divine law," (3) "to invoke and increase transgressions" (Rom

[4] Several New Testament passages reflect the belief of biblical times that the angels had a role to play in the giving of the Torah to the chosen people (see Deut 33:2 [Septuagintal version], Acts 7:38, 53, Heb 2:2).

7:7-11), and, (4) "to awaken a conviction of sin and guilt, and thus the need for salvation."[5] Numbers two and four seem to come closest to the truth in this context. Whatever the case might be, Paul is underscoring the inferior status of the law in Gal 3:19.

Confining Nature of the Law

The apostle advances still another argument to prove that the Mosaic law was never meant to be a vehicle for becoming a rightful heir to the promise of Abraham. As Paul sees it, the primary function of the Torah was simply to "consign all things to sin" so that "what was promised to faith in Jesus Christ might be given to those who believe" (3:22). Paul may have Deut 27:26 and Ps 143:2 in mind when he speaks of Scripture "consigning all things to sin." In other words, these two passages indicate that Scripture views all people as sinners who are in need of deliverance.

The term "consign" in Gal 3:22 is a translation of the Greek word *sygkleiô*, meaning "to make or keep someone a prisoner." That the apostle identifies the Torah with bondage is reiterated in Gal 3:23. He thinks of the law as that which "confines" (*froureô*) that is, holds one captive, keeps one locked up" (3:23b). The terminology that Paul uses to describe the purpose of the Mosaic law is normally reserved for those who are in prison. Paul is, in effect, warning the Galatians that adherence to the Torah results in confinement, the very antithesis of the promise of Abraham.

The apostle brings another metaphor into his argumentation concerning the subsidiary function of the Torah (3:24-25). He compares those who are under the law with those who are under a *paidagôgos* (custodian), a strict authoritative figure whose task in antiquity was to supervise a minor child both inside and outside the home.[6] The apostle's aim in using this

[5] See, for example, Ronald Y. Fung, *The Epistle to the Galatians*. NICNT (Grand Rapids, MI: Eerdmans, 1988), p. 159.
[6] See Arichea and Nida, *Galatians*, p. 81.

term is clear. It underscores both the confining nature of the law and its temporary status. The apostle repeatedly insists that the Mosaic law functioned only *until* Christ came (3:19, 23, 24, 25). For this reason, Paul divides all of history into two time periods; the era before the arrival of Christ when "we were confined under the law" (3:23), and the age following the coming of Christ when we "are no longer under a custodian" (3:25).

Even though the apostle regards the law as having but a secondary status and even though he contends that it cannot make one an authentic heir to Abraham's inheritance, Paul does not, by any stretch of the imagination, consider the Torah as inherently evil. On the contrary, he affirms in Gal 3:21 that if "a law had been given which could make one alive [that is, justified], then righteousness would indeed be by the law."[7] Having said this, the apostle quickly points out in Gal 3:22 that the law was *not*, in fact, destined to be a viable means to justification. Its purpose was merely to consign all things to sin. Inasmuch as the Torah did serve a divine purpose, albeit in a negative capacity, Paul can say in all intellectual honesty that the Mosaic law does not stand in opposition to the promises of God (3:21).

The apostle concludes his reflections on the law in Galatians 3 by concentrating on the person of Christ (3:25-29). He maintains that a dramatic change has taken place now that Christ Jesus has entered the picture. The era of the Torah's confining guardianship has been replaced by the era of faith. As Paul sees it, those who believe in Christ Jesus are no longer under the captivity of the law (3:25). Because of their union with the risen Lord, baptized Christians are free to participate in the blessing that was promised to the offspring of Abraham (3:16, 29).

[7] See Rom 7:12 where Paul claims that "the law is holy, and the commandment is holy and just and good."

New Life of Freedom

Galatians 3:27 is the only verse in the epistle in which the apostle mentions the Christian initiation rite of baptism (*baptizô*). In Hellenism the term *baptô* meant "to dip," "to dip into a dye," and, therefore, "to dye." The Greek word *baptizô*, an intensive form of *baptô*, conveys the idea of "immersing" and/or "washing" someone or something. This term was sometimes used in connection with one who perished by drowning.[8] A form of the word *baptizô* occasionally appears in ancient manuscripts to designate the process whereby a blacksmith dipped a piece of hot iron into water in order to temper it. Grammatically speaking, perhaps the most important aspect of *baptizô*, is that it in some way involves a significant change.

Baptism and the New Testament

The rite in which water was used as a sign of religious purification was well known in antiquity.[9] John the Baptist, for example, conducted his ministry in that part of the world where water was a rare commodity. In such dry surroundings, it is readily seen why water was particularly understood as a symbol of life, refreshment and purity. John recognized that he "baptized with water for repentance" (Matt 3:11) while the one who was to come, the Messiah, would baptize with the Holy Spirit.

There can be no question that Jesus was baptized by John the Baptist (e.g., Mark 1:9). Matthew associates the baptism of Jesus with the reception of the Holy Spirit and divine sonship (Matt 3:16-17). Interestingly enough, on at least one occasion Jesus made a direct connection between baptism and his own death (Mark 10:33-34, 38-39). According to the first evangelist, Jesus gave the apostles an explicit command to go "and

[8] See G.R. Beasley-Murray, "*Baptizô*," *DNTT* 1, pp. 144-150.
[9] See William F. Flemington, "Baptism," *IDB* 1, pp. 348-353, p. 348.

make disciples of all nations, *baptizing* them in the name of the Father, and of the Son and of the Holy Spirit" (Matt 28:19). The author of Acts informs his community that the rite of baptism was practiced by the first disciples of Jesus from the very first Pentecost onward (Acts 2:38).

The events surrounding the baptism of Paul are described at some length in Acts 9:1-18. Although Paul himself baptized a few people, he felt that his primary concern as an apostle was to proclaim the gospel (1 Cor 1:14-17). Paul was forced to address some questions regarding baptism in response to the troubled situation of the Christian community in Corinth (1 Cor 1:12-17). Within this context, the apostle informs the Corinthians that the one who baptized them is of little consequence. What is fundamentally important, however, is the one in whose name they were baptized, Jesus the Lord. Strange as it may seem, Paul makes reference to a custom in Corinth of baptizing someone on behalf of the dead (1 Cor 15:29).[10] The apostle simply mentions this tradition without condemning or encouraging it.

Theology of Baptism

Of all the New Testament writings, the letters of Paul contain the fullest exposition of the meaning of baptism. In the First Letter to the Corinthians, the apostle instructs those under his care that baptism is the vehicle by which one is incorporated into the life of Christ and into the Christian community (1 Cor 12:12-13). All who are baptized receive the divine gift of the Holy Spirit (Gal 4:4). According to Paul, Christian believers are so closely identified with the risen Lord by means of baptism that the apostle refers to them as the "body of Christ" (e.g., 1 Cor 12:27). Having been baptized by one Spirit, Christians are intimately bound to Christ and to one another (1 Cor

[10] See C.K. Barrett, *The First Epistle to the Corinthians*. BNTC (London, Adam & Charles Black, 1968), pp. 362-364, for an interesting examination regarding Paul's argumentation in 1 Cor 15:29.

12:13). Consequently, Paul proudly announces that, for those who are in Christ, all previous barriers which had formerly divided them have been removed. The members of the body of Christ must therefore realize that all prior distinctions between Jewish and Gentile Christians, slave and free, male and female, are a thing of the past (Gal 3:28, 1 Cor 12:13).[11]

Paul uses some very strong and mystifying language to describe the tremendous change that takes place in one who has come to believe in Christ Jesus and has undergone the rite of Christian initiation. The apostle's fundamental conviction is that those who have been baptized, have been immersed *into* the life of Christ. For that reason, Paul refers to Christians as those who are "in Christ Jesus" (3:26).

The apostle professes in Rom 6:3 that "all of us who have been baptized into Christ Jesus were baptized into his death." Since one who has died is freed from sin, those who have been crucified with Christ (Gal 2:20), by virtue of their baptism, are no longer enslaved by sin (Rom 6:6-7). Thus Christians must consider themselves as "dead to sin and alive to God in Christ Jesus" (Rom 6:11). Paul is confident that as "we have been united with him in a death like his, we shall certainly be united with him in a resurrection like his" (Rom 6:5).

The apostle's discussion in Gal 3:25-28 concerning faith and baptism is packed with theological insights. Paul heralds the good news that, through faith, all who have been baptized into Christ are children of God (3:26), have put on Christ (3:27), are one in Christ Jesus (3:28), belong to Christ (3:29a) and participate in Abraham's inheritance (3:29b). Indeed, the apostle has a rich vocabulary to describe the monumental change that has taken place in those who have professed their faith in Christ and have been baptized. This being said, one has

[11] See Bruce, *Galatians*, p. 187: "Paul makes a threefold affirmation [in Gal 3:28] which corresponds to a number of Jewish formulas in which the threefold distinction is maintained, as in the morning prayer in which the male Jew thanks God that he was not made a Gentile, a slave, or a woman."

the impression in reading Gal 3:25-28, and, for that matter, all of Paul's writings, that he is never completely satisfied with any one designation to explain this change. The apostle must therefore be content with simply illuminating different aspects of the benefits that Christ has won for humanity by virtue of his life, death, and resurrection. In addition to the nomenclature that appears in Galatians, which we have previously discussed, for example, "justification," "heirs of Abraham," "redeemed," and so forth, Paul also uses a variety of other designations to describe the substantial change that has occurred in those who have been baptized. A brief examination of such terminology will help us better understand Paul's argumentation in Galatians.[12]

Salvation

On a number of occasions the apostle makes reference to the salvific effect of Christ's death (e.g., Rom 1:16). The term "salvation" is a translation of the Greek word *sôtêria*, meaning "deliverance," "release," "preservation." This word connotes the act of being rescued from any sort of life-threatening danger that one might encounter in life. In the Hebrew Scriptures, God was thought of as the Savior of Israel (Isa 45:15). Paul's predominantly Gentile audiences would have been more familiar with the various pagan deities who were often viewed as salvific figures, for example, Zeus, Hercules, and Artemis. At times Roman emperors were also referred to as saviors.[13]

The apostle does not associate salvation with any pagan god or government official but exclusively with Jesus Christ (e.g., Rom 10:10, Phil 3:20). Paul declares that Christians are being saved because of the crucifixion of Christ (1 Cor 1:18). Those

[12] I am indebted to Joseph A. Fitzmyer, "Pauline Theology," *NJBC* II, pp. 1397-1402, who makes an informative survey of the effects of the Christ event as described by Paul in his letters. The content and structure of the following presentation is based, in part, on Fitzmyer's article.
[13] See John L. McKenzie, "Salvation," *Dictionary*, pp. 760-763, p. 761.

who have been baptized into Christ have been *saved from the devastating effects of sin*, including deliverance from divine wrath (1 Thess 1:10). That Christ has saved those who have been baptized from the tragic consequences of sin is alluded to in Gal 1:4 and 3:13. When an individual is rescued from some life-threatening situation by another, that individual usually feels obligated to the person who saved the individual's life. In a similar fashion, Christians owe a tremendous debt of gratitude to the one who saved them from the deadly effects of sin, namely, Christ.

Transformation

In 2 Cor 3:18, Paul describes the significant change that takes place in Christian believers in terms of a "transformation." The Greek word *metamorphoô* which appears in this verse, literally means "to change form," hence a fundamental change. This term is also used by the evangelists to depict the transfiguration of Jesus (e.g., Mark 9:2). The notion of transformation often appears in Greco-Roman mythology. There were a number of mythological stories in antiquity that portrayed both human beings and heavenly personalities as experiencing different kinds of transformations.

By using the term "transformation" in his writings, Paul wants to instill in his audience the notion that an *essential change* has taken place in one who has become a Christian. The apostle believes that those who profess their faith in Christ Jesus are being changed into the very likeness of Christ from one degree of glory to another (2 Cor 3:18). Paul assures the Philippians that on the last day, Christ will transform the earthly bodies of those who have been baptized to be like his glorious body (Phil 3:21).

The apostle describes in Galatians the transformation that takes place in those who came to believe in Christ. They were in a cursed condition (3:10) destined for corruption (6:8a) but now are blessed descendants of Abraham (3:14, 29) awaiting eternal life (6:8b). Assuredly, Paul's reflections on baptism indicate that the incredible change which takes place in those who have become Christian cannot be overemphasized.

Expiation

The apostle refers to the expiatory nature of Christ's death in Rom 3:25. The word "expiation" is a rendition of Greek *hilastêrion* and should be understood as "the means by which sins are forgiven." It conveys the sense of "wiping away" human transgressions. The Hebrew Scriptures describe the ritual in which all the sins of Israel were symbolically placed on a scapegoat who was then driven into the wilderness (Lev 16). The chosen people believed that by means of such a ritual, they were cleansed of their trespasses. Paul announces in Rom 3:25 that it is through the blood of Jesus that those who are in Christ are *absolved from their sins*, a forgiveness which was symbolized and foreshadowed by the scapegoat ritual.

The apostle pointed out to the Galatians in 3:13 that "Christ redeemed us from the curse of the law, having become a curse *for us*." In proclaiming that Christ died "for us" and that he became a curse "for us," Paul is not simply stating that Christ died "on our behalf" but rather that he died "in our place."[14] In other words, Christ took upon himself the burden of our sins so that we might purified (1:4, 2:20). Those who have put on Christ through baptism can be assured that they have been thoroughly cleansed from sin.

Reconciliation

The apostle offers some very moving reflections in 2 Cor 5:16-21 concerning divine reconciliation. The term "reconciliation" is a translation of the Greek word *katallassô*, a compound of the verb *allassô* (to alter), meaning to "put into a right relationship." Reconciliation has to do with establishing

[14] The fourth evangelists alludes to this point in John 18:39-40.

good relations between two parties who had been kept at a distance because of a previous conflict or misunderstanding. Within this context, the notion of "atonement" (at-one-ment) comes to mind. To be "at one" with another is to be in a harmonious relationship with that party. In the Hellenistic world, the term reconciliation was occasionally used in legal circles in connection with the relationship between a husband and wife (1 Cor 7:11). Moreover, it was sometimes used in the political realm to signify the change of relationship between two countries that had previously been enemies but were presently on friendly terms.[15]

Paul describes the tragic situation of humanity in Rom 5:10 before the coming of Christ, namely, that sinful human beings were considered as the "enemy" of God and in need of reconciliation. Now that Christ's salvific death has taken place, the apostle proclaims that the *relationship between those who are in Christ Jesus and God has been restored.* Through Christ, God has reconciled the world to Himself (2 Cor 5:19). The source of conflict between God and humanity has been removed. Regarding those who are united with Christ, the apostle affirms that God no longer holds their trespasses against them. Clearly this is reason to rejoice (Rom 5:11).

According to Paul, reconciliation should be understood as a gift from God that has ramifications for the way that Christians deal with one another. As God has reconciled Himself with them, so too must they must be reconciled with one another (2 Cor 5:19). That Christians are reconciled to the Father, is frequently alluded to in Galatians (most notably 4:6). By offering some specific advice concerning Christian conduct (e.g., 5:13, 6:2), the apostle demonstrates how the Galatians can live together in harmony as reconciled brothers and sisters in the Lord.

In the same manner that God the Father has taken the initiative in being reconciled to the world, Christians should

[15] See Herwart Vorländer and Colin Brown, "*katallassô*," *DNTT* 3, pp. 166-174.

likewise take the initiative in reconciling themselves with one another. To live in peace and harmony with the members of one's Christian community, especially with the members of one's own family, is a life-long task for all those who have been baptized into the life of Christ.

Glorification

Paul announces in Rom 8:30 that those whom God has justified have been glorified.[16] The word "glorified" is a translation of the Greek verb *doxazein*, meaning, "honored," "exalted." This term appears in the Hebrew Scriptures and is associated with the wonder and splendor of the divine presence (Exod 24:17, 40:34, Num 14:10). The apostle speaks of the glorification of Christians so that he can focus his attention on *the presence of God* which dwells in them, and on the *power* which is associated with that presence. Paul also links the notion of glory with the liberty which belongs to those who are children of God (Rom 8:21).

In a variety of ways the apostle demonstrates to the Galatians that the presence of God resides in baptized Christians. For example, Paul takes note of the fact that those who are in Christ have received the Holy Spirit (e.g., 3:14). Moreover, he points out to them that the life of the risen Lord abides in them (2:20). As "temples of the divine presence" (1 Cor 6:19), the very power of the Almighty resides in every Christian believer. Paul's reflections on the status of those who have professed their faith in the risen Lord, indicate that God has bestowed on Christians a great dignity, namely, participation in divine life.

Sanctification

The apostle declares in 1 Cor 6:11 that those who have been washed clean in baptism have been sanctified. The word "sanctification" is a translation of the Greek word *hagiasmos*, meaning

[16] See 1 Thess 2:12, 1 Cor 2:7, Rom 8:18

"holiness," "consecration," "dedication." This term connotes the idea of "being set apart." The biblical notion of sanctity is primarily concerned with the "dedication of persons for the service of God" as opposed to the "inner piety of an individual."[17]

Paul associates the will of God with the sanctification of those who belong to Christ (1 Thess 4:3). The apostle warns those Christian believers under his care that their sanctification is not a cause for boasting because they have not "earned" it. Rather, sanctification must be understood as a gift from God that was offered out of love (1 Cor 1:28-31). As one might suspect, Paul frequently uses the term "saints" (*hagioi*) to designate Christian believers (e.g., Rom 1:7, 1 Cor 1:2). They have been *set apart for the service of God and one another*.

The apostle's argumentation in Galatians suggests that the Galatians have been "set apart" because they have been liberated from the captivity of sin (e.g., 1:4, 3:13a). That the Galatians are called to be of service to others, even to non-Christians (6:10), is borne out by Paul's comments in Galatians 5 and 6. The sanctification of baptized Christians is manifested by their care and concern for others.

New Creation

In 2 Cor 5:17, the apostle refers to those who are in Christ as a "new creation" (*kainê ktisis*). This expression immediately calls to mind the creation accounts in Genesis (Gen 1 and 2). By applying the phrase "a new creation" to members of the Christian communities, Paul is emphasizing the "newness of life" that is associated with those who have been baptized. The change which occurs in one who has come to believe in Christ is so radical, that it seems as if one has been "re-created."

The apostle's comments in Gal 6:15 imply that the essential ingredient for becoming a new creation is one's attachment to Christ and not to the Torah. Paul's argumentation in Galatians

[17] See Fitzmyer, "Pauline Theology," Vol 2, p. 1401.

indicates that his reference to "a new creation," is meant to emphasize the aspect of "new life in Christ," and more specifically, the "new life of freedom," which those who have professed their faith in the risen Lord now enjoy. The apostle wants to point out to the Galatians in 3:23-29 that the most significant change that has taken place in those who have come to believe in Christ Jesus and have been baptized, is that they have been liberated. Baptized Christians are no longer confined, under constraint, nor under a custodian (3:23-24). On the contrary, they have an elevated status. They are children of God, united with Christ and each other, and authentic heirs to Abraham's inheritance (3:26-29). That Paul wants to focus his attention on freedom is especially brought out in Gal 5:1. This interior liberty is manifested in the life of Christians by the way in which they deal with one another, namely, as equals (3:28), whatever their race, social status, or gender.

Neither Male Nor Female

The apostle proclaims in Gal 3:28 that there is to be no distinction in the Christian community between Jew and Gentile, slave and free, male and female. Of these three categories, the one involving gender is still a topic of discussion for twentieth century Christians. Paul's claim regarding the equality of men and women is striking indeed. Nevertheless, one sometimes wonders if the apostle always remained faithful to his teaching concerning the radical equality of Christian believers. In 1 Cor 14:34-35, for example, Paul seems to infer that women have an inferior status in the Christian community. He very matter-of-factly states that "the head of every man is Christ, the head of a woman is her husband" (1 Cor 11:3). With this in mind, the apostle believes that "any man who prays or prophesies with his head covered dishonors his head, but any woman who prays or prophesies with her head unveiled dishonors her head" (1 Cor 11:4-5). Therefore,

Paul is convinced that a woman "ought to have a veil on her head" while praying. Moreover, he contends in 1 Cor 14:34-35 that "women should keep silence in the churches ... for it is shameful for a woman to speak in the church."

These negative comments notwithstanding, women played an active role in the apostle's evangelical ministry. Some of Paul's first Christian converts were women. The author of Acts informs us that a woman named Lydia was the first, along with the members of her household, to respond to the apostle's proclamation of the gospel in Philippi (Acts 16:14-15). There were also a number of people in Thessalonica who responded favorably to Paul's heralding of the good news, including many of the leading women (Acts 17:4).

The apostle is not afraid to refer to female Christians as his coworkers. Paul takes note of the fact that he worked side by side with women in the midst of his missionary activity (Phil 4:2-3). This is also attested to in Romans 16 where the apostle sends his greeting to a number of Christians, ten of whom are women. First of all, he commends his sister in Christ, Phoebe, a deacon (the apostle does *not* call her a deaconess) of the church at Cenchreae. Paul describes her as "a helper of many, and of myself as well" (Rom 16:2). He then refers to Prisca and her husband Aquila as "my fellow workers in Christ Jesus" (Rom 16:3).[18] Their Christian conduct was well known in "all the churches of the Gentiles" (Rom 16:4). The apostle is especially grateful to Prisca and her spouse for risking their lives on Paul's behalf (Rom 16:4). Then, using language that might surprise some modern day Christians, Paul refers to the female Junia as an apostle, as well as a fellow prisoner (Rom 16:7).[19]

[18] See 1 Cor 16:19.

[19] See Donald Senior, Convocation Address given at St. Meinrad School of Theology, May, 1991, p. 5: The female name "Junia" [Rom 16:7] has thrown translators into a dither for centuries, leading them to call her "Junias" even though this masculine form doesn't exist in Greek. See Allen C. Myers, "Junias," *EerdBib*, p. 613.

Was Paul's behavior always consistent with his teaching of the equality of male and female which he professed in Gal 3:28? Considering the male-dominated world in which the apostle lived, it is more surprising that he had any sort of positive outlook on women in regard to Christian ministry than that he should at times make some seemingly derogatory remarks concerning female believers. Like us, Paul had to live with the tension between his own cultural inheritance and the radical newness of the gospel. Perhaps the more important question that we should ask, is whether or not our behavior conforms with the good news of Jesus Christ and its emphasis on the equality of believers.

Born To Be Free

The apostle informs the Galatians in 3:25-29 of the freedom that baptized Christians now enjoy and of their privileged status as rightful heirs to the promise of Abraham. In Galatians 4 he proceeds to demonstrate that those who desire to place themselves under the law unknowingly revert back to their pre-redeemed condition, enslaved and in the unfortunate position of being illegitimate heirs to the patriarch's inheritance.

Paul calls to mind in Gal 4:1-2 some widely known facts about those who possess the right of inheritance. There was a legal practice in the Roman empire known as "guardianship for a minor."[20] In the process of ensuring that one's children would inherit one's estate, the head of the family would officially appoint a guardian for his children, with the understanding that they would be entitled to the father's inheritance after his death. Even though the children were, in fact, authorized beneficiaries of their father's estate, they did not have access to it until they had come of age. As minors, the children were placed under the stewardship of a guardian and a trustee, who conducted all

[20] See Betz, *Galatians*, 202.

necessary legal transactions on their behalf. This situation lasted until the appointed time, determined in the father's will, arrived. Then the guardianship was discontinued and the heirs were given free access to the inheritance. Paul points out to the Galatians a paradoxical situation. A legal heir who has not yet come of age is really no better off than a slave (4:1). After all, neither of them have access to any inheritance and neither of them are free from the custody of authoritative figures.

Slaves Once More?

The apostle makes a comparison ("so with us") between the status of legal heirs before they come of age and that of the Galatians before they became Christians (4:3). In keeping with the language that he used in 4:1, the apostle refers to himself and to the Galatians as *children* before they came to believe in Christ Jesus. At that time, they were, in effect, no better off than those under subjection. Again, in line with the terminology that he used in 4:1, Paul makes the surprising declaration that he and the Galatians were then "*slaves* to the elemental spirits (*stoicheia*) of the universe" (4:3).[21]

The meaning that the apostle intends to convey with the expression "elemental spirits of the universe" is unclear.[22] This phrase may be associated with pagan beliefs; it may allude to the supposed existence of personified forces such as demons, gods, and the like. Whatever may be the case, it is obvious that Paul has nothing positive to say about the elemental spirits of the universe (4:3, 9). Inasmuch as the apostle includes himself among those who were held hostage under these elemental spirits before acknowledging Christ Jesus in faith, he apparently uses this expression in a metaphorical way, namely, to designate "that which enslaves," be it idolatry, the law, sin, or whatever else.

[21] See Col 2:8, 20.
[22] See Andrew J. Bandstra, *The Law and the Elements of the World* (Amsterdam: Kampen, 1964), pp. 171-189.

Paul continues his discussion in Gal 4:4 by describing the way in which God rescued humanity from captivity. "When the time had fully come, God sent forth his Son, born of woman, born under the law, to redeem those who were under the law" (4:4). As a result of Christ's redemptive act (3:13) human beings are now in a position to become adopted children of God. They now cry out to God, "Abba, Father" (4:6).

The apostle quickly informs the Galatians of the ramifications of their being sons and daughters of God. Because of God's intervention, they have been set free from the enslavement of the "elements of the universe" and all that this represents. As children of God, they are now legitimate heirs to the divine inheritance, the promise of Abraham (4:7)

Paul reminds the Galatians that they were formerly enslaved in light of their idolatrous practices (4:8). He then drives home the main point of his discussion in Gal 4:9. Now that the Galatians have been liberated, how could they even consider turning "back again to the weak and beggarly elemental spirits," which would result in their being in bondage once again. The apostle's reference in Gal 4:10 to the "days, and months, and seasons, and years" is surely an allusion to the Mosaic law, with its special feasts and festivals, the Sabbath, Passover, and so forth. Paul is implying that if the Galatians give in to the teaching of the troublemakers and perform the works of the law in their misguided attempt to be justified, they will become slaves again just as had been before they responded to the good news of Jesus Christ. In effect, the Galatians would be turning back the clock to the time of their pre-Christian days by accepting the agitators' rendition of the gospel. Inasmuch as the Galatians have been designated as adopted children of God (4:5) and thus heirs to the promise, it is unthinkable that they return to their former status as slaves (4:9) and illegitimate heirs of the patriarch's inheritance.

Abba, Dad

The apostle's remarks concerning God the Father in Gal 4:6 may be the source of some confusion when understood in the context of the New Testament. Even though Jesus himself referred to God as Abba (Mark 14), he, according to the first evangelist, instructed his disciples in Matt 6:9 (Luke 11:2) to address God in prayer with the more formal term father (*patêr*). This being said, however, the apostle speaks of Christians as crying out to God, "Abba" (Gal 4:6, Rom 8:15).

The term Abba is a Greek transliteration of the Aramaic word for father. Ancient Aramaic manuscripts indicate that it was a familiar expression used by children to address their father, not unlike the contemporary expression "dad," or "daddy."[23] When one referred to one's father as Abba, a child-like sense of trust, intimacy, and tenderness was communicated. Although the Fatherhood of God was certainly not unknown in Judaism at the time of Jesus (e.g., 1 Chron 17:13, Ps 68:5, Jer 31:9), it was expressed in a more reserved and formalistic manner, with familiar language like Abba being avoided. Only Jesus, the Son of God would be "qualified" to refer to God in such a personal fashion.

According to Paul's argumentation in Galatians, baptized Christians are united with the risen Lord. The apostle testifies that those who have professed their faith in Christ have received the very Spirit of the Son of God into their hearts (4:6). Consequently, like the one with whom they are intimately bound, Christians too are enabled to address God in an intimately personal way, that is, as "Abba."

Personal Approach

Paul changes his tactics in Gal 4:12-20. In his attempt to persuade the Galatians to accept his rendition of the gospel, the apostle argues in these verses not with "his head" but with

[23] See John L. McKenzie, "Abba," *Dictionary*, p. 1.

"his heart."[24] He makes a personal appeal to the Galatians. In the beginning, they had shown great enthusiasm for Paul and for the good news that he proclaimed. The apostle reminds the Galatians of the circumstances in which he introduced Christianity to them. In spite of Paul's poor health, the Galatians did not consider him a burden but rather treated the apostle as a divine messenger (4:13-14). Paul recalls their hospitality with great affection. If possible, the Galatians would have plucked out their eyes and given them to him if need be (4:15). Having recalled such fond memories, the apostle groans, "What has happened that you now regard me as an enemy" (4:16)?

Paul then attacks the Judaizers in Gal 4:17 with an *ad hominem* argument. He questions the integrity of the agitators' motives for having "made much" of the Galatians for having paid attention to them and courted their favor. The apostle contends that the agitators have acted in such a manner simply for their own personal gratification, that is, so that the Galatians might "make much of them" (4:17). Paul recognizes that there is no harm in being "made much of" as long as its for a good purpose. However, the troublemakers have courted the Galatians' favor for an ill purpose. According to the apostle, his opponents have insisted that they separate themselves from Paul's rendition of the gospel and adhere to the Torah, so the Galatians might "make much" of the agitators.[25] Paul assumes the Galatians will realize that, unlike the motives of the Judaizers, his incentive for "making much" of the Galatians when he first preached the gospel to them was for a good purpose.

The apostle gives a heart-rending speech in Gal 4:19-20. He speaks to the Galatians with great tenderness and affection, referring to them as "my little children." Paul thinks of his relationship with the Galatians as that of a mother and her children. Using terminology normally associated with the birth

[24] See Charles B. Cousar, *Galatians* Interpretation (Atlanta, GA: John Knox, 1982), p. 98.
[25] See Bruce, *Galatians*, p. 212.

of a child, Paul describes in Gal 4:19 his present situation as a woman who must once again undergo the pangs of childbirth. "I am again in travail" (*ôdinô*) over you. Paul concludes his remarks in this section of the epistle by expressing sorrow that he cannot respond in person to the crisis situation in Galatia (4:20). The apostle's hope is that the Galatians will become as he is (4:12), namely, one who realizes that Gentiles becomes legitimate heirs to the promise of Abraham exclusively through faith in Christ.

By God's Grace, Free

Paul lashes out once more in Gal 4:21-31 against the troublemakers' use of Scripture. They may have first referred to the biblical narrative about the two children of Abraham, Ishmael and Isaac, in their efforts to sway the Galatians over to their camp.[26] As the agitators saw it, Gentiles who accepted the apostle's Torah-free gospel had the same status as Ishmael in that they no right to claim Abraham's inheritance. On the other hand, those who responded to the Judaizers' version of the good news and observed the Mosaic law were like Isaac, since they too had access to the patriarch's inheritance.

Paul bellows out a pointed question to those who affirm that adherence to the Mosaic law is a prerequisite for becoming a legitimate beneficiary to the blessing of Abraham. "Do you not hear what Scripture is telling you" (4:21)? In the following verses the apostle counters the troublemakers' teaching by providing what he considers the authentic interpretation of the story of Ishmael and Isaac. Paul notes that Ishmael was born "according to the flesh" while Isaac was born "through the promise" (4:23). In other words, Ishmael was conceived under ordinary circumstances, while divine intervention was required

[26] See C.K. Barrett, "The Allegory of Abraham, Sarah, and Hagar in the Argument of Galatians," Johannes Friedrich et al., eds, *Rechtfertigen. Festschrift für Ernst Käsemann* (Tübingen: Mohr, 1976), pp. 1-16, p. 9.

for the conception of Isaac as Sarah was advanced in years (Gen 17:17).

The apostle interprets this biblical story as an allegory (*allê-goumena*). According to his understanding, the two women, Hagar and Sarah, symbolize two covenants (4:24). Paul associates Hagar with Mount Sinai, an obvious allusion to the Torah which was presented to Moses on this mountain (Exod 19 - Num 10:11), and with Jerusalem. The apostle probably linked Hagar with Jerusalem because the agitators seem to have been in some way connected with this city.[27] As Hagar was a slave, all of her descendants are likewise born into slavery (4:24-25). Without mentioning Sarah by name, Paul associates her, with the "Jerusalem above," that is, with the Christian community. Those who have "Jerusalem above" for a mother are like Sarah and her offspring, namely, free. The apostle applies Isa 54:1 to Sarah, the barren one (Gen 11:30) who was made fruitful by the power of God (4:27).

Paul gives the implications of the biblical narrative in Gal 4:28-31. In sharp contrast to the troublemakers' heretical teaching, he insists that it is not the non-observers of the Torah who are children of slavery but those who "desire to be under the law" (4:21). Like Ishmael, they too are excluded from the inheritance. Assuredly, it is those who believe that the inheritance comes through faith in Christ alone that are likened to Isaac, the child of the promise. Paul's reference to the persecution of Isaac by Ishmael may be allusion to the pressure that agitators exerted on the Galatians to become observers of the Torah. Regarding Hagar and her son Ishmael, the child born into servitude, the apostle cites Gen 21:10: "Cast out the slave and her son." Paul's reason for citing this passage is readily seen. He wants the Galatians to "cast out" the troublemakers and their heretical doctrine from the Christian communities in Galatia. The apostle summarizes his discussion in Gal 4:31. Those who have responded to his rendition of the good news

[27] See Gal 1:17, 18; 4:25, 26.

are like the children of Sarah. They are free and they participate in Abraham's inheritance.

Concluding Remarks

In his endeavor to persuade the Galatians in Gal 3:15-4:31 that the troublemakers are teaching a corrupt form of the gospel, Paul is extremely creative. He illustrates that Gentiles become genuine heirs to the promise of Abraham by drawing upon principles from the legal realm concerning contracts and inheritance, his understanding of the Mosaic law, his theological reflections regarding faith and baptism, his strong feelings for the Galatians, and Scripture. The apostle puts forth a vast array of arguments to substantiate his Torah-free gospel so that if one type fails to convince the Galatians, another, he hopes, might win them over.

The Christian Contract

Paul focuses a great deal of his attention in Galatians on the covenant that was established between God and Abraham, namely, that both the patriarch and his descendants would be blessed (3:6-9, 14-18). The apostle looks upon this divine commitment in terms of a "legal contract." In numerous ways he has demonstrated that one participates in Abraham's legacy by believing in Christ without observing the Torah.

Paul's Christocentric interpretation of the Abraham narrative indicates that present day believers are spoken of in Scripture. According to the apostle's interpretation, the story in Genesis that portrays the circumstances surrounding the promise which God made to Abraham and his offspring, is not simply one which involves people who lived in the dim and distant past. In fact, this biblical narrative, which refers to the offspring of the patriarch, involves Christians of every age. Inasmuch as those who are united with Christ are legitimate heirs to Abraham's inheritance, those in the modern day world who profess their faith in Christ Jesus are also included with the offspring of Abraham mentioned in Genesis that God committed Himself to bless.

Free At Last

In the process of defending his position, Paul underscores the confining nature of the Torah. His argumentation in Galatians implies that those who are not in Christ are in some way held captive, be it by the Mosaic law, pagan worship, sin, or some other oppressive power. The apostle lumps together all such domineering forces of the world under the title of "the elemental spirits of the universe." Paul assures the Galatians that those who have acknowledged Christ Jesus in faith are no longer enslaved by these elemental spirits.

The apostle's discussion makes it clear that Christians are not held hostage by their past. They have been liberated. Because of their union with the risen Lord, those who are in Christ have been set free from the tragic consequences of sin. Within the Christian community, believers are encouraged by Paul to free themselves from the constraints of their own culture, which sometimes separates people into various categories according to race, social status, and sex, and treat one another on an equal basis. Those who have pledged to imitate Christ should follow his example by helping others, in any way possible, to free themselves from injustice, poverty, prejudice, ignorance, personal pain, and all other "elemental spirits of the universe" that keep human beings enslaved.

Foundation of Christian Living

Paul's reflections on the transformation that occurs in those who have faith in Christ and have been baptized, are both complex and profound. His comments on the theology of baptism invite Christian believers to re-examine their own understanding of this initiation rite. Unfortunately, all too many Christians simply view baptism as an event that took place long ago, without giving much thought to its ongoing effects.

Baptism is the foundational event in the life of those who have committed themselves to the risen Lord. Through this initiatory rite one enters into, and remains in, the life of Christ and his church. All the benefits that accompany those who are united with Christ through baptism, justification, salvation, sanctification, and so forth, continue to be active throughout their lives. The divine power and strength which is associated with the presence of Christ, unceasingly abide in the lives of baptized Christians. However, as Paul warned the Galatians, one can forfeit the benefits of baptism by not remaining faithful to the truth of the gospel.

The life of a Christian should be thought of in terms of living out one's baptismal promises. At the time of baptism, those who professed their faith in Christ solemnly pledged that Jesus is Lord. In effect, Christians have vowed that they would manifest the lordship of Jesus in their lives. They have pledged much but they receive much. Of all the benefits that Paul associates with baptism, the one that he emphasizes the most in Galatians is that of liberty. The apostle stresses that because of their union with the risen Lord, the Galatians have been freed from the captivity of sin.

CHAPTER SEVEN

FREEDOM, LOVE, AND RESPONSIBILITY (GAL 5:1-6:18)

Paul's campaign against the unorthodox teaching of the troublemakers reaches a crescendo in Galatians 5 and 6. Having overwhelmed the Judaizers' position with an unbelievable number of arguments, the apostle now sets out to illustrate in greater detail the ramifications of his understanding of the good news. He triumphantly proclaims the Christian declaration of independence: For liberty, Christians have been set free (5:1). Paul then proceeds to demonstrate once again that the decision to accept or reject his gospel of freedom is not to be taken lightly. It is, quite literally, a matter of life and death.

From the apostle's point of view, those who remain steadfast to his rendition of the good news and realize that Gentiles are justified exclusively through faith, are intimately bound with Christ (5:6, 24) and, therefore, reap an abundance of benefits. They have entered a new mode of existence (6:15), possess the "fruits of the Spirit" (5:22), and will enjoy eternal life (6:8). However, all who succumb to the perverted gospel of the agitators and insist that circumcision and fidelity to the Torah are obligatory in order to obtain righteousness, are separated from Christ (5:4). These unfortunate people are enslaved (5:1) and destined for corruption (6:8).

Lest there be some skepticism about his stance on moral behavior, Paul makes it abundantly clear that his law-free gospel is not to be construed as promoting dissolute living (5:13). He sternly warns the Galatians that the gift of freedom is not to be abused by yielding to the "cravings of the flesh"

(5:17). The apostle wants to impress upon his readers that Christian liberty must be understood within the context of love and responsibility. Earlier in the epistle, Paul informed the Galatians that it was out of love that Christ died for us (2:20). As Christ has freely given of himself in the service of others, so now the Galatians are called upon to give freely of themselves in the service of one another in a spirit of love (5:13).[1] Since they are sisters and brothers in the Lord, the apostle advises, the Galatians must recognize that they have a responsibility towards each other (e.g., 5:22, 6:6). Consequently, Paul encourages them to be attentive to the well-being of those around them.

In the midst of this discussion, the apostle does not pass up the opportunity to hurl a few more personal salvos at the troublemakers (5:10, 12). His comments regarding the agitators in this section of the letter are especially bitter. Paul goes so far as to wish them physical harm (5:12). Finally, taking the pen from the scribe, the apostle himself concludes the epistle (6:11-18).[2] Confident that he has answered all objections to the gospel which he first preached to the Galatians, Paul reiterates some of the main points of the letter. Even his final remarks are not free of contempt for the agitators and the trouble they have caused him (6:12-13, 17).

Christian Freedom

Paul waves the banner of freedom before the eyes of the Galatians in 5:1. In order to avoid all confusion regarding his understanding of Christian liberty, the apostle spells out in the last two chapters of the epistle what freedom entails for those who are in Christ and what it does not. Apparently Paul is

[1] Paul argues in a similar fashion in Rom 13:8-10.
[2] See also 1 Cor 16:21.

reacting, in part, to the troublemakers' accusation that his law-free gospel encourages immoral conduct.

Justification and Freedom

The present day reader of Galatians must be careful not to confuse the apostle's notion of freedom with that of 20th century democracies. In contemporary society, the word "freedom" is usually associated with the political realm. One who lives in a free country has freedom of movement, freedom of speech, freedom of religion, a voice in governmental affairs, and so forth. In most democratic countries, civil liberty has been obtained and preserved at a great cost, through the shedding of much blood. Even though many people in Western society are more apt to speak of rights than of duties, citizens of a free country, nevertheless, have certain responsibilities. They must obey the laws of the state, pay taxes, serve jury-duty, and so forth. Moreover, citizens in a free society are beckoned to take part in the defense of their country by joining the military, especially in time of war.

Political liberty is usually associated with freedom *from oppression* and with the freedom *to do whatever one desires* as long as one does not violate the rights of another citizen. In the realm of politics, freedom is understood in an "external" fashion. When Paul speaks of liberty in Galatians, however, his primary emphasis is on the "internal" freedom that those in Christ experience.

Interestingly enough, although the term "freedom" (*eleutheria*) is almost always used in the New Testament in a theological sense, it is never used in this fashion in the Septuagint. In the Hebrew Scriptures, the notion of freedom is spoken of only in the context of slavery. One who was free was not a slave (e.g., Exod 21:2, Lev 19:20). The political use of the term freedom never occurs in the Septuagint. In the Greek speaking world, however, the term freedom was primarily understood in a political sense.[3] The Galatians were well aware

[3] See Jürgen Blunck, "*eleutheria*," *DNTT*, 1, pp. 715-721; and John McKenzie, "Free, Freedom," *Dictionary*, p. 288.

of the fact that those who enjoyed the privilege of freedom in the Roman empire possessed certain rights and privileges.

The apostle focuses his attention in the epistle on the *religious* sense of the term freedom. Even though Paul does make reference to liberty in Gal 3:28 in the context of civil slavery, this is the exception and not the rule. More than any other New Testament author, the apostle uses the term freedom to describe the benefits that were obtained by Christ in light of his life, death and resurrection. In fact, Paul's argumentation in Galatians suggests that he understands justification primarily in terms of liberty (e.g., 1:4, 3:13, 5:1). In the course of defending his version of the good news, he offers some marvelous insights concerning his theology of Christian freedom. We now bring together the apostle's various comments in Galatians regarding the freedom that Christ has obtained for us.

Freed From...

As far as Paul is concerned, the Galatians were held hostage by sin before they came to acknowledge Christ Jesus in faith (Gal 3:22-23, Rom 6:20). In that pre-redeemed state they were incapable of unchaining themselves from the shackles of sin. The apostle informs the Galatians that Christ has liberated those who believe in him from the oppressive power of evil (5:1). Paul's argumentation illustrates that the redemption of humanity was not obtained without a high price, namely, the death of Christ (2:21, 3:13). Jesus bore the burden of our transgressions on the cross so that human beings might be free (3:13-14).

First and foremost, the apostle wants to make known to those under his care that they have been rescued from sin and its devastating effects (Gal 1:4, 3:13, Rom 6:18). Liberated from the alienating aspects of sin, they are now reconciled with God and with one another (2 Cor 5:18-19). Paul also assures those in Christ that they have been set free from the guilt and punishment which is associated with sin. In a manner of speaking, they have been freed from themselves (2:19). Moreover, the Galatians have been liberated from the captivity of the Torah (3:25) which had imposed a curse on all human beings in view of their transgressions (3:10, 19). Consequently, the apostle repeatedly hammers away at them that Gentiles are free from the obligation of observing the Mosaic law (2:4, 16). Furthermore, those who have professed their faith in Christ have been delivered from the "present evil age" (1:4), God's wrath (1 Thess 1:10), and eternal corruption (6:8).

Freedom For...

Even though Christians have been liberated from the enslavement of sin, Paul contends that their status, in a sense, remains that of a slave (Rom 12:11, Gal 1:10).[4] In other words, those who solemnly affirm that Jesus is Lord are *bound* to him and recognize him as the *master* of their lives. Inasmuch as they are intimately united with the risen Lord and with each other, members of the body of Christ must realize that they are not only slaves of Christ but also slaves of and for each other. Hence, the apostle's argumentation in the epistle indicates that the Galatians have been freed from the captivity of sin for a life of Christian ministry. They have not been called to exercise their freedom by gratifying selfish desires (5:16). Rather, their vocation as liberated Christians is to serve the Lord by ministering to one other (e.g., 5:14, 6:2). The inner reality of Christian freedom is to be manifested by charitable deeds. In serving others, those in Christ imitate their master who emptied himself and became a slave (Phil 2:7).

Happiness

Those who have been baptized into the new life of Christ have been liberated from the oppressive power of sin, so that they might find happiness. By happiness, I do not simply mean

[4] The Greek word *doulos* can be translated as "slave" or "servant."

"feeling good" physically nor the vague sense of general well-being. Rather, I define happiness as something much deeper. True happiness is finding value in oneself, in others, and in all of life. It is associated with coming to terms with a world in which sin, suffering, and death exist. Happiness is loving and being loved. It is enjoyed by those who freely share what they have with others. A person who struggles with the problems of human existence is not unlike an individual with a nagging toothache. Until the tooth is treated, one's attention is devoted exclusively to oneself and one's pain.[5] When an individual comes to believe in Christ Jesus, the "existential toothache" has been addressed. One's faith in Christ offers new hope. Those who have professed allegiance to the risen Lord have discovered new meaning in life. They detect the love of God in a remarkably different way. Baptized Christians are no longer burdened by their sinful past. They personally experience the compassionate mercy of God the Father. In light of the redemptive death of Jesus, they recognize the tremendous value they have in the sight of God who sent His beloved Son into the world for the salvation of humanity. Because of Christ's resurrection, their faith assures them that suffering and death do not have the last word. Those in Christ are confident that, as they have been immersed into the death of the Lord, they will also arise with him on the last day.

God bestows the gift of freedom on those who are united with His Son, not only for their own happiness but for that of others as well. Now that those in Christ enjoy the happiness which is associated with being justified, they are free to turn their attention outward and concern themselves with the needs of others. Liberated from the confinement of sin, they are indeed free to love others more fully. For all intents and purposes, Paul encourages the Galatians in the last two chapters of the letter to do what they can to make others happy.

[5] See John Powell, *Will the Real Me Please Stand Up?* (Allen, TX: Argus Communications, 1985), pp. 95-97.

In doing so he invites the Galatians to share in that divine joy that comes to those who conduct themselves in this charitable manner.

People often have the mistaken notion that happiness comes in having money, fame, good health, and so forth. If that were the case, then all rich people, all famous people, and all healthy people would be happy. That, obviously, is not the case. The alarming number of people who have turned to alcohol, drugs, immoral behavior, and the like, and the ever increasing number of those who have attempted suicide, many of them successfully, bear witness to the depth of unhappiness in Western society.

Perhaps we can say that Scripture is the "guidebook" for finding happiness in life. The author of Genesis informs us that human beings are made in the image and likeness of God. As such, we have been created out of love for love. Our Creator's fundamental concern is with our happiness. God has revealed to us that true happiness comes through Jesus Christ. With the salvation of the human race in mind, our Heavenly Father has offered His very self to humanity in a unique fashion, that is, in and through the person of His Son Jesus. Because of the way in which we were created, we find true happiness only by imitating the One in whose image we were made, namely, by sharing what we have, including our very selves, with others.

Christians have been called to a life of happiness. This is not a naive type of happiness that simply ignores all the pain and hardship in the world. On the contrary, those in Christ are well aware of the imperfect state of human existence. Nevertheless, Christians perceive the world in a different light in view of God's love for them and their love for Him. They are encouraged to follow the example of Jesus by displaying absolute confidence in the heavenly Father and doing whatever is in their power to alleviate the pain and suffering of others. Indeed, Christian happiness is based on their faith in the risen Lord. The world is in great need of happy people. Perhaps the best way of proclaiming the gospel of Jesus Christ is simply to live the good news and be happy, in the fullest sense of the word.

Free To...

By virtue of their unity with Christ, the Galatians are now free to participate in the blessing of Abraham which culminates in eternal life. Inasmuch as they have received the Spirit of God's Son, they are also free to address the Almighty in a warm and personal manner, namely, as Abba (4:6). As children of God, the Galatians belong to the one family of faith. Consequently, within the community of believers, they have been set free from the cultural divisions of society and therefore must consider one another as sisters and brothers in the Lord. The Galatians are thus free to love others, regardless of their race, social status, or gender (3:28).

Divine Liberty

Paul's discussion concerning Christian liberty also pertains to God's free initiative. Without any concern for the relatively advanced age of Abraham and his barren wife Sarah, God freely chose this elderly couple to play an integral part in salvation history. Moreover, God responded to the sinful situation of humanity with a loving gesture. He sent His Son into the world so that the human race might be redeemed. Paul's persecution of the church notwithstanding, God commissioned him to preach the good news to the Gentiles. Furthermore, even though the Galatians were steeped in pagan worship, God provided them with the opportunity to be united with His Son. God's love for human beings was never thwarted by their sinfulness. His love for them did not depend on their love for Him. In other words, in spite of humanity's ongoing rebellious attitude, God remains free to love. In all of this, Paul seems to encourage the Galatians to do likewise. He exhorts them to treat people lovingly and not as they might necessarily deserve.

Freedom and the Spirit

The apostle's theology of the Spirit plays a critical role in his discussion.[6] Paul reminds the Galatians that they received the Spirit when they first responded to his Torah-free gospel (3:3). Therefore, the Galatians should realize from their own personal experience that they received the Spirit by faith and not by observing the works of the law. As he does elsewhere in the letter, the apostle makes a close connection in Gal 5:5 between the Spirit and justification.[7] Likewise, he associates the Spirit with Christ (4:6), the blessing of Abraham (3:14), and adopted children of God (4:5-6). What Paul frequently alludes to in Galatians is specifically stated in 1 Cor 3:17, namely, that there is a direct link between the Spirit and liberty. Paul draws attention to the fact that all Christians were baptized by one Spirit into one body (1 Cor 12:13). Accordingly, they have been initiated into a new life in the Spirit (Rom 7:6). Within the Christian community, therefore, the distinction between Jew and Greek, slave and free, male and female, has been removed (3:28). The apostle contends that those who are led by the Spirit are not under the law (5:18). He guarantees the Galatians that all who "sow to the Spirit will from the Spirit reap eternal life" (6:8).

Spirit vs. Flesh

Paul insists that the "desires of the Spirit" are diametrically opposed to the "desires of the flesh" (5:16-17). He warns the Galatians that the cravings of the flesh stand in the way of those who aspire to "walk by the Spirit" (5:16). The apostle sharply contrasts the "fruits of the Spirit" (love, joy, peace, etc.) with the "works of the flesh" (fornication, impurity, licentiousness, etc.) in Gal 5:19-23. Paul appears to make a loose connection between "works of the flesh" and "works of the

[6] See Gal 3:2, 3, 5, 14; 4:6, 29; 5:5, 16, 17, 18, 22, 25 (2x); 6:8.
[7] See 3:2-5, 14.

law" (3:2-3). If this is in fact the case, then he seems to drive still another wedge between the possession of the Spirit, which is the mark of justification, and the observance of the works of the law.

The apostle mentions the term "flesh" (*sarx)* a number of times in Galatians (17 times) and, in spite of the various nuances that he gives this word, Paul usually seems to accentuate the *physical* nature of human beings. On occasion, the apostle also uses the word flesh in a pejorative sense (4:23, 5:19, 6:8).[8] As we have previously mentioned, the expression "works of the law" (e.g., 2:16) designates those acts which are performed in obedience to the commands of the Mosaic law; in particular, those acts which deal with circumcision and food laws. It is noteworthy that such ordinances of the Torah are concerned with *material* requirements.

There is good reason to believe that, in the mind of Paul, some similarity exists between "works of the law" and "works of the flesh." This similarity consists in the fact that they both appear to relate to a human being's *carnality*, and they both stand in opposition to the Spirit (2:2-3, 5:17).[9] The apostle is probably cautioning the Galatians in the epistle that if they are concerned with the precepts of the Torah that deal with material requirements, they should be aware of the realities that are associated with works of the flesh. Paul alerts the Galatians that the works of the flesh include such ungodly acts as idolatry, enmity, and dissension (5:19). Moreover, he compares one who is born according to the flesh with one who is born into slavery (4:23), and asserts that those who sow in their own flesh will reap corruption (6:8). The apostle pleads with the Galatians to walk in the Spirit and avoid the works of the flesh.

[8] See also Rom 7:25, 8:3, 8.

[9] See Herman Ridderbos, *The Epistle of Paul to the Churches of Galatia* (Grand Rapids, MI: Eerdmans, 1974), p. 114: "Paul brings the law and the flesh into relationship with each other here (Gal 3:3) because the law has its bearing upon all sorts of physical conditions and activities: upon circumcision, for instance."

Freedom and Commitment

Christian liberty is founded upon the believer's intimate unity with Christ. The way in which one enters into this unique relationship is through faith and baptism. Paul admonishes the Galatians that if they are to continue to enjoy the freedom that comes with being a legal heir to Abraham's inheritance, then they must remain faithful to their commitment to the risen Lord. The apostle castigates the Galatians for being on the verge of rejecting the truth of the gospel which he first proclaimed to them. He informs them of the tragic consequences of such behavior. Paul repeatedly points out to the Galatians that their life in Christ will come to an end if they yield to the troublemakers' teaching that adherence to the Torah is mandatory for obtaining righteousness. Furthermore, the apostle reminds the Galatians that those who take part in immoral behavior "shall not inherit the kingdom of God" (5:21).

Many people in today's society associate the notion of "commitment" with "confinement." They tend to dwell more on what is being given up by making a commitment than on the benefits that accompany it. Not so for Paul. He has a radically different understanding of commitment, understood within the context of one's baptismal vows. According to his way of thinking, one's commitment to Christ results in liberation. In light of this commitment, Christians are free to love and to live life to the fullest. Christian commitment gives direction and meaning to one's life. The believer's commitment to the risen Lord is such a fundamental reality in the life of a Christian, that all other religious commitments, marriage, religious life, priesthood, and so forth, are to be understood in light of this one. Christians are called to manifest their commitment to the Lord in charitable ministry, whatever their state in life might be. Indeed, the "uniform" by which Christians are to be identified is their freedom in dealing with others in a compassionate manner.

Opponents of Freedom

The apostle remonstrates that if the Galatians acquiesce in the agitators' rendition of the good news and opt for circumcision, they will have reneged on their Christian commitment (5:2). Paul then illustrates in greater detail why the Galatians will forfeit all the blessings that are associated with being a legal descendant of Abraham. The apostle very forcefully affirms that those who seek justification by means of the law are "severed from Christ" and have "fallen from grace" (5:4). For all practical purposes, Paul asserts that the Galatians would revert back to their pre-redeemed state, relinquish their Christian liberty, and "submit again to a yoke of slavery" (5:1) by paying heed to the agitators. If they, in fact, choose to do so, the apostle makes the incredible claim that Christ would be of no advantage to the Galatians (5:2).

Paul contests the compulsory observance of the works of the law in Gal 5:3 by arguing on the Torah's own terms. The apostle is of the belief and he is well versed in matters pertaining to the Mosaic law (1:14) that those who receive circumcision place themselves under the obligation to observe the whole law. However, as Paul has demonstrated in Gal 3:10, the failure to obey each and every precept of the Torah has drastic repercussions; it results in a curse. His argumentation in Galatians indicates that no one follows all the statutes of the Mosaic law because all have sinned. Therefore, those who seek to become children of Abraham by relying on the works of the law are excluded from the patriarch's blessing.

The apostle also downplays the relevance of the Mosaic law in Gal 5:5 by reaffirming his position that one receives the Spirit and is justified by means of faith. This being said, the apostle's comments in Gal 5:6 suggest that he has nothing against the observance of the law *per se*. Paul does, nevertheless, object to it as a means to obtaining righteousness. Consequently, whether a Christian is actually circumcised or not is of little consequence. What is fundamentally important is whether or not the believer's faith is "working through love" (5:6).

One can imagine the apostle shaking his head as he reflects upon the troubled situation in Galatia. Recalling that his converts to Christianity were doing so well when he last saw them, Paul wonders who was responsible for luring them away from the truth of the gospel (5:7). Whoever they were, the apostle prods the Galatians, they are certainly not to be regarded as emissaries of God (5:8). Unlike Paul's version of the gospel, the troublemakers' rendition of the good news did not originate with God the Father (1:15).

Although the agitators were relatively few in number, their heretical doctrine had contaminated many, if not all, of the Christian communities in Galatia (5:9). Nevertheless, the apostle is sure of his ability to persuade the Galatians to reject the distorted teaching of his adversaries. Even at this stage of the letter, he is supremely confident that the Gentile Christians in Galatia will listen to reason and "take no other view than mine" (5:10a).

Paul's tirade against the Judaizers continues with a passion in Gal 5:10-12. In view of his conviction that those who respond to the troublemakers teaching will suffer deadly consequences, the apostle directs some extremely sarcastic remarks towards his adversaries. First of all, he invokes judgment on their "ringleader" (5:10). In Gal 5:11 Paul insinuates that the agitators have spread vicious lies about his stance on circumcision. Regardless of what his opponents might have said about him, the apostle assures the Galatians that he does not preach circumcision. On the contrary, Paul has suffered persecution for that very reason. He testifies that the core of his missionary preaching is the crucified Christ and not circumcision. Carried away in the heat of the argument, the apostle expresses the hope that the troublemakers might castrate themselves (5:12). Immediately following these cutting remarks, Paul, the master of contrasting statements, exhorts the Galatians to conduct themselves in a loving fashion.

Christian Love

The apostle links the notion of love with that of Christian liberty in Gal 5:13. Thus he makes known to the Galatians that their freedom in Christ must be understood within the context of charitable service. It should not be used simply to gratify carnal desires. Rather, Christian freedom should be considered as a divine gift that provides the Galatians with the opportunity to love in a greater capacity. Paul therefore urges them to manifest their love for Christ by performing good deeds on one another's behalf. The apostle wants to instill in the Galatians the conviction that their vocation as Christians is to love. Assuredly, the more one knows about Paul's theology of love, the more one can appreciate the powerful message of Galatians.

Love Is...

For most people in the modern day world, the meaning of the term "love" is rather ambiguous. It may well be the most misunderstood word in the English language. Consider the following statements: "I love ice cream." "I love my friends." "I love mom and dad." "I love you." "I love God." "God loves human beings." Even though the word love is used in all of these sentences, it has a different nuance in each of them - hence, the confusion. J. Bruce Long's informative study of the notion of love in various societies sheds a great deal of light on the different meanings of the term love.[10]

According to Long, the various ideas of love can, in general terms, be reduced to three broad categories. First of all, there is "carnal love," which he defines as that which arises out of one's desire to enjoy an object of beauty "for one's own pleasure or gratification." Long refers to the Greek word *eros* (from which the English word erotic is derived) to signify this type of love.

[10] J. Bruce Long, "Love," *EncyclRel*, 9, pp. 31-40.

Secondly, there is "friendly love," a kind of love in which comradeship or affection is extended to another human being and is "motivated by feelings of altruistic generosity." This idea of love is designated by the term *philia* (from which the English word Philadelphia is derived, the city of brotherly love). Thirdly, there is "divine love," which is "manifested as self-giving grace." This type of love is represented by the word *agapê* (there is no English derivative of this term). Those who have *agapê* love for others are primarily motivated by the desire to promote the well being of their loved ones instead of their own personal gratification.

Mutual Self-Giving

Much can be learned about the makings of *agapê* love by reflecting on marriage. When a husband and wife begin their married life together, they are said to be "in love." The two of them seem to experience a special "thrill" whenever they are together. However, as the years go by, and children enter into the picture, and a certain routine of living sets in, a slow but sure change begins to take place. One sometimes hears the expression, "the honeymoon is over," to describe this change. The original excitement of sharing one's life with another has passed away. Many people in contemporary society mistakenly believe that at this stage in the marriage, the love which the spouses previously had for one another is gone. But, in fact, their love for each other is not dead. On the contrary, the spouses are now in a position to greatly deepen their love for each other.

If they are to come to terms with what is happening in their lives, each spouse must become more "other-centered." That is to say, if the marriage is to continue and to flower, both partners must become more attentive to the needs of the other. They must be more willing to give without necessarily expecting anything in return. To a greater extent they must find their happiness in making each other happy. Their motivation for remaining together as husband and wife and for sharing the joys and sorrows of life as a married couple must spring out of their mutual desire to promote the well being of the other. In other words, their love for each other must become less self-centered and more other-centered. To be sure, great sacrifice is often required to live in such a way. The great joy that accompanies *agapê* love makes it worth the while. Anyone who has experienced true *agapê* love has discovered the "thrill" of loving an individual pure and simply for the individual's own sake. Those who have been married ten years, twenty years, thirty years, and longer know what *agapê* love is or they would not still be married. One of the great "side-effects" of a loving marriage is that once husband and wife begin to experience real *agapê* love for each other, they naturally seem to offer that unselfish love to those around them. Such love makes life worth living.

Indeed, the best way to understand *agapê* love is to see it in action. Several years ago a woman had a stroke in which she became completely incapacitated. The woman lost all ability to communicate in any manner. Her husband had to feed her, clothe her, clean her, and so forth. When asked how he was coping with such a difficult situation, the husband simply remarked: "I consider it a joy to take care of my wife." He participated in that divine joy which comes to those whose fundamental concern is with the welfare of others.

Unconditional Love

The early church preferred to use the term *agapê* to articulate its understanding of the good news of Jesus Christ. The various New Testament authors portray Jesus as one who radicalized the concept of human love. He provided an extraordinary example of what it means to love unconditionally. Usually, when one person has a deep and unselfish love for another, that individual is assumed to have a similar type of love for the person in return. Jesus, however, demonstrated *agapê* love for those who not only did not love him in return but were, in fact, hostile towards him, to the point of putting him to death. Concerned with the well being of others even as he hung on the cross, Jesus implored his heavenly Father to forgive those who were responsible for his death (Luke 23:34). The passion and death of Jesus act as a stark reminder of the great sacrifice that is sometimes demanded by *agapê* love.

When Paul proclaims in Gal 2:20 that Jesus died for him out of love, he uses the term *agapê*. Likewise, when the apostle speaks of "faith working through love" in Gal 5:6, he uses the word *agapê*. When Paul encourages the Galatians to be servants of one another through love (5:13) and to love one another as they love themselves (5:14), he uses the word *agapê*. Assuredly, the apostle is encouraging the Galatians to love others as Christ has loved them, that is, unconditionally.[11]

Not Agapê

Paul's discussion in Galatians demonstrates that it is not only important for Christians to know what *agapê* love entails but also what it does not. When one remarks, "I love ice cream," one does not intend to convey the notion of selfless love but rather the idea that it gives one physical pleasure. However, when a person tells another, "I love you," one would hope that this person has in mind the love which is associated with genuine friendship and/or the unconditional love spoken of in the New Testament. Unfortunately, this is not always the case. Consider the scenario that often takes place in entertainment. Man meets woman, man goes to bed with the woman, man says, "I love you. What's your name?" In this context, "I love you," simply means, "You make me feel good." In effect, these two people seem to have used each other primarily for self-centered pleasure without much thought for the well being

[11] For a rather in-depth study of the notion of Christian love, see Anders Nygren, *Agape and Eros* (New York, NY: Harper Torchbooks, 1969).

of the other. Paul warns the Galatians that this kind of selfish conduct is not consistent with the truth of the gospel. Consequently, he beckons those in Christ to love others in a selfless manner (5:13, 19).

Agapê Spirituality

These reflections regarding *agapê* love can shed some light on the believer's relationship with Christ. One must be careful that one's love for God in Christ is not self-centered. Perhaps without realizing it, people are motivated to pray and to perform good deeds by somewhat selfish reasons, for a "spiritual reward of some sort." If the love that Christians have for God is to deepen, it must become more other-centered. They must seek to imitate Jesus whose primary incentive for praying and for doing works of charity was love. Those who express *agapê* love for God are motivated to action primarily by their love for Him alone. Christians are called to love God for His own sake. Moreover, they must be concerned with the sanctification of others as well with the sanctification of themselves. They have a response to those who remark, "I don't go to church and I don't pray because I don't get anything out of it." To such a comment, Christians reply that their fundamental reason for praying privately or with a community is not simply to receive something, but rather to express something, namely, their love for God.

Love is the Greatest

There is ample evidence in New Testament to substantiate the claim that Paul is the theologian of Christian love *par excellence*. In the course of persuading various Christian congregations to accept his point of view, the apostle often reflects upon *agapê* love. He speaks of the love of God the Father and Christ for humanity (e.g., 2 Cor 13:14, Gal 2:20), the love of Christians for God the Father and Christ (e.g., 2

Cor 5:14, Phil 1:9), and the love of Christians for one another (e.g., Rom 12:9, Gal 5:13).

God has manifested His love for humankind in a most remarkable fashion. He has given of His very self in the person of Jesus Christ so that humanity might be liberated from the slavery of sin (4:4). That our heavenly Father loves human beings for our own sake is borne out by the fact that His Son died for us even while we were still steeped in sin (Rom 5:8). In view of our unity with the beloved Son of God (Matt 3:17), Christians are now entitled to be referred to as "God's beloved" (Rom 1:7, 12:19). The love of Christ now compels them to seek out the well-being of others in charitable service (2 Cor 5:14). Following the example of Jesus, such loving service is not to be limited to those who are in Christ but must also extend to non-Christians as well (5:10), including even those who are hostile towards them (Rom 12:14-21)!

The apostle considers love to be a gift from God (1 Cor 12:31), one of the fruits of the Spirit (5:22). In a rather poetic way Paul describes in Rom 5:5 the connection between this divine gift and the Spirit. "God's love has been poured into our hearts through the Holy Spirit." Motivated by their love of God in Christ, those who have committed themselves to the risen Lord are encouraged to forgive those who have repented of their wrongdoing (2 Cor 2:5-8), and that includes themselves. The apostle is convinced that love is *the* ingredient for the building up of the body of Christ (1 Cor 8:1).

Paul considers love to be the most powerful force in the universe. He is convinced that there is absolutely nothing in heaven or earth that can separate us from the love of God in Christ Jesus (Rom 8:38-39). As far as the apostle is concerned, everything works out for the best for those who love God (Rom 8:28). Paul promises those who love God that He has something in store for them which is beyond their wildest dreams (1 Cor 2:9). As we have previously mentioned, the apostle informs the Galatians that their faith in Christ must be expressed through acts of charity (5:6). As a result of this belief, Paul exhorts those under his care to do all things out of love (1 Cor 16:14). The apostle is well aware of the fact that his love for others sometimes compels him to discipline and to firmly correct them for their own good (2 Cor 2:4).

1 Corinthians 13

Paul presents a somewhat lengthy exposé on *agapê* love in 1 Corinthians 13. This is a truly marvelous piece of Christian literature. As the apostle sees it, the gifts of the Spirit were not bestowed on certain individuals so that they could brag about their unique God-given talents or lord it over others (which some Corinthians were apparently doing). Rather, they were given these divine gifts to build up the church and to assist others.

According to Paul, all charisms must be understood within the context of love. Christian ministry devoid of love is meaningless (1 Cor 13:1-3). Paul drives home this point by insisting that even if one has the supernatural gift of speaking in tongues or of prophecy, or has an incredibly strong faith, or even suffers martyrdom, it is all for nought if love is not present.

The apostle proceeds to illustrate that *agapê* love involves more than just an intellectual activity or a "warm feeling" about someone. Paul defines love in terms of "doing" (1 Cor 13:4-7). As in Galatians 5 and 6, the apostle offers some specific advice in 1 Corinthians 13 regarding his understanding of love and Christian conduct. Those in Christ must be patient and kind but not jealous, arrogant or rude. They should not insist on "getting their own way," nor be resentful or irritable. Interestingly enough, Paul's reflections on *agapê* love in 1 Cor 13:4-6 all have to do with promoting harmony in the Christian community. According to the apostle, love is to be the driving force that draws people together.

Paul compares the self-centered behavior of Christians with that of children (1 Cor 13:11). He encourages those in Christ to "grow up" and to leave their childish ways behind them.

For all practical purposes, the apostle instructs them to make more of an effort to be other-centered in their day to day conduct. In conclusion, Paul realizes that faith, hope, and love are basic realities in the life of the Christian. This being said, he considers only love to be everlasting and the greatest of the three.[12]

Charity Begins at Home

The apostle's comments regarding love in 1 Corinthians 13 are especially applicable to those who are engaged in Christian ministry. One may have a charism for preaching, teaching, singing, organization, planning liturgy, or the like, but without love these divine gifts are empty. God has freely given these talents to His people so that the Christian community might be uplifted. Paul's list of do's and don'ts concerning how those in Christ are to love one another ring just as true today as they did some 2,000 years ago. All who follow his advice promote harmony and peace in their homes as well as in their own local churches.

Christian Responsibility

There is a decided shift in Paul's argumentation in Gal 5:13 - 6:10. Up until this point, most of his discussion has been dedicated to proving that Gentiles become children of Abraham by means of faith without observing the Torah. Now, however, the apostle turns his attention to the moral implications of his version of the good news. In this section of the epistle Paul reminds the Galatians that their relationship with Christ has a direct bearing on their own personal conduct. The apostle's comments in Gal 5:13 - 6:10 indicate that the Christian

[12] Paul's reflections on love in 1 Cor 13:8 and 13 are somewhat similar to those of the author of 1 John who equates God with love (See 1 John 4:16).

freedom which the Galatians enjoy is not without responsibility. An eminently practical and pastoral missionary, the apostle spells out in these verses what that responsibility involves.[13]

In addition to presenting various high-minded theological arguments concerning the significance of the death and resurrection of Jesus in Galatians, Paul also offers some down-to-earth advice regarding proper Christian conduct.[14] He cautions the Galatians that they are not at liberty to follow every personal whim. The apostle instructs them to avoid all immoral behavior and concern themselves instead with charitable deeds. Paul has previously demonstrated that there are no restrictions concerning the equality of believers (3:28). Nevertheless, the apostle warns the Galatians that there are restrictions concerning their personal conduct.

Paul informs the Galatians that those who have been called to a life of Christian freedom have a wonderful opportunity to exercise that liberty by attending to the needs of others in a spirit of love (5:13). The apostle warns them not to abuse their freedom by using it as an opportunity to simply satisfy the cravings of the flesh. In this context, Paul associates the term "flesh" with that which is evil and threatens one's moral life.[15] This being said, there is no reason to believe that the apostle considers the physical aspect of human beings to be sinful *per se*. On the contrary, he sometimes speaks of the body in sacred terms, that is, as a temple of the Holy Spirit (1 Cor 6:19).

Life in the Flesh

In order to avoid any misunderstanding regarding immoral behavior, Paul lists a rather lengthy catalogue of vices which are to be shunned: fornication, impurity, licentiousness, and the like.

[13] Paul often concludes his letters by urging those under his care to conduct themselves in a Christlike manner. See, for example, 1 Thess 5:12-22, 1 Cor 16:13-14, Phil 4:8-9.

[14] See 1 Cor 5:9, 6:9-10, 2 Cor 6:6-7, Rom 13:13.

[15] See John Barclay, *Obeying the Truth. A Study of Paul's Ethics in Galatians* SNTIW (Edinburgh, T. & T. Clark, 1988), p. 110.

The apostle insists that "those who belong to Christ Jesus have crucified the flesh with its passions and desires" (5:24). Paul's comments in this verse imply that those who take part in lewd conduct have *not* died to the flesh and have thus demonstrated that they are *not* "in Christ" (5:21). The apostle forewarns the Galatians that all who gratify purely self-centered desires will pay the price for their corrupt behavior and reap spiritual death (5:8).

Paul also admonishes the Galatians not to relate to one another in an arrogant manner. In light of their unity with the risen Lord, all Christians must be treated with dignity and respect. Consequently, the apostle entreats the Galatians to abstain from jealousy, dissension, selfishness, self conceit, and so forth. Unlike the fruits of the Spirit which bring people together, these vices of the flesh drive people apart. Moreover, the apostle feels compelled to alert the Galatians against the dangers of backbiting. He considers this type of behavior to be ultimately self-destructive (5:15). In view of these considerations, one wonders whether the Galatians were in special need of such exhortation since they already seem to have been experiencing some fierce dissensions within their communities (5:15, 20, 26).

Life in the Spirit

Paul urges the Galatians to give evidence in their daily lives that they are "walking in the Spirit" (5:25). Interestingly enough, the apostle does not link the fruits of the Spirit with miraculous gifts in Gal 5:22-23 as he did earlier in 3:5. Rather, Paul associates the gifts of the Spirit with those virtues which promote harmony and understanding in the Christian community. Thus the apostle exhorts the Galatians to be kind, good and patient (5:22), share all good things (6:6), love one another (5:14), bear one another's burdens (6:2), and gently correct those who have wronged them (6:1).[16] The Galatians are

[16] Judging by his comments in Galatians, it appears that once again we have a case of Paul not following his own advice, namely, to be gentle with those who have wronged you.

further instructed to act in a loving manner towards all people as well as towards those who are of the household of faith (6:10).

For all practical purposes, Paul informs the Galatians that they fulfill the law through works of mercy and not through the observance of specific precepts of the Torah, such as those pertaining to circumcision and dietary regulations (5:14). In a similar fashion the apostle contends that the Galatians fulfill the "law of Christ," which is presumably the "law of love," by helping one another with the burdens of life (6:2). Paul comments in jest that there is no law against such behavior (5:23). On a more serious note, however, he prays that the Galatians will not grow weary of being attentive to the well-being of each other. The apostle promises those who remain steadfast to the truth of the gospel and conduct themselves accordingly that they will reap untold benefits.

Personal Responsibility

Even though Paul stresses the importance of helping others, he does not intend for individual Christians to neglect their own welfare. The apostle invites the Galatians to reflect on their own personal situation. They should examine themselves to see if they have mistreated other members of the Christian community (6:1). Paul encourages them to excel in the art of humility (6:3). He challenges the Galatians to be introspective. They are urged to reflect upon the strengths and weaknesses of their ministry within the church (6:4). In all of this, Paul reminds the Galatians that Christians have a responsibility to themselves (6:5).

Surely it is no accident that the apostle cites Lev 19:18 in Gal 5:14 ("You shall love your neighbor as yourself") immediately after exhorting the Galatians to serve one another in love. By referring to this passage from the Hebrew Scriptures, the apostle implies that one cannot communicate *agapê* love to others if one does not express *agapê* love for oneself.

Therefore, for example, if the Galatians are to be truly compassionate and forgiving of one another, as Paul exhorts them to be in Gal 6:1, then they must first be compassionate and forgiving of themselves.

Last Words and Testimony

The apostle now brings his argumentation to a close. His remark in Gal 6:11 concerning the size of the letters in which he is writing is meant to draw attention to his final comments.[17] Paul remains obsessed with the troublemakers to the end. Once again in 6:12-13 he accuses them of having ulterior motives for preaching their heretical doctrine to the Galatians (4:17).

True to the sharp tenor of the entire epistle, the last verses also end on a sarcastic note. The agitators had focused a good deal of their attention on the "marks of circumcision." The apostle, however, boasts not of his own circumcision, but of the physical scars that he has endured for the sake of the gospel.[18] In view of these "marks of Jesus" (6:17),[19] Paul adjures his readers not to bother him any more.

The final words of the letter are, so to speak, a hidden prayer that the Galatians might accept the apostle's rendition of the good news (6:18).[20] Paul has previously warned them that all who yield to the teaching of the Judaizers have "fallen from

[17] See Betz, *Galatians*, p. 314: Paul's writing in large letters in Gal 6:11 is a practice that would be comparable to the variation in letters (italics, capitals, boldface) in modern printing.

[18] Paul lists some of the ways in which he has suffered for the sake of the gospel in 2 Cor 11:23-28.

[19] See Merrill Tenney, *Galatians: The Charter of Christian Liberty* (Grand Rapids, MI: Eerdmans, 1986), p. 209, who sees an illusion to slavery in Gal 6:17. A slave was usually marked with the brand of his master, or was identified by some distinguishing scar to show to whom he belonged.

[20] Likewise in Gal 1:3

grace" (5:4). Now the apostle prays that the grace of our Lord Jesus Christ might be with the Galatians (6:18). Of course this will only occur, according to Paul's argumentation, if they accept his teaching.

The apostle has completed the task of defending his understanding of the gospel. The time is at hand for the Galatians to make a decision. They must decide for themselves whether they are to remain steadfast to the gospel that the apostle first preached to them or capitulate to the teaching of the troublemakers. Having stated his case, Paul has no doubt whatsoever that the Galatians will reject the erroneous doctrine of the agitators and accept his point of view (5:10).

Concluding Remarks

The apostle has demonstrated in Galatians 5 and 6 that all who respond to his version of the good news and recognize that Gentiles participate in Abraham's inheritance exclusively through faith in Christ open up the doors to an entirely new world of freedom. Paul considers the liberty which has been bestowed on those who have come to believe in the risen Lord as a gift of the Spirit and something marvelous to behold. The apostle assures the Galatians that there is a tremendous improvement in the quality of one's life as a result of this divine gift.

Christians have been set free from the paralyzing effects of sin and are thus in a position to experience inexpressible happiness. As those who are united with Christ, they share in the possession of the Spirit. Christians therefore have the "right" to call upon God as Abba. Consequently, they have the opportunity to experience in a new way that wonderful freedom from anxiety which comes to those who have a childlike confidence in divine providence. Paul guarantees the Galatians that if they remain steadfast to the truth of the gospel, they will not only reap benefits in this life but will also enjoy eternal bliss in the life to come. However, the apostle warns the Galatians in the strongest terms that if they should shift their allegiance to the Judaizers and opt against his Torah-free gospel, they will be doomed to a life of interior slavery and will have to encounter the wrath of God on the last day.

Born To Serve

Paul informs the Galatians that Christian freedom should not be understood in isolation. Rather, it must be viewed in conjunction with love and responsibility. Christ did not obtain liberty for those who believe in him for a life of unbridled passion but for a life of love and charitable service. As there is freedom of movement in dancing, yet with the discipline of the beat, so too is there Christian freedom with the discipline of love and responsibility.

Christian liberty did not come cheaply. Jesus humbled himself, took the form of a slave, and died upon the cross so that those who believe in him might be set free from the confinement of sin (Phil 2:6-8). Those in Christ are, in effect, challenged by the apostle to imitate Jesus who, even though he was the very personification of freedom, did not use that freedom as an opportunity to satisfy selfish desires. On the contrary, he dedicated his life to the service of others. Christians must view their new life of freedom as providing them with the opportunity to follow in the footsteps of Jesus, honoring God by being attentive to the needs of one another.

The Divine Romance

Paul's discussion in Galatians contains some beautiful insights concerning his understanding of *agapê* love. Jesus is presented as the personification of this generous type of love. Indeed, he exemplified God the Father's love for humanity. God so loved human beings that He gave them the perfect gift of pure love by sending His beloved Son into the world. It was

God's way of saying, "I love you" to the human race. The incarnation seems to reinforce the belief that love seeks equality. God became like human beings so that they might become like Him. God who is free and loving desires that all human beings be free and loving through the mediation of His Son.

Jesus manifested the depth of God's love for humanity especially in his willingness to forgive others. On the cross he demonstrated that no sin is so big that it cannot be forgiven. Even those who committed the ultimate crime of murdering the Son of God were not beyond divine forgiveness. Paul himself, who violently persecuted the church, was also the recipient of God's compassionate mercy. There is no such thing as an "incurable spiritual disease." God's love is much greater than human sinfulness. Perhaps the greatest way that Christians can demonstrate their appreciation for being forgiven by God is to freely forgive those who have sinned against them (Matt 6:12).

Jesus always dealt with people in a loving and respectful way. Despite all cultural and religious pressures, Jesus always remained free to love others. Christians are obligated to follow the example of Jesus whose primary vocation was to love. The apostle's argumentation in Galatians implies that one's motive for doing charitable deeds should not simply arise out of one's desire to "earn" salvation nor to "pay back" God for what He has done for humanity. Rather, one should be motivated to a life of loving service by the love of God alone. Ultimately, the best way to respond to divine love is to love in return. Christians express this love for God in Christ by being attentive to the needs of others. Whether at church, at home, at work, or at play, the respect and the care that Christians show for each other is to be their hallmark. All who manifest such Christian values in their day to day living proclaim the gospel of Jesus Christ.

The Holy Family

According to Paul's way of thinking, the Son of God must be viewed not only as the mediator between God and human beings but also between human beings and themselves. Through Christ Jesus, God's love has made it possible for all of heaven and earth to freely gather together into one glorious holy family. Within this one family in Christ, the sons and daughters of God are confronted with a tremendous task, namely, to love one another as Jesus has loved them. Paul's argumentation in Galatians indicates that Christian freedom enables those in Christ to realize more fully their capacity to love.

The Demands of Love

The apostle makes known to the Galatians that their life in Christ involves much more than simply a one on one relationship with the risen Lord. As Christians, they can not ignore the needs of others. Paul insists that those in Christ have a responsibility not only to themselves and to Christ, but to other Christians and to non-Christians as well, including those who may not like them and, perhaps, are even antagonistic towards them. All who are united with the Lord must express their faith in Christ and their love for him through charitable acts on behalf of others.

Augustine seems to have been of the same mind-set as Paul when he commented: "Love and do what you will."[21] Like the troublemakers in Galatia, some people might have the mistaken impression that such a belief inevitably leads to illicit behavior. Just the opposite is true. To base one's behavior on the principle of love is extremely demanding, especially when one considers the biblical notion of *agapê* love, namely, unconditional, selfless love.

[21] See Erich Przywara, ed., *An Augustine Synthesis* (New York, NY: Sheed and Ward, 1945), p. 341.

Before we conclude this section, a word of caution is in order concerning love. Christians must have a balanced understanding of *agapê* love. Love does not mean letting others take advantage of you, putting up with physical or other types of abuse, or placing yourself in a possibly dangerous situation, such as picking up a hitchhiker in a remote part of town late at night, and the like. Moreover, as every person who is involved in Christian ministry must discover, love does not mean always saying yes when asked to take part in some activity, however noble it might be. Christians must be careful to temper their notion of *agapê* love with wisdom. Jesus himself instructed his followers to be as wise as serpents (Matt 10:16).

Ever Vigilant

Paul warned the Galatians about the dangers of yielding to the self-centered desires of the flesh. Nevertheless, as we have previously noted, the apostle has a favorable attitude concerning the human body. His writings indicate that he has a tremendous respect for the corporal nature of human beings. Nowhere is this more evident than when he reflects on what the author of the Fourth Gospel refers to as "the Word become flesh" (Gal 4:4, Phil 2:6-7, John 1:14). Furthermore, Paul's comments concerning the resurrected body in 1 Corinthians 15 are also significant in this regard.

Christians should consider themselves as caretakers of their bodies. They must attend to their physical needs as well as their spiritual needs. Nevertheless, Christians must be ever vigilant not to be carried away by today's seemingly greed driven, self-centered society which often places its exclusive attention on the physical needs of the human person. The importance of prayer and the support of the other members of the Christian community with similar values cannot be overstressed in this respect. Fidelity to the Christian lifestyle sometimes requires great courage and great sacrifice. However, one's love for God in Christ provides one with the strength for such an admirable task.

Journey of Faith

Love presupposes freedom. God has liberated those who are in communion with His Son Jesus so that they might be free to love Him, others, and themselves. God does not force this freedom on human beings; He invites them to participate in it. One enjoys Christian liberty through faith in Christ apart from the Mosaic law. As Paul has so forcefully demonstrated, faith is not divorced from good works. Those in Christ are called to display their faith in Christ through acts of charity and not by observing the precepts of the Torah.

The one whose new life in Christ began on the road to Damascus has provided Christians of all times with a "roadmap" for their journey of faith. The apostle urges those who believe in the risen Lord to walk in the Spirit by manifesting their faith in Christ through love. Paul does not base his advice on mere intellectual reasoning or on secondhand information. Rather, the apostle is a spiritual guide who has experienced the sacred mysteries of which he is writing. In a most radical fashion Paul has experienced divine freedom, *agapê* love, and Christian responsibility. The life and writings of the apostle provide the church with an outstanding example of a person who is on fire with the love of Christ and who, in spite of all adversity and hardship, was, like his master, free to love.

POSTSCRIPT

All human beings have a natural craving for freedom and love. According to Paul's understanding of the Christ event, real freedom, in the deepest sense of the word, comes exclusively to those who have faith in the risen Lord. Only those who have been liberated from the enslavement of sin by Christ Jesus are truly free and thus have the capacity to love God, others, and themselves, to the fullest. The apostle's argumentation in Galatians indicates that one's external circumstances do not necessarily affect one's interior freedom. Consequently, a Christian might suffer from poverty, poor health, and even be imprisoned, as was Paul (Phil 1:7, Philmn 1), and still enjoy Christian liberty. On the other hand, one may have great wealth, power, fame, and so forth, and yet be entrapped by sin, and all of its horrendous side effects.

Whatever situation those in Christ might find themselves in, whatever dark past they may have experienced, Christians are free to love. The gospel of liberty that Paul proclaimed was and remains a counter-cultural teaching. In a "me-oriented" world, the apostle went against the prevailing winds of society and informed the Galatians that they have been liberated to live a full life of unconditional love, as opposed to an empty lust-filled existence. Paul makes it crystal clear that there is no room for alienation of any sort within the Christian community. Regardless of the way that society often pigeonholes people because of race, social status, gender, poverty, poor health, and the like, Christians must always strive to treat one another as equals.

Zeal for the Gospel

Paul was not only enthusiastic about the good news of Jesus Christ because God the Father had personally revealed His Son to the apostle and had commissioned him to proclaim the gospel to the Gentiles. He was also excited about the divine message because Paul recognized its liberating power. The apostle was so confident about the importance of the good news that he was willing to endure untold suffering on its behalf. This confidence also provided him with the strength to continue to herald the gospel even though he knew that it might result in hardship and persecution for those who responded favorably to it (e.g., 1 Thess 1:6). Paul's life, ministry, and martyrdom demonstrated that the gospel was not only worth living for, it was also worth dying for.

Present day Christians, in particularly those who are involved with the teaching and preaching of the gospel, must never underestimate the power of the message that they have been entrusted to proclaim in word and deed. Assuredly, those who accept the good news of Jesus Christ will vastly improve the quality of their lives in this world and the world to come. This belief helped Paul to remain steadfast to the truth of the gospel despite all obstacles. Hopefully it will do the same for contemporary Christians who are engaged in various ministries.

The Divine Caretaker

All who have pledged allegiance to the risen Lord and have sworn to follow in his footsteps are invited to place their unshakable trust in divine providence. Oftentimes Christians become discouraged with the everyday routine of life, meetings, church bureaucracy, scandals, controversy, and so forth. Paul's remarks in Galatians act as a constant reminder that the God who transformed the tragedy of the crucifixion into the glory of the resurrection will always watch over the church whose members are united with his Son.

Christian Identity

The troublemakers' conviction that Gentile believers obey at least some of the commandments of the Mosaic law is fraught with difficulties. Not only does such a way of thinking insinuate that Christ died in vain (2:21), but it also may lead to the mistaken notion that Christianity can be reduced to the performance of specific deeds. Paul aggressively argues in Galatians that the identifying character of a believer is one's faith in Christ. That being said, the apostle's discussion in the epistle demonstrates that faith is inexplicably bound to charity. Indeed, faith in Christ expresses itself through love (5:6). One's life in Christ does not merely involve the doing of a few certain activities but rather entails an entire way of living.

Christians are urged to manifest their faith in the risen Lord and their love for him through a life of dedicated service. Twentieth century believers must be careful to avoid the mistaken notion that one fulfills all obligations connected with one's baptismal commitment to Christ by simply doing particular acts, such as going to church on Sunday, praying, almsgiving, and so forth, as important as these might be. Those in Christ also express their faith in the risen Lord, for example, by good moral conduct and by the charitable way in which they deal with others. Christianity is a very demanding religion that affects every aspect of the believers' lives.

The overriding importance that Paul places on faith is not unique in the New Testament. In this respect, it is interesting to note that Mary, the mother of Jesus, is alluded to in Gal 4:4. Luke goes to great pains in his gospel to demonstrate that Mary's preeminence is to be attributed not so much to her physical relationship with Jesus as to her great faith and her willingness to do God's will (Luke 1:38, 8:20-21, 11:27-28). Like the apostle, the author of the third gospel makes a strong connection between believing and responding to the word of God.

Greater Love Than This...

Perhaps the most important task which lay before Paul was to let others know just how really good God is. The apostle informed those under his care that through the life, death, and resurrection of Jesus, God has revealed to humanity the depth of His love for the human race. Having experienced divine liberty and compassion, Paul invited others to share in the grandeur of that same glorious freedom and love. Christians are exhorted to communicate God's tremendous love for the human race. Unfortunately, for whatever reason, all too many people have kept God's love hidden. Those who are united with Christ should be continually reminded that they have it in their power to be a vehicle of God's grace and benevolence. Paul's exhortation to the Galatians continues to inspire Christians: Do good to all people, especially to those in the Christian family (6:10).

The United Way

Paul often emphasizes the communal dimension of Christianity in his writings. All the members of the body of Christ are bound together by their faith in the risen Lord and by their concern for the welfare of the Christian community at large. Individual believers are to focus their attention not only on their own sanctification but that of all the members of the universal church as well. In light of this unity of believers, Christians have a holy obligation to be aware, as much as possible, of the needs, the sufferings, and the joys, of other members of the church, be they in a different part of the neighborhood or a different part of the world. Those in Christ have a special vocation to pray for one another. All should view their respective roles in life and their particular journey of faith in terms of a contribution to the uplifting of the body of Christ, be one a parent, religious, teacher, hermit, or some such. Moreover, the Christian community has a universal responsibility for the well-being of the human family. Ultimately, Christian believers are concerned with nothing less than the salvation of the world.

Mystical Union

The Christian faith is founded upon the belief that God and humanity came together in the person of Jesus Christ. In some mysterious way, the infinite and the finite, the mortal and the eternal, were joined together in one human being. Through Jesus, God has revealed Himself and has demonstrated His unconditional love for humanity. Therefore, all that Jesus taught, all the miracles that he performed, his crucifixion, and his being raised from the dead, must be viewed in light of God the Father, who sent His only-begotten Son into the world so that the human race might be saved.

Paul occasionally alludes to the mystery of the incarnation in his writings (Gal 4:4, Phil 2:6-7). Like all Christians, the apostle, in a sense, was forced to wrestle with this sublime mystery, that is, the coming together of humanity and divinity. Assuredly the risen Lord identifies closely with each member of the church (e.g., Acts 9:4). As one who has been united with the Son of God, the apostle describes the tension that he experiences in Gal 2:20. Even though Paul recognizes that "it is no longer I who live, but Christ who lives in me," the apostle nevertheless realizes that he still lives "in the flesh."

By means of his communion with the risen Lord, Paul believed that he participated in divine life. This being said, however, the apostle nonetheless grappled with his own humanity (2 Cor 12:7-10) and all of its shortcomings. In a similar fashion, contemporary Christians must contend with the mystery of the incarnation. To be sure, the incarnate Christ dwells within baptized believers. Still and all, the lures of the flesh are often present and, at times, seem stronger than ever. Paul reminds the Galatians in Galatians 5 and 6 that there is an ongoing battle between the "flesh" and the "spirit." Christians should not be surprised by this sometimes seemingly continuous struggle. The apostle exhorts those under his care to persevere and "walk in the spirit." The saintly person is not necessarily the one who is always successful in this regard but rather the one who depends on God's mercy and is not afraid to "try again."

Giving Your All

Paul's love for God in Christ was not simply an intellectual affair. The apostle was one of those rare persons who gave God his "all." Like the great saints who followed him, St. Francis of Assisi, St. John of the Cross, St. Teresa of Liseux, and so forth, Paul was an individual who followed the command of Jesus and loved the Lord our God with all of his heart, with all of his soul, and with all of his mind (Matt 22:37).

The apostle realized that God the Father sees "something" very special in every Christian, that is, the life of His Son. Because of his faith in Christ and his baptism, Paul knew that his life was intimately bound to that of the risen Lord and to his heavenly father. Few people would argue that the way to a parent's heart is through his/her children. The same is true in the divine realm. The way to the "bosom of the Father" is through His beloved Son Jesus (John 1:18, 13:23).

Paul perceived that Christ Jesus had given of himself completely on his behalf (Gal 2:20). The apostle sensed that Christ had offered the apostle divine love, divine life, and divine salvation. Love compelled Paul to love in return. The selfless way in which the apostle expressed his love for the Lord enkindles in Christians of all times the desire to do likewise.

Joy to the World

That God united Himself with humanity through Jesus so that the world might be redeemed (4:4-5) is indeed good news. That God unites Himself in Christ to every baptized Christian is fantastic news and cause for rejoicing. In the second chapter of the third gospel, Luke describes the coming of Jesus into the world as "tidings of great joy." Unquestionably, these same words can also be used to express the happiness that is experienced by those who have been bound to the Son of God through their faith in Christ.

Christian living need not be devoid of joy. On the contrary, Paul informs us in Galatians that one can detect the presence of the Holy Spirit through joy-filled members of the Christian community (5:22). Consequently, a "sad believer" is a contradiction in terms. Those who are involved in Christian ministry are called to be "ministers of joy." It is their task to communicate to others, Christian and non-Christian alike, the joy which is associated with the gospel of Jesus Christ and its emphasis on divine love and liberty.

Realizing a Dream

Martin Luther King's dream of liberty and equality is not simply a vain hope. Paul is convinced that all who come to believe in the risen Lord and place their unwavering trust in him are "free at last." Liberated from the oppressive power of sin, those in Christ are free to love. God intended that His sacred gifts of liberty and love be continually expressed and shared by Christian believers.

Our sojourn of faith is one in which we discover daily the wonders of divine freedom. The apostle promises us that this journey will eventually result in eternal bliss. In the meantime, great courage and sacrifice are often required to live out our Christian liberty. True as this may be, however, we have the divine guarantee that the glorified Christ is deep within us, ever present to strengthen us in this venerable quest.

INDEX OF PERSONS

Achtemeier, P.J. 57
Andressen, C. 112
Arichea, D.C. 100, 166

Bandstra, A.J. 180
Barclay, J. 210
Barclay, W. 69
Barrett, C.K. 32, 139, 169, 184
Beare, F.W. 79
Beasley-Murray, G.R. 168
Becker, U. 62
Betz, H.D. 17, 35, 57, 89, 163, 179, 213
Bligh, J. 33, 141
Blunck, J. 191
Bokenkotter, T. 8, 9
Boring, E.M. 15
Borowitz, E.B. 32
Brown, C. 101, 174
Brown, R.E. 70, 88
Bruce, F.F. 18, 31, 89, 90, 139, 170, 183
Burrows, M. 141
Burton, E. 33

Carcopino, J. 12
Cervantes, L.F. 14
Chadwick, H. 8, 14
Christ, K. 11
Chrysostom, John 64, 111
Coenen, L. 56, 83
Collins, R.F. 4, 56, 82, 86
Cousar, C.B.183

Davies, A. 86
Davies, W.D. 105, 126
Dinkler, E. 112
Dodd, C.H. 142
Donfried, K. 88, 102
Donin, H.H. 106, 107
Drane, J.W. 20, 31
Duncan, G.S. 87
Dunn, J.D.G. 45, 91, 109

Ebeling, G. 110
Edwards, W.D. 150, 152
Ehrman, B.D. 87
Esser, H.-H. 57

Fee, G.D. 79
Ferguson, E. 10, 12, 13
Fitzmyer, J.A. 16, 73, 104, 116, 141, 171, 176
Flemington, W.F. 168
Fransen, P. 57, 58
Friedrich, G. 62
Friedrich, J. 32, 139
Fung, R.Y. 78, 166

Gardner, J.F. 14
Goetzmann, J. 82
Grant, R.M. 9, 11
Günther, W. 72
Guthrie, D. 93, 147

Hays, R.B. 155
Hamerton-Kelly, R. 126
Hendriksen, W. 41
Hensell, E. 4
Hooker, M.D. 117, 118
Howard G. 123, 124, 125
Hübner, H. 128
Hultgren, A.J. 75

Johnson, L.T. 10, 11
Jeremias, J. 134

Käsemann, E. 32, 139
King, Martin Luther 3, 227
Klein, G. 112
Koester, H. 13
Kümmel, W.G. 19, 28

Lambrecht, J. 99
Latourett, K.S. 9
Lightfoot, J.B. 16
Long, J.B. 202

Longenecker, R.N. 19
Lüdemann, G. 7
Luther, Martin 38
Lyonnet, S. 147

McGinn, B. 21, 50
McKenzie, J.L. 41, 48, 72, 76, 87, 150, 171, 182, 191
Merrigan, T. 5
Michel, O. 103
Miller, J.L. 148
Miller, M.S. 148
Moo, D.J. 107, 109
Moule, C.F.D. 70
Mundle, W. 70
Mussner, F. 34
Myers, A.C. 138, 178

Nida, E.A. 100, 166
Noth, M. 143
Nygren, A. 205

O'Connor, J.M. 20
O'Neill, J.C. 20
Paoli, U.E. 13

Pick, B. 22
Pöhlmann, W. 32
Przywara, E. 217

Räisänen, H. 82, 108, 114, 117, 119
Reuman, J. 88
Ridderbos, H. 48
Rendall, M. 143
Rengstorf, K.H. 53
Ridderbos, H. 48, 198
Roetzel, C.J. 39
Rollins, W.G. 13
Rowell, J. 194

Sabourin, L. 147
Sanders, E.P. 105, 119, 126, 127, 128
Schillebeeckx, E. 12, 17
Schoeps, H.-J. 115
Senior, D. 27, 178
Smit, J. 20
Stamm, R.T. 141
Stendahl, K. 82, 84, 85
Stuhlmacher, P. 32

Tenney M. 213

von Eicken, E. 44
Vorländer, H. 174

Wardman, A. 11
Watson, F. 113, 114, 119, 120, 121, 122
Wengst, K. 9, 12
Werblowsky, R.J.Z. 53
Wilckens, U. 110, 114

Yates, R. 164

INDEX OF SCRIPTURAL REFERENCES

Genesis
1:2 116
1:26 45
2-3 45
2:16-17 46
3:5 46
3:6 46
3:6-18 122
3:7 46
3:9 46
3:10 46
3:11-12 46
3:16 80, 85
3:16-19 47
3:19 47
3:28 80
4:8 47
5:21 80
11:30 184
12:1-3 136
12:3 31, 124, 136
12:4 136
12:7 163
15:6 135
17:1 137
17:10-13 32
17:10-14 106, 134
17:14 32
17:17 184
17:17-21 137
18:18 31, 136
21:2 137
21:10 184
22:1-2 137
23:11-12 137
34 47

Exodus
6:6 147, 148
19 184
20:19 164
21:2 190
21:30 147, 148
24:17 174
40:34 174

Leviticus
9:1-24 147
16 172
18:5 32, 111, 124, 125, 143
18:12 113
19:2 106
19:18 51
19:20 190
25:47-55 147
25:48 148

Numbers
10:11 184
14 174
16:10 72

Deuteronomy
5:5 164
5:23-27 164
6:4 114
15:12 72
21:22-23 144
21:23 76, 114, 117, 118, 144, 145, 152
27:26 32, 99, 108, 111, 112, 114, 131, 143, 156, 165

1 Chronicles
17:13 181

Psalms
22:1 152
143:2 165

Isaiah
45:15 170
49:1 83
54:1 184

Jeremiah
1:6 83
31:9 181

Habakkuk
2:4 143, 156

2 Maccabees
7 32

Matthew
2:1-18 54
3:11 167
3:16-17 167
3:17 206
6:9 181
6:10 55
6:12 215
10:2 87
10:16 217
16:19 87
22:37 225
26:17 107
26:38 151
26:69-75 96
27:26 151
27:32 151
27:39-43 150
28:18-20 43
28:19 168
28:19-20 8

Mark
1:9 167
1:21 107
3:16 87
9:2 171
10:33-34 167
10:38-39 167
11:11 107
11:15-19 65
15:15 151
15:34 152
15:44 151

Luke
1:38 222
1:46-55 86
1:68-79 86
2:1 7
2:21 107
6:14 87
8:20-21 222
11:2 181
11:27-28 222
23:34 157
23:46 152
24:34 87

John
1:14 217
1:18 225
1:40-42 87
3:8 58
3:16 152
13:23 225
19:12-16 54
19:17 150
19:19 150
19:23 150
19:29 150

Acts
1-12 87
1:13 87
1:21-22 43
2:38 168
4:36-37 89
5:30 144
7 8
7:58 21
7:58-60 74
8:1 74
8:3 74
9:1-2 74
9:1-18 168
9:2 8
9:15 124
9:21 80
9:27 89
10:39 144
11:25-26 89
11:26 53
11:29 89

12:1-2 8
13:1-3 89
14:12 11
15:7-8 25
16:6-7 17
16:14-15 177
16:22 151
17:4 177
17:18 24
18:3 24
18:23 17, 21
19:23 8
21:23-26 84
21:39 21
21:40 22
22:4 8
22:5 74
22:24 151
22:25 12
22:28 12
23:14 24
23:16 21
24:14 8
25:10-12 13
25:25-26 53
25:26 12
26:9 75
26:10 74
26:11 74
26:14 22
26:28 53
28:6 11

Romans
1:2 59
1:3 44
1:3-4 118
1:7 175, 206
1:16 170
1:18-32 11
1:18-3:18 49
2:6 48, 102
2:7-11 102
2:8 48
2:9 48
2:17-24 122
3:5 48
3:20 112
3:20-22 113
3:23 48, 111, 125
3:24 59
3:25 45, 172
3:27 114
4:14 162
4:19 135
4:22 135
4:23-24 135
5:5 206
5:7-8 49
5:8 206
5:10 102, 173
5:11 173
5:12 48, 111
5:17 101
5:18-19 45, 48
5:20-21 122
6:5 169
6:6-7 169
6:11 169
6:14 48
6:18 191
6:20 191
7:1 115
7:6 116, 196
7:7-11 164
7:12 113
7:15 25
8:7 48
8:15 181
8:21 174
8:28 27
8:38-39 206
9-11 85
10:4 115, 124
10:5 124
10:8-9 103
10:10 170
10:17 103
11:28 85
11:11-30 121
11:31-33 85
12:3 104
12:9 206
12:11 192

12:14-21 206
12:19 206
14:10 102
14:14 121
16:2 177
16:3 177
16:4 177
16:7 177
16:22 19

1 Corinthians
1:1 43
1:2 41, 175
1:3 57
1:3-4 26
1:11-12 66
1:12-17 168
1:14-17 168
1:18 170
1:23 45
1:28-31 175
2:9 206
3:9 43
4:1 43
5:19 60
6:11 174
6:19 174, 209
6:20 148
7:11 173
7:15 60
7:23 148
8:1 206
9:1-18 21
9:1-23 42
9:2 44
9:20 120
9:21 121, 123
10:25 121
11:3 176
11:4-5 176
11:23 50
11:24-26 45
11:27 51
12 28
12:9 25
12:12-13 168
12:13 169, 196
12:27 168
12:31 206
13 26
13:4-6 207
13:4-7 207
13:11 207
14:34-35 176, 177
15:2 63
15:5 87
15:8 79
15:9 23
15:10 43
15:22 45
15:29 168
15:51 51
15:51-57 51
15:54-55 52
16:14 207
16:19 177
16:21 19
16:23 26

2 Corinthians
1:23 88
2:4 207
2:5-8 206
2:13 90
3:6-9 122
3:12-18 86
3:14-16 122
3:18 171
4:7 26
5:14 105, 206
5:14-15 45
5:17 175
5:18-19 191
5:19 173
5:20 43
7:6 90
7:6-16 90
7:13 90
8:6 90
8:16-17 90
8:23 90
10:10 22, 23
11 23
11:6 23

11:23-25 80
11:23-33 22
11:24 120
11:26 9
11:32-33 24
12:1-4 25
12:7-8 22
12:7-10 26, 224
12:11 43
12:12 44
12:18 90
13:14 205

Galatians

1:1 18, 28, 40, 42, 43, 52, 53, 60, 78, 152
1:1-2 40
1:1-4 35, 42
1:1-5 39, 40
1:1-10 39, 65
1:1-2:14 35
1:1 42
1:2 16, 17, 27, 39, 40, 50, 56, 61, 64, 72
1:3 12, 40, 42, 53, 56, 57, 59
1:3-4 41, 42
1:4 11, 41, 42, 49, 52, 54, 59, 72, 77, 148, 171, 172, 175, 191, 192
1:5 42
1:6 18, 30, 34, 42, 59, 60, 61, 72, 77
1:7 30, 34, 57, 61, 62, 63
1:8 18, 63, 95
1:8-9 29, 34, 63, 102, 122
1:9 18, 63
1:10 13, 22, 31, 34, 42, 65, 192
1:11 35, 42, 60, 64, 72, 78
1:11-12 70
1:11-2:14 69
1:12 70
1:13 22, 59, 74
1:13-14 30, 75
1:13-16 77
1:14 75, 199
1:15 42, 59, 70, 200
1:15-16 22, 28, 30, 35, 42, 43, 78, 83, 89
1:16 44, 70, 125
1:16-2:14 34
1:17 34, 43, 88
1:17-24 30
1:18 34
1:18-20 88
1:18-24 120
1:19 73
1:22 88
1:23 8
1:24 23
2:1 89
2:1-2 88
2:1-14 30
2:1-21 125
2:2 88
2:2-3 197
2:3 27, 107, 121
2:4 64, 90, 192
2:5 28, 62, 63
2:6 91, 102
2:7 62
2:7-10 43
2:8 23
2:9 33, 77, 91, 93
2:10 25, 91
2:11 18, 77, 121
2:11-14 31, 108, 109
2:12 15, 63, 79, 92
2:13 27
2:14 92, 99
2:14-21 133
2:15 111
2:15-21 99
2:15-4:31 35
2:16 29, 38, 76, 79, 83, 99, 103, 104, 105, 107, 109, 113, 122, 129, 153, 192, 197
2:17 29, 100, 111
2:17-21 99
2:18 100
2:19 100, 108, 192
2:19-21 100, 111
2:20 22, 26, 37, 81, 100, 104, 169, 172, 174, 204, 205, 224, 225
2:21 100, 101, 110, 122, 127, 133, 152, 155, 191, 222

3:1 17, 18, 31, 133, 152
3:1-5 131, 133
3:1-13 153
3:1-14 131, 132, 133, 156, 160
3:2 31, 102, 134, 154, 155
3:2-3 197
3:2-5 135
3:3 122, 154, 196
3:4 29
3:5 25, 31, 44, 134, 154, 155, 210
3:5-6 154
3:6 132, 134, 135, 136
3:6-9 131, 134, 154, 156, 185
3:7 31, 102, 131, 132, 133, 135, 136
3:8 124, 125, 135, 136, 156, 157
3:9 102, 136, 156
3:10 15, 62, 63, 83, 101, 105, 107, 108, 111, 112, 114, 122, 131, 138, 143, 145, 148, 154, 156, 171, 192, 199
3:10-13 84
3:10-14 131
3:11 110, 143, 156
3:11-12 15, 143
3:12 111, 112, 113, 124, 131, 143, 148, 156
3:13 29, 76, 77, 111, 114, 115, 117, 118, 122, 144, 145, 146, 147, 148, 152, 153, 156, 171, 172, 175, 180, 191
3:13-14 125, 157, 191
3:14 62, 77, 84, 125, 133, 153, 154, 155, 156, 171, 174, 196
3:14-18 185
3:15 29, 35, 72, 160, 162
3:15-4:31 160, 161, 185
3:15-17 162
3:15-18 160, 162
3:16 131, 132, 160, 162, 163, 166
3:16-17 132
3:16-18 161
3:17 108, 135, 162, 164
3:18 162
3:19 102, 108, 164, 166, 192
3:19-20 164
3:19-22 160
3:21 102, 110, 112, 166
3:22 153, 165, 165. 166
3:22-23 191
3:23 13, 101, 165, 166
3:23-24 176
3:23-29 176
3:24 166
3:24-25 165
3:25 166, 192
3:25-28 169, 170
3:25-29 166, 178
3:26 42, 102, 169
3:26-28 13, 133
3:26-29 176
3:27 167, 169
3:28 14, 15, 53, 63, 125, 169, 176, 178, 191, 209
3:29 102, 133, 163, 166, 169, 171
3:31 127
4:1 179
4:1-2 29, 160, 161, 178
4:1-7 122
4:3 13, 179
4:4 7, 44, 49, 84, 168, 180, 206, 217, 224
4:4-5 55, 225
4:5 180
4:5-6 196
4:6 41, 42, 72, 173, 180, 181, 195, 196
4:7 180
4:8 16, 11, 101, 180
4:9 179, 180
4:10 31, 180
4:11-15 18
4:12 35, 72, 183
4:12-20 160, 161, 181
4:13 17, 18, 34
4:13-14 182
4:13-16 22
4:14 17, 18, 34
4:15 182
4:16 33, 35, 161, 182
4:17 34, 182, 212
4:18-20 18
4:19 35, 182, 183
4:20 29, 30, 182, 183

4:21 29, 183, 184
4:21-23 148
4:21-31 160, 161, 183
4:22-25 13
4:22-31 15
4:23 183, 197
4:24 184
4:24-25 107, 184
4:25 34
4:26 34
4:27 184
4:28 35
4:28-31 184
4:29 122
4:31 35, 184
5 and 6 65
5:1 7, 13, 176, 188, 189, 191, 199
5:1-6:10 35
5:1-6:18 188
5:2 15, 16, 18, 79, 107, 109, 199
5:2-3 31, 108
5:3 108, 112, 199
5:4 18, 31, 34, 57, 109, 110, 188, 199, 213
5:5 199
5:6 109, 110, 188, 199, 200, 204, 206, 222
5:7 200
5:8 200, 210
5:9 61, 200
5:10 33, 189, 200, 206, 213
5:10-12 200
5:11 35, 120, 121, 200
5:12 30, 34, 189
5:13 35, 173, 188, 189, 201, 204, 205, 206, 208, 209
5:13-6:10 20, 21
5:13-14 37
5:14 51, 86, 192, 204, 210, 211
5:15 61, 210
5:16 104, 192, 196
5:16-17 196
5:16-21 172
5:17 189, 197
5:19 197, 205
5:19-21 11
5:19-23 196
5:20 210
5:21 18, 210
5:22 188, 189, 206, 210, 226
5:22-23 210
5:23 211
5:24 188, 210
5:25 210
5:26 61, 210
6:1 35, 210, 211
6:2 173, 192, 210, 211
6:3 61, 211
6:4 211
6:5 211
6:6 104. 189, 210
6:8 62, 101, 102, 171, 172, 188, 192, 197
6:10 73, 86, 175, 208, 211, 223
6:11 212
6:11-18 19, 189
6:12 16, 31, 34, 107
6:12-13 34, 189, 212
6:13 122
6:15 109, 110, 175, 188
6:16 56, 84
6:17 18, 24, 30, 77, 189, 212
6:18 12, 35, 77, 212, 213

Philippians
1:7 220
1:9 206
2:6-7 217, 224
2:6-8 214
2:7 192
2:11 54
3:5 105
3:6-9 127
3:8 79
3:20 170
3:20-21 13
3:21 171
4:2-3 177
4:7 60
4:21-22 72

Colossians
2:8 179
2:20 179

1 Thessalonians
1:4 41
1:6 8, 54, 221
1:10 102, 192
2:2 62
2:5 88
4:3 175
4:13-18 51
4:15 26, 51
4:17 25
5:8 103

1 Timothy
3:16 118

Titus
1:4 90

Philemon
1 220
9 21
11 23

James
2:18-26 38

1 Peter
3:16 37
4:16 53

1 John
4:10 37

INDEX OF SUBJECTS

Abba 182, 214
Abraham 131-133, 134-138, 155, 157, 161, 184, 186, 196
Adam 45-47, 116
adelphoi 71-72
agapê 203-209, 215, 217
agapê spirituality 206
allegory 185
anti-Semitism 84-85, 86
apostle 27-28, 29, 42-45, 69-70, 93
atonement 174
authority 95
baptism 50, 73, 102, 168-171, 188
  theology of 169-171

Barnabas 89-90
blessing 154-156
brothers and sisters 72-74

call 82-85, 123
charis 56, 209
Christ-centered 78-81
Christian identity 222
Christos 39
church 50, 56, 65-67, 177
circumcision 92, 135
commitment 199
condemnation 138
conversion 82-83
covenant 162-164
covenantal nomism 126-127
co-workers 27
cross 158-159
crucifixion 146, 150-153

death 156-157
diathêkê 163
dikaioô 101
doxazein 175

eirênê 56
ekklêsia 56
eros 202
expiation 172

faith 99-104, 125, 141, 142
flesh 197-198, 210, 211
freedom 37-38, 51, 62, 67, 69, 96-97, 130, 146, 184, 187-188

Galatia 16-18
Galatians:
  authorship 18-19
  integrity 19-21
  purpose 30-35
  salutation 39-40
  structure 35-36
  text 19-21
Gentiles 77-78, 92, 123, 132, 154, 157
gift 56-60
glorification 175
gospel 62-63
grace 45, 57-60, 70, 184

Habakkuk 141-142
Hagar 185
hagiasmos 175
happiness 193-195
hilastêrion 173
holiness 106-107
holy family 217

Jesus 52-54
  death of 48, 54
journey 219
joy 226-227
Judaism 14-15, 75, 83, 105, 128
Judaism and Christianity 85-86
judgment 48, 51
justification 101-103, 130, 133, 138, 191-192

ideology 120-122

koine Greek 10

last day 51
law:
curse of 137, 145
works of 107-109
letter writing in antiquity 39-40
love 49-52, 162, 202-209

manumission, 148-149
Mary, the mother of Jesus 223
Messiah 116
Moses 116, 165-166
mutual self-giving 203-204
mystical union 225

new creation 176-177

paidagôgos 166
Paul:
apostleship of 27, 28, 42, 44, 93
biographical information 74-75
identity of 21-26, 41-42
and the law 109-123
persecution 74-78
Peter (Cephas) 87-89, 90-93, 95
Peter and Paul 95-96
philia 203
pistis 103
pistis Xristou 125
promise 163

reconciliation 173-175
redemption 146, 148
responsibility 102, 209-210, 212-213
resurrection 48
revelation 36, 70-71
Roman empire 9-15
and idolatry 10-11
and immoral behavior 11
and stratification 12-15
romance, divine 215-216

salvation 126, 171-172
slavery 13, 147, 180
sanctification 175-176

Sarah 185-186
sarx 198
self-righteousness 112-113
sin 45, 48, 67, 193
original 47
sociological approach 119-123
sôtêria 171
Spirit 155-156
sygkleiô 166

Titus 90
Torah 31, 76-77, 81, 84, 97, 99, 105-108, 126, 144, 164-168, 186, 200
and Christ 117-119
annulment of 115-117
failure of 140-145
transgression of 110
transformation 172-173
troublemakers 30-34, 38, 61, 63-65, 125, 129, 138, 161, 181, 200

will of God 54-55
women 14, 178-129

ORIENTALISTE, P.B. 41, B-3000 Leuven